PRAEGER LIBRARY OF U.S. GOVERNMENT DEPARTMENTS
AND AGENCIES

The
Federal Trade
Commission

The
Federal Trade
Commission

Susan Wagner

PRAEGER PUBLISHERS
New York · Washington · London

PRAEGER PUBLISHERS
111 Fourth Avenue, New York, N.Y. 10003, U.S.A.
5, Cromwell Place, London S.W.7, England

Published in the United States of America in 1971
by Praeger Publishers, Inc.

© 1971 by Praeger Publishers, Inc.

Library of Congress Catalog Card Number: 72–95695

This book is No. 28 in the series
Praeger Library of U.S. Government Departments and Agencies

Printed in the United States of America

Preface

Has the Federal Trade Commission worked? That is the question I asked myself when I began work on this volume in what now seems some long-forgotten past. Actually, it was little more than three years ago. But then there was no popular consumer movement to speak of. Ralph Nader was simply "that man who went after General Motors." The student movement had not blossomed into an all-out attack on the Establishment. Lyndon Johnson was still President. An American Bar Association study group had not suggested that the country might be better off without the FTC if the agency didn't shape up pretty quickly.

As I struggled to come to grips with the complex legal and economic concepts underlying the work of the FTC, there were moments when it occurred to me that I should perhaps be asking myself a more immediate question: Will the agency survive long enough for me to publish a book on the subject? The answer to that question is still in doubt. But the FTC has a renewed lease on life under its new Chairman, Miles W. Kirkpatrick, who has expressed the conviction that the job of preserving the American free competitive economic system and protecting the consumer against fraud and deception in the market place can and should be performed by the agency created by President Woodrow Wilson in 1914 to deal with the "trust problem."

But can the FTC work? Certainly, it has failed in many respects. Yet critics have so far failed to win support for any of their alternatives.

It is easy to make a scapegoat of federal regulatory agencies, which stand in a vulnerable position somewhere between the White House and Congress. Shouldn't we, rather, ask ourselves why the agency has been denied sufficient funds to do a real job, why Congress has pre-empted the field in the few instances when the FTC stepped forward boldly, why the White House has undercut its operation with appointment of mediocre political hacks, why the people of the United States have failed to rise up and demand adequate consumer protection or protection against economic concentration?

Would it be too much to hope that today's students, as a future generation in power, will assume their responsibilities as citizens and provide the needed support? If they do, they will not be alone. There are many, both inside and outside government, inside and outside the FTC, who would like to see the American free enterprise system fulfill its promise.

My thanks go to the many patient people—too numerous to name—who were kind enough to assist in the task of understanding the peculiarly American system of antitrust and trade regulation.

Washington, D.C.
January, 1971

Contents

LIST OF CHARTS

A selection of photographs follows page 88.

The
Federal Trade
Commission

I

The "Trust Problem"

Corporate mergers, phony get-rich-quick schemes, deceptive textile labels, price wars—all these practices fall within the purview of the Federal Trade Commission (FTC), for the FTC acts as watchdog of fair play in the American market place. It seeks to preserve the benefits of a free economy by maintaining competition. Second oldest of the major independent federal regulatory agencies, the FTC was established in 1914 under the Federal Trade Commission Act passed by Congress at the request of President Woodrow Wilson after a long political fight arising out of what was then called the "trust problem." Wilson envisaged an agency of experts to protect businessmen from unfair acts by competitors. Consumer protection was not one of the agency's original jobs. Nor did Wilson foresee the Commission's adjudicative function, which was written into the enabling legislation by Congress.

In the more than fifty years since the FTC began life on a modest scale in the offices of the Department of Commerce and Labor, the agency has gone far beyond the role envisioned by its founders. It would be unrecognizable to them today in

3

the power it exercises over business practices. From the limited Wilsonian concept of a guardian agency for business, the FTC has evolved into a powerful quasi-judicial body, seeking, in the words of Judge Learned Hand, "to discover and make explicit those unexpressed standards of fair dealing which the conscience of the community may progressively develop."

Most of the Commission's activities can be divided into two broad categories—those designed to combat restraint of trade (antitrust) and those aimed at eliminating deceptive business practices. The FTC, as the federal government's catch-all business- and consumer-protection agency, is unique in the broad spectrum of industry over which it wields authority. Its jurisdiction extends throughout the entire industrial complex, involving a welter of nomenclatures, technologies, manufacturing procedures, and methods. Congress gave it regulatory power over nearly all of manufacturing, mining, wholesaling, retailing, and most of the service trades. Only such businesses as banks, common carriers, and electric utilities, subject to the control of other agencies, fall outside its jurisdiction. Although the FTC has been the subject of attack and criticism ever since the first years of its life, it has amassed a record of investigation and enforcement that, in quantity at least, probably towers over that of any other administrative agency.

THE GROWTH OF BUSINESS GIANTS

In his first message to Congress, in 1889, President Benjamin Harrison called for antitrust legislation. He labeled monopolies "dangerous conspiracies" that tended to "crush out" competition. His request, which led to passage of the Sherman Antitrust Act the following year, was made against the background of a long and bitter struggle in which the opponents of monopoly turned to the federal government much as the proponents of railroad regulation had before them.

In the United States by the end of the nineteenth century, the techniques of capitalism had tamed a continent and created a proud industrial power. But, at the same time, the agrarian economy dependent upon the individual had given way to impersonalized industry and a trend toward concentration of industry into fewer business entities. The traditional forms of business organization—sole proprietorship and the partnership—had been replaced by the corporation. As entrepreneurs recognized the advantages of companies that could control their sources of supply, means of production, and marketing outlets, trusts and then holding companies developed. The concept of economic freedom was twisted to justify the heedless pursuit of self-interest. Many fortunes were founded on such practices as rate wars, predatory price discrimination, industrial espionage, sabotage, and commercial and political bribery.

Nothing demonstrates better the permissive climate of the late 1800's and the astounding opportunities open to aggressive businessmen than the story of John D. Rockefeller and Standard Oil. When Rockefeller began to refine petroleum at Cleveland, Ohio, in 1865, the oil industry was in its infancy. Within two decades, Standard Oil, the company he founded, had acquired control over almost 95 per cent of national oil production. Rockefeller's giant combine had virtually taken over the industry with the help of discriminatory railroad rates and a system of rebates granted by the railroads to Standard Oil on its own oil shipments—and those of its competitors.

The railroads were notorious for their discriminatory dealings with clients. By the 1870's, price discrimination against both individual shippers and geographical areas had become widespread. Intense and vigorous competition highlighted by bitter rate wars had given birth to the railroad pool, which enabled a number of railroads to work together to divide up the market, with each line given exclusive rights to carry goods and passengers in certain territory. Profit sharing, the use of patents, and other matters were worked out in pool agreements, too. The disadvantage of the pool was that it depended on voluntary adherence by the companies involved; there was no way of enforcing compliance.

Attorneys for Rockefeller's oil interests, frustrated by the unreliability of pool arrangements, decided to apply the technique of the common law trust to their companies and affiliates to form a giant corporation that would be assured of continued dominance in the oil industry. Trusts were formal, highly developed combinations of firms in which stockholders in the separate corporations gave up their shares and voting rights to trustees in return for trust certificates in the new organization. Trusts could thus enforce agreements and control any number of corporations. The original trust agreement establishing Standard Oil of Ohio was signed in 1882. By 1887, trusts in the whisky, sugar, lead, and cotton industries had been formed, as well. Working through a trust, individual business leaders could gain control of virtually an entire industry, control that extended over all aspects of the business from procuring raw materials to assuring sales. When the courts began to move against the trusts in the late 1800's, holding companies, which purchased controlling interest in subsidiary corporations, replaced trusts as the primary method of gaining and maintaining industry-wide control.

During the second half of the nineteenth century, many entrepreneurs sincerely regarded competition as a destructive rather than a constructive force. They bent their energies toward minimizing economic rivalry, and competition was sharply curtailed in many industries. These men, in effect, abandoned competitive free enterprise as an ideal. But not all Americans viewed this development with equanimity. Many feared that concentrated economic power could lead to the abuse of that power for selfish interests. As the trend toward concentration gathered momentum, many investors, businessmen, producers of raw materials, and consumers suffered serious injury. Bankruptcy was widespread, with independent businesses driven out of the field by the giants. As the frontier disappeared, so, too, it seemed, did opportunities for new enterprises. There developed a strong fear that democracy itself might be endangered. The sprawling corporation or stockholding trust could no longer be ignored.

THE ANTITRUST MOVEMENT

As early as 1876, the Greenback Party warned against the dangers of an aristocracy of wealth. The demand for enactment of a law to curb the power of industrial combinations figured in the Presidential campaign of 1884, when Grover Cleveland was elected the first Democratic President since the Civil War. In 1887, with passage of the Interstate Commerce Act, the government instituted regulation of the railroads, which had by then become a hated symbol of monopoly, especially among farmers. The Interstate Commerce Act outlawed the pool, the rebate, and geographical price discrimination and set up the Interstate Commerce Commission (ICC), the first federal regulatory agency, to enforce the Act's provisions.

But the monopolies remained, and the clamor for antitrust legislation continued. Standard Oil led the combinations that antagonized the public, and Bell Telephone was reaching similar eminence. Early in 1888, as a concession to those crying for reform, Congress authorized an investigation of the four trusts in the whisky, sugar, lead, and cotton industries. And in the Presidential election of that same year, the platforms of both major parties included antitrust planks. President Harrison's call for a federal antitrust law followed.

An antitrust bill, introduced by Senator John Sherman of Ohio, was passed by Congress with only one dissenting vote. Although the bill was so changed in committee that it bore little resemblance to the one Senator Sherman introduced, it was given his name. President Harrison signed the legislation into law on July 2, 1890. The Sherman Antitrust Act was designed "to protect trade and commerce against unlawful restraints and monopolies." It outlawed "every contract, combination in the form of a trust or otherwise, or conspiracy, in restraint of trade or commerce among the several states or with foreign nations." In concept, the new law was a relatively simple piece of legislation based on English common law, the body of legal decisions handed down by the courts in individual cases. The Act's real significance was that it made restraint of trade and monopolization offenses against the federal government, which meant that offenders could be prosecuted by federal officials.

The nineteenth century thus drew to a close with at least the hope that the Sherman Act would be an effective anti-monopoly weapon. That hope proved illusory.

The Failure of the Sherman Act

The Sherman Act contained a deceptively simple mandate. For one thing, no provisions were made for adequate enforcement. For another, the scope of the law was ambiguous. If taken literally, the Act barred every combination or contract that hampered or prevented unlimited trade. It thus fell to the courts to spell out the exact meaning of the law, and this they were cautious about doing. In the first case taken before the Supreme Court, in which the government sought to make the American Sugar Refining Company, which controlled 98 per cent of the sugar industry, divest itself of stock in four formerly independent refiners, the court ruled that sugar refining was manufacturing and that the Sherman Act applied only to commerce, of which manufacturing was not part. In five successive cases, the law was interpreted literally to mean that any restraint of trade was illegal.

A third and perhaps more important reason for the Sherman Act's ineffectiveness was its timing: it was passed on the eve of a great merger movement. By 1904, approximately 5,000 independent producers had been absorbed by some 300 large corporations. United States Steel alone had eliminated about 600 independent producers and, by the turn of the century, controlled two-thirds of the nation's steel output. Economic historians are agreed that the Sherman Act, as enforced and interpreted in its early years, did little to slow, or even guide, this movement. It was terminated, at least temporarily, by the stock market slump of 1903–4 and by the momentary exhaustion of merger possibilities. But the movement had shaped the structure of many American industries. Uncontrolled merger activity at the turn of the century created many of the hard-core oligopoly industries that still pose serious problems for public policy–makers.

The trusts, too, were falling into the hands of groups that threatened to merge the whole of American industry into a supertrust. When the opportunities in a particular industry had been exploited, the bankers and promoters combed the ground over again. Trusts themselves were consolidated. Pyramids were built on pyramids. The Rockefeller combine included oil, railroads, and other interests. J. P. Morgan controlled the steel and shipping trusts, the electrical supply trust, the rubber trust, and a score of smaller combinations. Morgan and Rockefeller were themselves allied by close ties. A congressional committee found in 1912 that the banking houses dominated by J. P. Morgan and William Rockefeller interests held 341 directorships in railroads, shipping, utilities, banks, express companies, coal, copper, iron, steel, and insurance, with aggregate resources of $22 billion. The trusts concentrated in the hands of a few power over the fortunes of millions. The nation was teetering on the brink of economic monarchy.

Antimonopoly sentiment, meanwhile, had been gathering steam. It proved strong enough in 1892 to bolster a third party in a national election, the Populist Party, a reform group composed largely of western farm interests. Its party platform stated: "The fruits of toil of millions are boldly stolen to build up colossal fortunes for the few, unprecedented in the history of mankind; and the possessors of these in turn despise the Republic and endanger liberty. From the same prolific womb of governmental injustice we breed the two great classes— tramps and millionaires." Although the Populists did not do as well in the election as many feared, their appearance and drawing power gave indication of growing national resentment of the concentration of wealth and economic power in the hands of a few.

The assassination of President William McKinley in 1901 promoted Theodore Roosevelt to the White House. Although Roosevelt earned a reputation as the "great trustbuster," he was actually more in favor of regulating the trusts in the public interest than of destroying them. Nevertheless, Roosevelt excoriated "malefactors of great wealth," supported legislation toughening the Interstate Commerce Commission's regulation of railroads, and brought a number of Sherman Act suits to the courts. He also took one step toward regulation of business that foreshadowed creation of the FTC.

THE BUREAU OF CORPORATIONS

With Roosevelt's Attorney General, Philander C. Knox, pressing for the creation of a fact-gathering commission to collect data on American corporations, Congress, in 1903, established the Bureau of Corporations in the Department of Commerce and Labor. The Bureau had no regulatory powers, but it could make investigations of corporations engaged in interstate commerce and publish the information so acquired. Looking back, Roosevelt said that the Bureau was one of the great achievements of his Administration.

The Bureau carried out its task of gathering, sorting, and disseminating information. Still, it could not achieve the goals envisioned. It was, after all, merely an extension of the executive, bound to conform to the policy of any given administration and dependent on voluntary compliance with its requests for information. There was a degree of cooperation between business and the Bureau, but, without compulsory measures, the flow of information was slow.

THE CRY FOR NEW ANTITRUST LAWS

Then came the Supreme Court decisions in the *Standard Oil* and *American Tobacco* cases. Both had been argued during the administration of William Howard Taft by Attorney General George W. Wickersham. The government won unanimous decisions in both when the Court ordered the oil and tobacco trusts dissolved. In addition, the Court adopted a rule-of-reason measuring stick to determine what constituted illegal activity among businesses. The former strict interpretation of the Sherman Act was abandoned in favor of the traditional concept established in common law that only contracts or combinations effected solely to restrain trade were prohibited. Chief Justice Edward D. White expressed the view that Congress had never intended to outlaw all agreements that might lessen competition, since many normal and usual business arrangements have some restraining effect. Rather, in *Standard Oil of New Jersey* v. *United States,* he explained that illegal contracts were those in which restrictive agreements had been

> such as to justify the conclusion that they had not been entered into or performed with the legitimate purpose of reasonably forwarding personal interest and developing trade, but on the contrary were of such a character as to give rise to the inference or presumption that they had been entered into or done with the intent to do wrong to the general public and to limit the

right of individuals, thus restraining the free flow of commerce and tending to bring about the evils, such as enhancement of prices, which were considered against public policy.

The public was outraged at the rule-of-reason provision. Within twenty-four hours after the Court handed down its decision in the *Standard Oil* case, Senator Francis G. Newlands, of Nevada, chairman of the Senate Committee on Interstate Commerce, declared on the floor of the Senate:

> The question therefore presents itself as to whether we are to permit in the future the administration regarding these great combinations to drift practically into the hands of the courts and subject the question as to the reasonableness or unreasonableness of any restraint upon ... trade ... to the varying judgments of different courts upon the facts and the law, or whether we will organize, as the servant of Congress, an administrative tribunal similar to the ICC, with powers of recommendation, with powers of correction similar to those enjoyed by the ICC over interstate transportation.

On July 8, 1911, Senator Newlands introduced a bill designed to require the registration of interstate corporations. Commenting on the Newlands bill in hearings before the Senate Interstate Commerce Committee, Herbert Knox Smith, then commissioner of Corporations, said:

> The one imperative change now required in our policy towards the "corporate problem" is a change from our present system of treating that problem through occasional prosecutions to a system which will treat it with continuous administrative action. We should advance from a negative policy to a positive constructive policy; from mere occasional prohibition to permanent regulation and prevention.

The Newlands bill did not ripen into statute, but the trust problem became a major issue in the Presidential campaign of

1912. All three political parties advocated remedial legislation to strengthen the antitrust law by enumerating illegal business practices. Antitrust was much debated during the vitriolic campaign. Neither the Wilson Democrats nor the Roosevelt (Bull Moose) Progressives found much good in the Republican achievements. But all three Presidential candidates, including Republican incumbent Taft, agreed that something had to be done. Wilson accused Roosevelt of having come to terms with the monopolists. In a speech entitled "The Old Order Changeth," Wilson charged that industrial society had been closed to the would-be entrepreneur. All markets had been organized, he said, "to shut out beginners, to prevent new entries in the race, to prevent the building up of competitive enterprises that would interfere with monopolies which the great trusts have built up." What the United States needed above everything else, he asserted, was "a body of laws which will look after the men who are on the make rather than the men who are already made."

The Republicans and Progressives wanted to place in the hands of an administrative agency many of the functions exercised by the courts, but Wilson did not endorse the concept of a federal administrative agency at that time. A few years before, Roosevelt had suggested that corporations with contracts that might be in restraint of trade be permitted to submit them for approval to the commissioner of Corporations. But others favored creation of a federal regulatory body that would have greater control over businesses. Among them was Louis Brandeis, the Boston lawyer whom President Wilson later named to the Supreme Court. Brandeis believed that a new enforcement technique was required to banish the specter of monopoly from the American scene. He placed his faith in an administrative agency.

The Senate Committee on Interstate Commerce, after two years of hearings on the trust problem, issued a report in February, 1913, advocating formation of a commission with authority to take over the investigative work of the Bureau of Corporations, to pass on the legality of combinations in restraint of trade, and to aid the courts in dissolving any combinations found unlawful. The report continued:

> It is believed that through the intervention of such a body of men the legislative policy with respect to combinations and monopolies could be vastly more effective than through the courts alone, which in most cases will take no cognizance of violations of the law until months or years after the violation occurs, and when the difficulty of awarding reparation for the violation is most insurmountable.

Lending his voice to the mounting chorus in favor of a regulatory agency, Senator Newlands told Congress in 1913:

> The railroad question is practically settled; the settlement of the trust question has hardly commenced. Had we submitted the administration of the antitrust act to an impartial quasi-judicial tribunal similar to the ICC instead of the Attorney General's office, with its shifting officials, its varying policies, its lack of tradition [and] record of precedent, we would by this time have made gratifying progress in the regulation and control of trusts.

WILSON PROPOSES A TRADE COMMISSION

Woodrow Wilson was sworn in as President on March 3, 1913. In his State of the Union message the following December, he called for new antitrust legislation. He spelled out some of his ideas in a speech to both houses of Congress on January 20, 1914. The speech was in part an elaboration of the thesis he had hammered away at during the Presidential campaign—the need for explicit legislative definition of the policy and meaning of antitrust law. "Surely, we are sufficiently familiar with the actual processes and methods of monopoly and of the many hurtful restraints of trade," he told the lawmakers, "to make definition possible, at any rate up to the limit of what experience has disclosed. These practices, being now abundantly disclosed, can be explicitly and item by item forbidden by statute in such terms as will practically eliminate uncertainty, the law itself and the penalty being made equally plain."

Wilson, influenced by Brandeis and others, went on to request the creation of a commission with broad powers to investigate trade practices, make findings regarding the significance of the practices, and prohibit those which tended to promote monopoly. "The opinion of the country would instantly approve of such a commission," Wilson told Congress. He added:

I would not wish to see it empowered to make terms with monopoly or in any sort to assume control of business, as if the Government made itself responsible. It demands such a commission only as an indispensable instrument of information and publicity, as a clearing house for the facts by which both the public mind and the managers of great business undertakings shall be guided, and as an instrumentality for doing justice where the process of the courts or the natural forces of correction outside the courts are inadequate to adjust the remedy to the wrong in a way that will meet all the equities and circumstances of the case.

Wilson had gone to Congress at an auspicious time, for the legislative body was in a mood to do something about the trusts. Numerous bills were introduced under the auspices of two schools of political thought. One adhered to the Rooseveltian concept that would have permitted cartelization of enterprises under a federal law. This group wanted an agency that would not only take action in the negative sense of Sherman litigation but would also perform a positive licensing function. The other school, the one backed by Wilson, wanted to foster the kind of environment in which competition could thrive. The Wilson school believed that business combinations would gain the upper hand unless effective legislation was coupled with the supervisory role of a federal agency.

Representative James H. Covington, of Maryland, introduced a bill he believed carried forward the Wilson goals. He said that the President had recommended "the creation of an interstate trade commission as an instrument of information and publicity, and as a clearing house for the facts by which both the public mind and the managers of great business undertakings should be guided." Opposition to the Covington bill arose immediately. The Progressive Party claimed that publicity would only mitigate the disease. The "corporate problem" was known. Why bore the country with details? Action was what was needed. Congressman Victor Murdock, a Kansas newspaperman who served twelve years in Congress and was later named an FTC Commissioner, declared that "the underlying philosophy of the pending measure—the Covington bill—is a sort of childlike belief in the potency of publicity; and, let me say, we in Congress seem to have a pathetic reliance upon publicity and its powers and a singular indifference to our experience in the past with the failures of publicity to correct."

In the course of congressional deliberations over the legislation, attempts to define certain phrases in the Sherman Act were abandoned. So, too, were efforts to enumerate all but a few specific unlawful practices. The legislators were convinced that as soon as twenty illicit practices had been defined, twenty more would crop up. As a result, the final legislation did not contain an "explicit legislative definition of the policy and the meaning of existing antitrust laws," as had been requested by President Wilson and desired by business. It merely supplemented and augmented the Sherman Act.

THE ANTITRUST LAWS OF 1914

What finally emerged from Congress in 1914 was not one law, but two—the Clayton Act and the Federal Trade Commission Act. The first enumerated four specific practices and declared them illegal; the second covered the field with a broad prohibition against "unfair methods of competition" and provided for an agency to spell out standards of competition. Both bills were passed with Democratic and Progressive party support of large majorities and signed into law by President Wilson on October 15, 1914.

With the passage of the new legislation, there were three antitrust laws and two enforcement agencies. The Sherman Act, the basic antitrust statute, would be administered by the nation's legal arm, the Justice Department, which utilizes the services of federal attorneys, economic analysts, and investigators. The new Federal Trade Commission was to administer the FTC Act, and both agencies were to enforce the Clayton Act.

The Federal Trade Commission Act, in addition to setting up the Commission, provided for substantive regulations of industry. Its key section, Section 5, held that "unfair methods of competition in commerce are hereby declared unlawful." The phrase "unfair methods of competition" had been chosen by the draftsmen of the new law because they wanted an elastic term, which would embrace not only known unfair trade practices but those which future generations of rogues might dream up.

The Clayton Act, companion law to the FTC Act, was designed "to supplement existing laws against unlawful restraints and monopolies." It began as an omnibus antitrust bill introduced by Representative Henry D. Clayton, of Alabama. When passed by Congress on June 5, 1914, it enumerated four unfair methods of competition. The provisions were intended to prevent practices that, it was feared, would not fall within the scope of the Sherman Act. The key substantive parts are sections 2, 3, 7, and 8, which proscribe certain price discriminations and tying and exclusive dealing contracts and impose restrictions on intercorporate mergers and directorates if they are anticompetitive in effect.

The antitrust legislation of 1914 did not purport to cover the whole field of monopoly and restraint of trade. But it turned America back along the road to free competition following a period in which the trusts were tolerated, even celebrated. The tradition of pluralism had proved too deep to be washed away by the excesses of a burgeoning capitalism. American politics had been shaped by the belief that the individual citizen should exercise maximum control over his own development. The antitrust and trade regulation laws were passed as a political act of faith. Important additions were to come, but the basic links in the chain of antitrust law had been forged.

II

An Agency to Preserve Competition

The men who drafted the 1914 antitrust legislation envisioned the Federal Trade Commission as an independent administrative agency that would adapt the law to current commercial practices, whatever they might be. Section 6 of the FTC Act authorized the new agency to "gather and compile information concerning, and to investigate from time to time the organization, business, conduct, practices, and management of any corporation engaged in commerce, excepting banks and common carriers." The FTC was thus to combine the functions of publicity and prosecution. Not only would it investigate and publicize, it would also prosecute and judge. Moreover, court review of agency orders was limited. Commission findings, if supported by substantial evidence, were to be binding on the courts.

Congress also concluded that the administration of the new policies should be placed in the hands of an impartial nonpartisan body of men thoroughly experienced in the intricacies of commerce. There were to be five Commissioners, appointed by the President and confirmed by the Senate, with staggered, seven-year terms. The impartiality of the Commissioners was to be assured by a provision requiring that not more than three of the five be members of the same party, a reflection of the congressional desire to remove the Commissioners as much as possible from political influence.

THE FIRST COMMISSIONERS

Five months elapsed after enactment of the FTC Act before President Wilson completed his selection of the first Commissioners. Joseph E. Davies, a Wisconsin lawyer whose distinguished career of public service led eventually to appointment as U.S. Ambassador to the Soviet Union, was the first selected. As commissioner of Corporations, a position with which Wilson had rewarded him for successfully leading the Democratic campaign in the West during the 1912 Presidential election, he was a logical choice.

The other slots were more difficult to fill. Davies and Wilson discussed at length qualifications for membership on the Commission. Three of the Commissioners should be lawyers, Wilson decided, and two, businessmen of broad experience. They should come from different parts of the country, as well. Wilson's major concern, however, was with general principles of the law rather than with finding men whose personalities and talents were suitable for their tasks. His nominations also ran into opposition in the Senate.

Edward N. Hurley, an Illinois manufacturer of farm equipment, was the second Democrat appointed. With only a secondary school education, Hurley had made a success in business and wound up as president of the Illinois Manufacturers' Association. The third Democratic appointee was William J. Harris, a Georgia insurance executive who was made director of the Bureau of the Census after serving as chairman of the Democratic Committee of Georgia. During confirmation hearings in the Senate, Hurley was said to have reactionary tendencies, and Harris came under fire for having run for governor of Georgia while serving in the census post.

On the Republican side, Wilson selected William H. Parry, an editor and publisher of Oregon newspapers, and George Rublee, a Wisconsin lawyer who had practiced law in Chicago. Rublee's appointment was opposed by Senator Jacob H. Gallinger of New Hampshire, no doubt because Rublee had managed the campaign of Gallinger's opponent in his senatorial election. After serving a recess appointment, Rublee, who was one of Wilson's most able appointees, was forced to retire.*

THE EARLY YEARS

The Federal Trade Commission came into existence on the day the first Commissioners were sworn into office, March 16, 1915. Davies was elected Chairman of the Commission. The Bureau of Corporations, merged into the FTC, provided a nucleus of experienced staff and, incidentally, a place to work. For some time, the FTC operated out of the Bureau's former offices in the Department of Commerce and Labor, but the space proved inadequate. Hearings were held in the Chairman's office, except on the occasions when the Treasury made other space available. The first annual report of the Commission, which covered the period from March 16 to June 30, 1915, complained that "the Commission has been hampered seriously in its work by limitation in appropriations, especially in the matter of quarters." Working conditions were still cramped the following year. According to the 1916 annual report, "the inadequate quarters which the Commission obtained was a serious physical impediment to the proper performance of its duties."

* A recess appointment is one made by the President without Senate confirmation. Such an appointee retains the position until he or a successor is confirmed by the Senate.

The staff of the new agency was organized into three departments— administrative, legal, and economic. The secretary of the Commission directed the administrative machinery, and, during an experimental period of organization, chiefs or boards of review headed the legal and economic departments. Rules of Practice, said to be the handiwork of George Rublee, established the Commission's casework approach to determining unfair competition.

During the first four months of its existence, the Commission held a series of 114 conferences with industry leaders to explore how it should best operate. Altogether, it heard 171 persons. Louis Brandeis, who had worked on the enabling legislation, warned against giving advisory opinions to business. He feared the Commission would be trapped into approving action it might later wish to disavow. Forty complaints were processed during this period, and the Commission established its policy of investigating each case before issuing a complaint. Once organized, the Commission went ahead with policy statements, conference rulings, disposal of complaints, and preparation for new investigations authorized by Congress. On-going Bureau of Corporations investigations, such as those into the lumber, beet sugar, fertilizer, and petroleum industries, were taken up by the FTC.

But the agency was not permitted the luxury of slow development. When the United States entered World War I in 1917, President Wilson called on the FTC to make studies of the prices of food and materials related to the war effort— a task for which the agency was not yet ready. One study, the meat-packing investigation, grew to historic proportions. (See Chapter V.) Several others brought the Commission almost as much notoriety.

One of the most important of these investigations concerned what were known as Blue Sky cases, so named after a Kansas law directed at speculative schemes with "no more basis than so many feet of blue sky." The investigation began shortly after U.S. entry into the war, when the Treasury Department asked the Commission to investigate wildcat stock sales that were threatening Treasury attempts to sell Victory Loan bonds to the public. The Commissioners, uncertain whether the FTC had jurisdiction, yielded to pressure from the Treasury Department and set up machinery to carry out an investigation. Soon, the FTC was deluged with cases, and the evidence gathered was turned over to the Department of Justice for criminal prosecution. In the course of its probes, the Commission found that manipulation of stocks on the exchanges caused greater losses to the Treasury than the sale of the wildcat stocks. When these findings were disclosed, the FTC offered Congress bills to regulate these practices, giving the FTC jurisdiction. Such bills were introduced year after year. Finally, in 1934, the Securities Exchange Act was passed, with regulation of stock sales vested in the newly created Securities and Exchange Commission.

Four years after the FTC was created, its jurisdiction within international trade was established. In 1918, Congress passed the Export Trade Act, known as the Webb-Pomerene Act, exempting export trade associations from the antitrust laws. Within certain limits, the Act authorized cooperative activity among American exporters for the purpose of promoting foreign trade. It expressly forbade the members of such associations to interfere with the exports of nonmembers and to take joint action in making sales in the domestic market. Associations were directed to file their charters, by-laws, agreements, and other data with the FTC and to make periodic reports to the agency. The FTC was not authorized to issue orders of cease and desist in these matters, but it could investigate association activities and recommend readjustments.

Although several important investigations were launched and much FTC policy established in these early years, the Commission got off to a slow start, in large part because of internal differences. The Commissioners themselves disagreed on the agency's responsibilities. In addition, none of the Commissioners served long enough to nurse the FTC through its infancy. The record of Commissioners from 1915 to 1920 lists eleven men. Parry and Hurley spent only two years each on the Commission. Parry died in office. Harris and Davies each served about three years, leaving the Commission to seek elective office. Rublee, who had never been confirmed by the Senate, was forced out after only one year. (See Chart I.)

The second round of appointees proved more effective. Two Wilsonian liberals, Victor Murdock, an ex-congressman, and William B. Colver, a newspaper executive, filled the vacancies left by Parry and Hurley. They formed an aggressive triumvirate with Huston Thompson of Colorado, who took the place of Davies as Chairman in 1919. Thompson, a former assistant attorney general, immediately stepped up investigations of unfair trade practices.

FROM ACTIVE TO PASSIVE

With a fresh line-up on the Commission in the early 1920's, its liberal members sought to launch a bold attack on monopoly and restraint of trade, but they were thwarted on two fronts—in Congress and in the courts.

At first, Congress merely ignored the FTC's pleas for money to halt the high turnover rate among its staff. Then, after the FTC entered the maelstrom of politics with its investigation of the meat-packing industry, the agency came under attack. Irate congressmen called for an investigation of the FTC, alleging that it must be filled with socialists. As a result, Commission investigators and economists were quietly discharged, appropriations for contemplated future investigations were denied, and jurisdiction over the meat-packing industry was transferred to the Department of Agriculture.

That unpleasant experience was followed by adverse court

Chart I

The Succession of Commissioners at the Federal Trade Commission

DATE OF CHART: OCTOBER 1970

THE SUCCESSION OF COMMISSIONERS

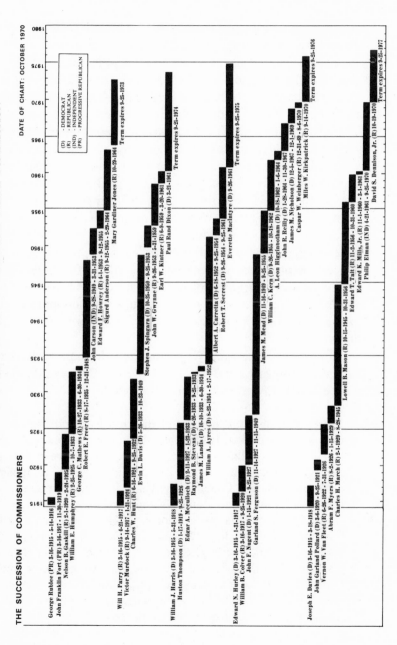

(D) - DEMOCRAT
(R) - REPUBLICAN
(IND) - INDEPENDENT
(PR) - PROGRESSIVE REPUBLICAN

George Rublee (PR) 3-16-1915 - 5-14-1916
John Franklin Fort (PR) 3-16-1917 - 11-30-1919
Nelson B. Gaskill (R) 2-1-1920 - 2-24-1925
William E. Humphrey (R) 2-25-1925 - 10-7-1933
George C. Mathews (R) 10-27-1933 - 6-30-1934
Robert E. Freer (R) 8-17-1935 - 12-31-1948

John Carson (IND) 9-28-1949 - 2-31-1953
Edward F. Howrey (R) 4-1-1953 - 9-12-1955
Sigurd Anderson (R) 9-12-1955 - 2-29-1964
Mary Gardiner Jones (R) 10-29-1964   Term expires 9-25-1973

Will H. Parry (R) 3-16-1915 - 4-21-1917
Victor Murdock (R) 9-14-1917 - 1-31-1924
Charles W. Hunt (D) 6-16-1924 - 9-25-1932
Ewin L. Davis (D) 5-26-1933 - 10-23-1949

Stephen J. Spingarn (D) 10-25-1950 - 9-25-1953
John W. Gwynne (R) 9-26-1953 - 5-31-1959
Earl W. Kintner (R) 6-9-1959 - 3-30-1961
Paul Rand Dixon (D) 3-21-1961   Term expires 9-25-1974

William J. Harris (D) 3-16-1915 - 5-31-1918
Huston Thompson (D) 1-17-1919 - 9-25-1926
Edgar A. Mcculloch (D) 2-11-1927 - 1-23-1933
Raymond B. Stevens (D) 6-26-1933 - 9-25-1933
James M. Landis (D) 10-10-1933 - 6-30-1934
William A. Ayres (D) 8-23-1934 - 2-17-1952

Albert A. Carretta (D) 6-18-1952 - 9-25-1954
Robert T. Secrest (D) 9-26-1954 - 9-25-1961
Everette MacIntyre (D) 9-25-1975   Term expires 9-25-1975

Edward N. Hurley (D) 3-16-1915 - 1-31-1917
William B. Colver (R) 3-16-1917 - 9-25-1920
John F. Nugent (D) 1-15-1921 - 9-25-1927
Garland S. Ferguson (D) 11-14-1927 - 11-15-1949

James M. Mead (D) 11-16-1949 - 9-25-1955
William C. Kern (D) 9-26-1955 - 10-18-1962
A. Leon Higginbotham (D) 10-18-1962 - 1-6-1964
John R. Reilly (D) 1-28-1964 - 11-30-1967
James M. Nicholson (D) 12-5-1967 - 12-1-1969
Caspar W. Weinberger (R) 12-31-69 - 8-6-1970
Miles W. Kirkpatrick (R) 9-14-1970   Term expires 9-25-1976

Joseph E. Davies (D) 3-16-1915 - 2-18-1918
John Garland Pollard (D) 3-6-1920 - 9-25-1921
Vernon W. Van Fleet (R) 6-26-1922 - 7-31-1926
Abram F. Myers (R) 8-2-1926 - 1-15-1929
Charles H. March (R) 2-1-1929 - 8-28-1945

Lowell B. Mason (R) 10-15-1945 - 10-31-1956
Edward T. Tait (R) 11-2-1956 - 10-31-1960
Edward K. Mills, Jr. (R) 11-1-1960 - 2-1-1961
Philip Elman (IND) 4-21-1961 - 9-25-1970
David S. Dennison, Jr. (R) 10-19-1970   Term expires 9-25-1977

decisions. In *FTC* v. *Gratz*, the first Commission case decided by the Supreme Court, the Court ruled in 1920 that the FTC could not proceed against conduct that was not regarded as illegal under common law or the Sherman Act. Deciding an FTC case against the Curtis Publishing Company in 1923, the Supreme Court said: "Effective competition requires that traders have large freedom of action when conducting their own affairs. Success alone does not show reprehensible methods, although it may increase or render insuperable the difficulties which rivals must face." These and similar decisions forced the agency's work, during its formative years, into certain unyielding categories: actions against monopolies and regulation of those practices in restraint of trade that were clearly predatory and those regarded as opposed to good business morals because they had been held fraudulent, oppressive, or deceptive by the courts prior to 1914. As the FTC shifted its emphasis from major assaults on monopoly to the policing of unfair practices, however, it began to fare better in the courts.

Nevertheless, the agency's performance in those early years was disappointing. In *The Federal Trade Commission,* published in 1924, Gerard C. Henderson wrote:

> There is a constant complaint of the crowded condition of the Commission's docket. It takes months to bring a case to a hearing, and additional months to reach a decision. At the end of the fiscal year 1922, there were 231 applications for complaints docketed with the Commission which had been on hand an average of four months and eight days. These were cases in which formal complaints had not yet been issued. At the same time there were pending 257 cases in which formal complaints had been issued. The largest number of formal complaints ever disposed of in a single year was 166, the average being much lower. . . . Yet the Commission has an annual appropriation close to a million dollars, and a personnel, as revealed by its first annual report, of over 300 employees.

Obstructed by the courts and cowed by Congress, the FTC thus retreated to "cooperative" and "voluntary" regulation and spoke of itself as merely an administrative and fact-finding body. The Wilsonian policy of pitiless publicity was discarded; the Commission entered a quiescent era.

The change in national leadership in 1924 brought change to the Commission, too. President Calvin Coolidge's let-business-alone policy was reflected in the kinds of men he chose as Commissioners. In 1925, with the appointment of William E. Humphrey, an Ohio congressman, the Commission had a Republican majority for the first time. With Humphrey came changes in objectives, policies, and procedures. To the new Commissioner, the FTC had become "an instrument of oppression and disturbance instead of a help to business," and he intended to reverse that trend. Increasingly, the FTC's work was assigned by Congress and consisted chiefly of "studies." One of these, the public utilities investigation of 1928, produced a report that laid the foundation for the Public Utility Act of 1935.

The Humphrey Affair

If any one figure stands out in the history of the FTC, it is William E. Humphrey. For the better part of eight years, he ruled the agency autocratically and wielded tremendous power, much of it negative in the opinion of New Deal President Franklin D. Roosevelt. Roosevelt wanted to shift FTC activity away from the laissez-faire approach of the Coolidge era to a more vigorous antitrust policy. In an attempt to do so, he requested the resignation of Humphrey, then Chairman of the FTC, in July, 1933. The President stated his reasons in a letter. "I do not feel," he wrote, "that your mind and my mind go along together on either the policies or the administering of the Federal Trade Commission and, frankly, I think it best for the people of this country that I should have a full confidence." The President, regarding the FTC as part of the executive, believed its policies should accord with those of the New Deal.

Humphrey refused to resign, contending that he could be removed only for cause set forth in the statute, namely, inefficiency, neglect of duty, or malfeasance in office. Humphrey told the *New York Times* on October 10, 1933: "This action is going to be made a party issue. The President and his political friends are attempting to inaugurate the spoils system in a Federal agency which, under the law, is declared bi-partisan in every way."

In November, 1933, the Comptroller General ruled that Humphrey was no longer entitled to his salary as Commissioner. Humphrey then took the matter to court, alleging that he had been improperly removed from his government job. The Court of Claims ruled against him. But on May 27, 1935, shortly after Humphrey had died, the Supreme Court overruled the Court of Claims. The high court said that the President's removal power applied only to purely executive officers and did not extend to the independent regulatory agencies, where removal was limited to reasons specified in the agency's organic statute. The Court concluded that "it is quite evident that one who holds his office only during the pleasure of another cannot be depended upon to maintain an attitude of independence against the latter's will."

The New Deal Period

The Great Depression fostered a regulatory experiment in which the government attempted to establish rules of fair competition as guidelines for the conduct of business. Congress enacted the National Industrial Recovery Act (NIRA) at the beginning of the New Deal to stimulate economic recovery and reduce unemployment. Under its provisions, actions taken by businessmen in compliance with approved codes were exempt from the provisions of the antitrust laws. During the brief life of the National Recovery Administration (NRA), which was created by the Act, the FTC filed several complaints alleging violations of codes, but the agency's role in such instances was uncertain. Had the NRA survived, the FTC would doubtless have diminished in importance. As it turned out, however, the Supreme Court, on May 27, 1935, declared the NIRA Act unconstitutional. The FTC promptly dismissed complaints it had issued charging violations of the codes.

During the NRA period, antitrust went into eclipse. So did the FTC. President Roosevelt, who might have picked the agency as an instrument of his new policy, had apparently been discouraged by his attempt to dislodge Commissioner Humphrey. The FTC sank into the quagmire of political cronyism. The so-called Tennessee Gang was put into its corridors by Edward Hull "Boss" Crump and Senator Kenneth D. McKellar, both of whom practiced politics as they knew it back home—you do something for a congressman, and he assures you of an appropriation for the next year. Senator McKellar was chairman of the Senate appropriations subcommittee with jurisdiction over the regulatory agencies, and Roosevelt allowed him to install his friends at the FTC. One of the first of them was Ewin L. Davis, a former congressman, who served as a Commissioner from 1933 until his death in October, 1949. It was Davis who first hired, as a trial lawyer, Paul Rand Dixon, a fellow Tennessean who many years later was to be appointed Chairman of the Commission by President John F. Kennedy.

Two Decades of Expanding Power

After the demise of the NRA, there was a revival of antitrust and a revitalization of the FTC. The Depression had shaken the judiciary's faith in business. Although the courts continued to apply the competitive standard to cases, they approached the task in a different spirit. Trade associations not only lost favor with the Supreme Court; they became suspect. The corporation was discouraged from expanding, either by growth or merger. From 1924, when the Supreme Court told the Commission not to direct "fishing expeditions" into private papers of business corporations on the chance of finding evidence of illegal activity, to 1948, when it said the "courts should not lightly modify Commission orders," the judicial pendulum had swung from right to left.

Concurrent with the change in the Court's position, FTC appropriations were increased and its ventures into the realm of consumer protection gained favor. Although only 43 FTC orders from a total of 82 reviewed by the courts up to 1931 were upheld either entirely or substantially, the courts upheld 22 of the 29 FTC orders involving false advertising. This relatively high batting average indicates that FTC prohibition of deceptive advertising was becoming the most generally approved of its functions.

Near the end of the 1930's, a series of adverse court decisions that demonstrated the confining boundaries of the FTC's authority furnished the stimulus for major expansion of the Commission's jurisdiction. That expansion came about through the Wheeler-Lea Act of 1938, which reflected a growing preoccupation with unfair and fraudulent trade practices in contrast to the earlier emphasis on antitrust. The Act added to Section 5 of the FTC Act a prohibition against deceptive as well as unfair practices in commerce, a broadening of the statute to protect the consumer as well as the merchant or manufacturer from suffering at the hands of dishonest businessmen. The Commission could thereafter proceed against unfair or deceptive acts without reference to competitive effect.

The Wheeler-Lea amendment also strengthened the Commission's hand in dealing with false advertising of food, drugs, cosmetics, and other consumer commodities and devices and gave weight to its enforcement procedures by providing, among other things, definite and substantial civil penalties for violation of orders to cease and desist from illegal practices.

The second major step in the evolution of the Commission's powers came with passage of the Wool Products Labeling Act in 1939, which for the first time authorized the Commission to formulate substantive rules governing practices in a particular industry. Addition of the Fur Products Labeling, Flammable Fabrics, and Textile Fiber Products Identification acts in the 1950's indicated congressional satisfaction with this specialized form of regulation.

In 1950, as part of repeal of the special oleomargarine tax, Congress, almost by inadvertence, increased the forcefulness of FTC cease-and-desist orders by stating that each day of continuing violation of a final order shall be deemed a separate violation. In 1950, too, the antimerger section of the Clayton Act was strengthened when Congress passed the Celler-Kefauver Antimerger Act, which closed the loophole by which many mergers had been brought about, without running afoul of the law, through purchase of assets rather than of stock.

During this period, the Commission's jurisdiction over interstate commerce was broadened by a series of court decisions that reflected a trend toward obliterating the line between interstate and intrastate commerce. Lower courts as well as the high court, liberally applying the "stream of commerce" theory to a wide variety of situations, brought many activities fairly local in nature within the reach of the FTC. The courts have held that such strictly intrastate activities as hiring employees and financing the purchase of automobiles come within the FTC's jurisdiction when they are part of a larger scheme to sell merchandise in interstate commerce. Moreover, the courts have moved steadily away from the doctrine prevalent in the 1920's that the sale of goods from an intrastate stock replenished from time to time out of state does not constitute interstate commerce. A recent decision affirmed without comment an FTC order against false advertising by a Pennsylvania department store that delivered some of its merchandise to customers in New Jersey. Following the spirit of these court decisions, Congress, too, has granted the FTC and other regulatory agencies jurisdiction over matters "affecting" rather than strictly "in" interstate commerce.

STABILIZING THE PENDULUM

Since the late 1950's, the FTC has emphasized industry guidance and voluntary procedures. President Dwight D. Eisenhower's second appointee as Chairman, Earl W. Kintner, an Indiana Republican who had served as FTC general counsel before being elevated to the Commission in 1959, made a special effort to publicize the work of the Commission. As general counsel, he had launched a program of issuing statements on industry guides to the public, thousands of copies of which were distributed throughout the country. Kintner also called the first consumer conference at the FTC.

Chairman Paul Rand Dixon, serving throughout the administrations of John F. Kennedy and Lyndon B. Johnson, attempted to steer a middle course by mixing industry guidance, voluntary procedures, and litigation. The burly, blunt-spoken Democrat had joined the FTC first in 1938, then moved to Capitol Hill in 1957 to serve as staff director and chief counsel for the Senate Monopoly Subcommittee, of which fellow-Tennessean Estes Kefauver was chairman. In that capacity, Dixon took part in investigations of alleged administered prices in the drug, bread, auto, and steel industries. Then, in 1961, President John F. Kennedy appointed Dixon to the FTC and made him Chairman, a position he held longer than any of his predecessors. Dixon's eight years topped by three the record of his closest runner-up, Garland Ferguson.

Dixon placed improvement of FTC-business relations high on his list of accomplishments, asserting that he had tried to make the agency the servant of the legitimate business community as well as the consumer. He also claimed to have abandoned the antitrust "numbers game"—the piling up of a record number of cases—in favor of industry guidance and voluntary compliance, with legal action reserved for the few.

Commissioner Philip Elman, a former Justice Department official appointed to the Commission by President Kennedy in 1961, kept up a running criticism of the agency's case-by-case approach during this period. He favored, instead, industry-wide regulation. Consumer advocate Ralph Nader criticized, among other things, Dixon's emphasis on voluntary procedures and the agency's concentration on trivia.

In answer to critics such as Nader, Dixon could point to the FTC attack on the tobacco industry, the crackdown on automobile tire advertising, the challenge to coffee industry pricing policies, acceleration of consumer protection, and moves in the antipoverty field. There were also a few tough antitrust rulings and some new laws, such as truth-in-lending and truth-in-packaging, which expanded the agency's work.

Nevertheless, toward the end of Dixon's tenure as Chairman, criticisms of the FTC began to mount as the consumer movement gained momentum. Ralph Nader's student investigators, known as "Nader's Raiders," descended on the Commission and then issued a scathing report on their findings in January, 1969. Such was the storm created by this report that major newspapers called for complete overhaul or even abolition of the agency. The result has been efforts at reform from within and without the agency. In May, 1969, the American Bar Association (ABA), at the request of President Richard M. Nixon, appointed a study group made up of law-

yers and economists to examine the FTC. Their report—brief
and critical—was issued five months later.

In this atmosphère, California State Finance Director Caspar W. Weinberger, a Harvard Law School graduate and
moderate Republican, was picked by Nixon to take over the
reins of the FTC. He was sworn in on January 13, 1970. Weinberger moved, as his first order of business, to mend internal
wounds within the Commission and to present a public image
of the agency as a strong supporter of consumer interests. But
scarcely had he begun than he was tapped by Nixon to go to
the newly reorganized Office of Management and Budget.
Nevertheless, the mood of reform was on the agency. The
critical reports prepared by Nader's Raiders and the ABA,
combined with Weinberger's vigorous reorganization efforts,
marked what appeared to be the beginnings of a new era for
the "old lady of Pennsylvania Avenue."

III

The Organization of the FTC

In the years following the Civil War, commercial intercourse among the states mushroomed. Congress could hardly have been expected to concern itself with the day-to-day regulation of it. The states, faced with the growth of industry and commerce earlier in the nineteenth century, had already begun to turn certain functions over to *ad hoc* regulatory commissions. It was argued at first that the states were trying to delegate their law-making authority in violation of the separation-of-powers principle. The courts said these commissions were, in effect, instrumentalities of the legislature. But later, seeing the practicality of the arrangement, they held that the power exercised by commissions was not legislative but quasi-legislative and, hence, acceptable. When certain commissions were given functions akin to adjudication—to hold hearings and hand down judgments dealing with conflicts and controversial issues—this kind of activity was not prohibited by the Constitution, the courts said, because it was not really judicial; it was quasi-judicial. This question of legal semantics had thus been resolved by the time Congress began to delegate a good part of its authority to associated bodies.

The independent regulatory commission was one such arm of Congress. "Independent" in this context refers to independence from the executive, not absolute independence. The regulatory agencies are responsible to Congress and subject to its oversight. Congress passes the laws they administer and appropriates operating funds. But Congress grants them wide discretion to make rules and issue orders. Their members are appointed by the President, but the political balance required by law makes it difficult for the executive to direct policies. Sometimes described as the fourth branch of government, they are creatures of the other three and enjoy powers partaking of each.

Congress, in other words, determined on a course of creating independent agents to whom it would delegate a limited amount of legislating authority—namely, the filling in of legislative detail within a broad framework of congressional standards and declarations of policy. Section 8 of the Constitution empowers Congress "to regulate commerce with foreign nations, and among the several states, and with Indian tribes." Section 5 of the Federal Trade Commission Act, which stipulates that unfair methods of competition are unlawful, is a refinement of the power granted Congress under the Constitution. The independent regulatory agent—in this case, the FTC —is delegated authority and power by the Act to fill in and implement legislative details to establish the precise meaning of the phrase "unfair methods of competition." This it is to do by quasi-judicial action and by quasi-legislative process, including rule-making proceedings.

THE FTC—A SPECIAL CASE

The FTC is a special kind of independent agency. Whereas the others regulate a particular industry, the FTC is charged with regulating a vast array of American business not otherwise the subject of special federal regulation. It does not award licenses or set rates. It has nothing to give any particular industry in that sense. In addition, the Commission shares its jurisdiction with another governmental entity—the Justice Department's Antitrust Division. There were presumed to be numerous benefits in such concurrent jurisdiction. The underlying idea was succinctly stated by Senator Newlands, who, in introducing the original FTC bill, said: "The need has long been felt for an administrative board which would act in these matters in aid of the enforcement of the Sherman antitrust law, which would have precedents and traditions and a continuous policy and would be free from the effect of such changing incumbency as has in the nature of things characterized the administration of the Attorney General's office."

The Justice Department, as a general matter, has concerned itself almost exclusively with hard-core and clear-cut cases. The Commission, on the other hand, has been more willing to move into gray areas to fill the interstices of the Clayton Act. In doing this, the Commission relies on its economic expertise.

The Erosion of Independence

Since the creation of the first independent regulatory agencies, there has been an almost endless stream of legislative and judicial erosion of their independence.

Among the plethora of statutes enacted solely for housekeeping purposes, many subsequently proved to have considerable impact on the substantive work of the agencies. The first was the Budget and Accounting Act of 1921. That Act specified that henceforth the budgets and requests for appropriations of all governmental units, with the exception of the legislative and executive units, shall be submitted to the Bureau of the Budget (now the Office of Management and Budget) created by the Act. These budgets and requests for appropriations would be included in the nation's budget submitted by the President to Congress each year. Congressional debate indicates that passage of the Act reflected increasing concern over governmental economy. The United States had experienced its first budgetary deficit in 1918. To remedy this situation, it appeared necessary to wipe out duplications in government service, to eliminate inefficiency, to stop unnecessary work. Such were the motives prompting passage of the Act. The question remains whether Congress intended to curtail regulatory independence as, in fact, it did.

In practice, the Act resulted in a degree of control over agency programs that was certainly not envisioned by Congress. An agency's appropriation request is now reviewed by the Office of Management and Budget (OMB), which follows policies and priorities established by the President and not necessarily by Congress. To the extent that Presidential and congressional aims coincide, congressional intent will be fulfilled; to the extent that they differ, congressional intent will take a back seat.

Another development affecting the independence of regulatory agencies was passage of the Judges Act of 1925. The purpose of this Act was to collect in one statute the provisions of the law relating to appellate jurisdiction of the Supreme Court. At the same time, the Act sought to reduce this jurisdiction due to the backlog of cases before the Court. This was accomplished by the simple expedient of broadening the Court's authority to issue writs of certiorari, thus increasing the Court's discretion as to the cases it will hear. At that time, by leave of the Attorney General, the FTC and the ICC prepared their own requests for writs of certiorari and argued their own cases before the Supreme Court. In the case of the ICC, this practice, which had been codified in 1913, was reaffirmed by the Judges Act. At the same time, however, it was denied to the FTC by implication. Now, all independent agencies, with the exception of the ICC, do not ask the Supreme Court to grant a writ of certiorari directly but channel their requests through the Attorney General.

Sometime during the mid-1930's, the practice originated of submitting legislative proposals to Congress via the Bureau of the Budget. Franklin Roosevelt inaugurated the procedure, although there does not seem to be any statutory authority for it. In fact, it would appear to run contrary to the mandate of Section 6(f) of the FTC Act, which requires the Commission to submit, together with annual and special reports, recommendations for legislation directly to Congress. When the Commission is requested to report on specific legislative proposals, such reports are now cleared by the Office of Management and Budget before being submitted to the appropriate congressional committee. At the OMB, reports and recommendations receive clearance in light of the President's policy objectives.

Passage of the Federal Reports Act of 1942 put another crimp in the activities of the regulatory agencies. That Act was passed because the nation was engulfed in a blizzard of governmental questionnaires and paperwork concerning rationing, output, and prices to ensure successful prosecution of World War II. The Bureau of the Budget was given power to review proposed requests for information with a view to eliminating unnecessary and presumably duplicate reports. The Act enables the OMB to exercise considerable control over the investigative functions of the agencies.

ORGANIZATION AND REORGANIZATION

With every change in administration, there have been calls for reorganization of the regulatory agencies. Perhaps the most sweeping came in the late 1940's.

In 1947, the Hoover Commission was organized to report on governmental operations, with particular emphasis on efficiency. Its report, dated March 3, 1949, was to have a far-reaching impact on the independence of the regulatory agencies. For one thing, it changed the status of their chairmen.

Up to that time, with the exception of the Federal Communications Commission, whose organic statute provides for the appointment of its chairman by the President, the agencies selected their chairmen from among their members, generally, on an annual rotating basis. In addition, the agencies themselves decided how to handle intra-agency administrative detail.

The Hoover Commission recommended that, in the interest of efficiency and to "enable the President to obtain a sympathetic hearing of broader consideration of national policy which he feels the Commission should take into account," the FTC Chairman, like those of the other regulatory agencies, should be appointed by the President and should be given more administrative authority over his agency. These recommendations were written into the Reorganization Act of 1950. The Chairman was given authority: (1) to appoint and supervise personnel, (2) to distribute the workload among such personnel, and (3) to determine the use and expenditure of funds. The rationale behind this departure from past practice was that it would relieve the Commissioners from burdensome administrative chores such as ruling on the salaries of the char force and, theoretically at least, would free them to devote their energies to questions of policy.

There has been a continuing controversy as to whether the FTC should be organized along functional lines or by type of case. Prior to 1950, the structure reflected function. There were two principal bureaus—a Bureau of Legal Investigation to investigate and work up complaints and a Bureau of Litigation to handle court work. But the Hoover Commission advised President Harry S Truman as follows:

> Since different bureaus of the Commission are responsible for different stages of its cases and are relatively autonomous, this creates problems of coordination between bureaus on both general programs and particular matters. . . . A prime example

relates to the investigation and trial of cases.... One bureau collects a miscellany of facts, often unrelated to any particular theory of the case, and turns the data over to the trial lawyers to be fitted into a case that will stand up in the courts. In non-routine cases, and particularly in antimonopoly cases, there should be a close knitting of the investigation and trial aspects.

The Hoover Commission suggested that the agency reorganize along program lines, with one bureau to handle antimonopoly work and another to handle deceptive practices. This suggestion was adopted. But, following a management survey in 1954, the Investigation and Litigation bureaus were reconstituted. Then came the Landis Report of 1960.

Before taking office, President-elect Kennedy asked James M. Landis, a former Harvard Business School dean who had served briefly as an FTC Commissioner during the New Deal, to make a study of the regulatory agencies. With respect to the FTC, his report stated:

> Here, as in the case of the Interstate Commerce Commission, the Civil Aeronautics Board and the Securities and Exchange Commission, the powers of the Chairman should be increased and the Commission's authority to delegate decision-making implemented by Presidential Action under the Reorganization Act. . . . The responsibility for concentration on a particular area should be the responsibility of the Executive and not the Federal Trade Commission.

In a seemingly contradictory statement, the report added, "There has also been too much of the morale-shattering practice of permitting executive interference in the disposition of cases and controversies delegated to the agencies for decision." The Landis Report became the basis for Reorganization Plan No. 4, which went into effect in 1961. With respect to the FTC, it merely broadened the Chairman's authority, particularly in the assignment of work among Commission personnel and individual Commissioners.

At the beginning of the Kennedy Administration, the FTC returned to a program scheme of organization. The principal bureaus were the Bureau of Restraint of Trade and the Bureau of Deceptive Practices. There were four others: Economics, Field Operations, Textiles and Furs, and Industry Guidance. After Paul Rand Dixon was named Chairman on March 21, 1961, he made a reorganization of the staff. In a gesture aimed at bringing greater cohesiveness and over-all planning to the agency's work, he appointed a program review director, who was told to study the economy, select problem areas, and prepare plans calculated to resolve the problems. The new director never did come up with any recommendations, and, for a year or so at the end of Dixon's term as Chairman, the position was vacant.

By the late 1960's, too, the FTC had come under strong criticism from many quarters, including Ralph Nader and the American Bar Association. President Nixon's appointee as Chairman, Caspar W. Weinberger, was directed to "revitalize" the agency. As a first step, he requested the Budget Bureau to make a management survey, and then, on June 8, 1970, he announced a major reorganization to become effective on July 1. (See Chart II.) Under the reorganization, three of the operating bureaus—Field Operations, Textiles and Furs, and Industry Guidance—were abolished. The Bureau of Restraint of Trade was replaced by the Bureau of Competition, with seven divisions, and the Bureau of Deceptive Practices was replaced by a Bureau of Consumer Protection, with nine divisions. An Office of Policy, Planning, and Evaluation was set up to develop studies, reports, and recommendations on how and where the FTC should allocate its resources. The Bureau of Economics retained the same tasks and the same designation. As part of his program, Chairman Weinberger also said that the Commission would expand its field offices with the intention of initiating cases in the field. Two new positions within the Commission were created—an economic adviser to

CHART II

THE ORGANIZATION OF THE FEDERAL TRADE COMMISSION

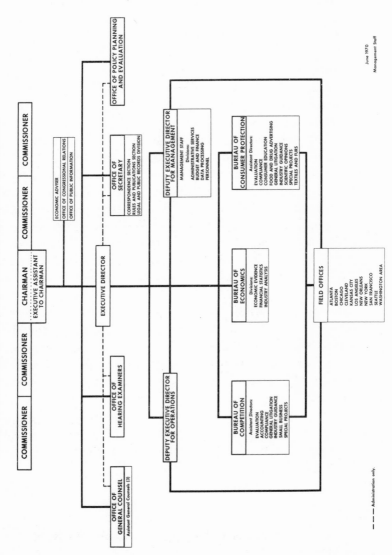

June 1970

Management Staff

- - - - Administration only.

help educate the staff and a congressional relations officer to work with Congress on legislation. Along with the Office of Public Information, these two officials report directly to the Commission through the Chairman's office. Two other new positions—deputy executive director for Operations and deputy executive director for Management—were put under the executive director, the Commission's chief administrative officer, to strengthen the agency's management and internal administration.

"In the transfer of responsibilities, field operational problems will be resolved by the deputy executive director for operations to the extent that they cannot be resolved by the bureau directors to whom the field offices will report on operational matters," the FTC said in an announcement of the reorganization. "The functions of the bureau of textiles and furs go to the bureau of consumer protection, and the guides and rules functions of the bureau of industry guidance are shifted to the bureaus of competition and consumer protection."

Seven assistant directorships were created in the Bureau of Competition: accounting, compliance, evaluation, general litigation, industry guidance, small business, and special projects. Nine assistant directorships were created in the Bureau of Consumer Protection: compliance, consumer education information, evaluation, food and drug advertising, general litigation, industry guidance, scientific opinions, special projects, and textiles and furs. The Office of the General Counsel was given responsibility for the Commission's program of giving businessmen advisory opinions.

Administrative Set-up

The Chairman sits at the top of the administrative pyramid, although power is vested equally in each of the Commissioners.

James M. Mead, a New York Democrat, was the first Chairman appointed by the President. He took his oath of office on November 16, 1949. Forty-seven Commissioners have served on the FTC since its creation in 1915. Although the statute provides for a term of seven years, only seventeen stayed that long. Eight held office for a decade. The five-member Commission is the final authority on all matters coming before the tribunal. Acting on a majority vote, it sets general policies, revises budget estimates, and allocates funds in addition to performing its adjudicative function in deciding cases appealed to the Commission.

Each Commissioner has a staff of three assistants who have, with one exception, all been lawyers. The FTC's first woman member, Mary Gardiner Jones, a New York lawyer and former member of the Justice Department's Antitrust Division who was named to the Commission by President Johnson, opted in favor of two lawyers and one economist. Until 1961, the Commission called on a special group of staff lawyers to help research and write opinions. Opinions are now written by individual Commissioners.

Complaints that have reached the Commission level are assigned to individual Commissioners by the secretary of the Commission, who tries to balance the workload of each member. Each Commissioner studies the case he is assigned and makes a report in the form of a memorandum circulated to his four colleagues. The Commissioners, meeting in executive session (other meetings are public), then decide how to dispose of the case. They can agree with, modify, or reject the recommendation of the staff or the Commissioner who has been assigned the case. A majority of the five members constitutes a quorum.

Acting in a capacity similar to that of clerk of court, the secretary takes minutes of Commission meetings and serves as custodian of the Commission's seal, property, papers, and records. He signs Commission orders and coordinates all liaison with Congress and other government departments and agencies. His office maintains a current index of opinions, orders, statements of policy and interpretations, staff manuals, and instructions that affect members of the public. The secretary is responsible, too, for seeing that all mail received by the FTC is answered. This duty alone imposes a heavy burden on the agency, which, with its consumer activities, receives more than 8,000 letters and other requests for action a year.

The Chairman, subject to the guidance and approval of his four colleagues, appoints an executive director as chief operating official of the FTC. Functioning somewhat like an executive vice-president of a corporation, the executive director exercises executive and administrative supervision over all the bureaus, offices, and staff. His authority is limited to administrative matters where the secretary and general counsel are concerned, however, since they work directly for the Commission.

The general counsel, the Commission's chief legal officer, is responsible for representing the Commission in the federal courts, drafting legislation, preparing legal memoranda, and advising the Commission on its rules and the current status of the law.

Although court trial work comes under the supervision of the general counsel, the Commission delegates the initial performance of its adjudicative functions to hearing examiners. Hearing examiners play an independent judicial role characteristic of the regulatory agencies. Their main task is fact-finding. They hold hearings on complaints that have been contested by respondents and issue initial decisions, which may be reviewed by the Commission on its own motion or appealed by the staff or the respondent. Hearing examiners are hired under the authority of the Civil Service Commission to assure independent status.

FIELD OFFICES

At the base of the administrative pyramid are the FTC's field offices, which play a key role in the Commission's work.

Attorneys in eleven field offices—in Atlanta, Boston, Chicago, Cleveland, Kansas City, New Orleans, New York, Los Angeles, San Francisco, Seattle, and Falls Church, Virginia— are responsible for obtaining evidence in cases where there may have been possible violation of law, for evaluating this evidence, and for making initial recommendations for action to the Commission. Field attorneys may also draft complaints and try cases of a regional nature.

Prior to the reorganization of 1970, in addition to the field offices, the FTC maintained ten field stations to carry out its textile and fur regulatory work. The reorganization made use of these field stations as well as the larger field offices to broaden the FTC's attack on fraud and deception practiced against consumers. Consumer-protection specialists have taken over the inspection work in the wool, textile, and fur industries in addition to carrying out a wide variety of enforcement activity and providing guidance to consumers, consumer groups, state and local officials, and the business community. As part of Weinberger's reorganization, consumer-protection coordinating committees were set up under the auspices of the field offices to serve as sounding boards for consumer complaints and to provide more effective coordination of the efforts of all three levels of government.

How Much Clout?

The FTC is a small agency by any standard. Richard Harwood of the *Washington Post* wrote in March, 1966: "What can be done by a miniature bureaucracy of fewer people (1140) and a smaller budget ($14 million) than the Railroad Retirement Board, which need only mail out pension checks on time?"

The combined annual budget of the FTC and the Justice Department's Antitrust Division in 1968 came to $23 million, the highest amount ever appropriated. With this sum, the two agencies were charged with collecting data, initiating investigations, and enforcing laws dealing with deceptive and anti-competitive practices in an $850 billion economy. In fiscal 1970, the FTC had a budget of $20.9 million and a staff of 1,330 employees, including nearly 500 attorneys, the largest single professional category, and some 40 economists.

One of the outstanding characteristics of the regulatory or administrative agencies is the sheer volume of business they do, however trivial much of it may be. During fiscal 1969, for example, the FTC received 11,927 applications for complaint, initiated or reopened 626 investigations, closed or completed 954 investigations, took 5,768 corrective actions, approved 215 consent orders, issued 221 orders to cease and desist, took 511 voluntary compliance actions, issued 128 advisory opinions, completed 2,093 compliance actions, and issued 8 trade regulation rules and guides. At year end, there were 1,664 investigations pending and 38 complaints awaiting litigation. During the month of August, 1968, the Commission received 911 letters of complaint, of which 615 came directly from the public and 66 were referred from the White House, 96 came from members of Congress, 45 from other federal agencies, 58 from state agencies, and 31 from consumer groups.

IV

FTC Tools: Industry Guidance and Law Enforcement

The Federal Trade Commission was never intended to act as a business policeman, ready and able to bring every violator of law to justice. It was created, rather, to provide explicit and intelligible guidance to businessmen on how to avoid those unfair methods of competition and deceptive acts and practices which would undermine the economic system. President Wilson originally conceived of the FTC as primarily a fact-finding body that would give advice and definite guidance to business. Congress added legislative and adjudicative authority with Section 5 of the FTC Act, which empowered the agency to conduct investigations, hold hearings, and issue cease-and-desist orders.

From the beginning, the FTC adopted a case-by-case approach to the application of the trade laws. This was done in the expectation that such an approach would clarify the laws and that, under threat of a lawsuit, those engaged in illegal action would mend their ways. The FTC for many years pursued a policy of suing as many firms as it could. In the process, it built up a formidable body of case law. By publicizing each case at every stage of prosecution, it educated business and the public on Commission policy. But the Commission soon realized that it was unable to sue every violator and came to rely on industry guidance as a preventive measure—on the theory that an ounce of prevention is worth a pound of cure. The FTC utilizes a variety of guidance techniques designed to fit different needs—trade practice rules for entire industries, guides covering particular problems common to many industries, trade regulation rules clearly defining the Commission's interpretation of the statutes as they apply to particular trade practices, and advisory opinions concerning proposed actions by individual businessmen or organized groups.

THE TRADE PRACTICE CONFERENCE

One of the first guidance procedures initiated by the FTC was called the Trade Practice Submittal. This procedure was first used in 1918 to deal with the numerous complaints about misleading branding of gold shell and gold-plated and gold-filled finger rings. It seemed impractical to proceed against each manufacturer, one by one, since the practice in question was industry wide, so the Commission, after consultation with industry leaders, called an all-industry conference at which rules covering the marking of gold content for rings were agreed upon. The first formally designated trade practice submittal came a year later, following a conference of book and writing-paper industry leaders.

The trade practice conference, as the procedure was renamed, developed and enjoyed substantial growth in the years that followed, with some twenty conferences held in the first six years of the Commission's existence. After 1926, when a separate division was set up within the agency to handle trade conferences, both the procedure and the rules surrounding them became more standardized.

GUIDES

An alternate, industry-wide voluntary compliance procedure known as the guides program was instituted in 1955. The guides, like many trade practice conference rules, are interpretive statements without the force of law, but they do serve to put businessmen on notice as to how they may avoid violating the law. The two procedures, though closely related, were handled separately in the agency until 1967. Both kinds of guidelines are now known as industry guides. Today, there are 175 guides in effect, including the older trade practice rules. They range across a broad segment of American business. Some cover specific industries—tires, furniture, jewelry, hosiery, hearing aids, phonograph records. Others cover general practices such as deceptive pricing and deceptive advertising of guarantees.

Guides are promulgated in different ways. Sometimes the Commission acts on its own initiative when it sees a need; at other times, interested parties apply. Guides have also been drafted by Commission staff as a result of informal conferences with industry or as a result of public hearings in which industry grievances are thrashed out. But, in any event, interested and concerned parties are given a chance to comment on proposed guides before they are approved by the Commission.

TRADE REGULATION RULES

The post-1960 Commission showed impatience with and skepticism about the willingness of businessmen to comply voluntarily with its guides. As a result, the guides program was augmented by the trade regulation rules procedure, which was adopted on June 1, 1962, one year after Chairman Dixon took over, as an experiment in industry-wide enforcement and a departure from the case-by-case approach to industry problems. The rules are intended to determine in a single proceeding issues that crop up over and over, such as whether cigarettes are harmful to health. Although industry guides are purely advisory, trade regulation rules represent the conclusions of the Commission and thus inform businessmen about practices that the Commission considers unlawful. The rules may be used in subsequent litigation.

In 1914, during the course of Senate debate on the antitrust legislation, Senator Newlands made it clear that he expected the Commission to use discretionary rule-making power. The final laws unequivocally echoed his view. Nevertheless, for the first fifty years of its life, the FTC had written no substantive rules except in a few instances in which they had been expressly authorized by such laws as the Fur Products Labeling Act. In 1964, following issuance of the U.S. Surgeon General's report on the effects of cigarette smoking, the FTC moved to use its rule-making power by issuing its proposed *Trade Regulation Rule for the Prevention of Unfair or Deceptive Advertising and Labeling of Cigarettes in Relation to the Health Hazards of Smoking.* The tobacco industry attacked the Commission's authority to make such industry-wide rules, but the question was never tested in the courts. In this case, Congress quickly took the matter out of the hands of the FTC.

Under the trade regulation rules procedure, the Commission publishes a notice of its intention to issue a rule dealing with a particular practice. Businessmen are then given an opportunity to present their views at hearings. Most of the rules deal with specific deceptive practices such as misrepresentation of the size of TV picture tubes, exaggerated claims for analgesics, failure to disclose that reclaimed motor oil has been previously used, or claims that dry cell batteries are leakproof.

Advisory Opinions

For the first forty-eight years of the Commission's existence, advice was given to businessmen on the legality of a proposed course of action only by members of the Commission staff and was not binding on the Commission itself. The need for advance rulings, especially for new methods of promotion, was obvious. In what was described as an effort to give the businessman something "more than the menace of legal process," the Commission reversed its historical position on June 1, 1962, when it initiated the practice of rendering formal, advisory, binding opinions. The advisory opinion procedure is designed to give businessmen, especially small businessmen who cannot afford to retain legal counsel, speedy answers to their questions. The FTC offers this kind of guidance not entirely from unselfish motives: it hopes to be spared the necessity of bringing lawsuits against numerous small enterprises.

Cautious by training, the legal experts at the FTC set conditions under which advisory opinions will or will not be rendered. The Commission will not attempt to give advisory opinions in cases that require extensive investigations— almost all *per se* monopoly and restraint-of-trade cases. If the agency were to undertake extensive fact-finding only to give advice, it would be burdened with extensive work for the sole benefit of the person presenting the question. Its opinions therefore tend to remain in the orbit of fair methods of competition. Neither will the FTC give advisory opinions if the plan of action is already in operation or if the activity is covered by existing federal agency programs.

Several trade associations have requested and obtained advisory opinions from the Commission covering such activities as issuing codes of ethics, setting product standards, and suggesting codes governing the members' dealings with their customers.

Advisory opinions may be rescinded by the Commission. In this event, the recipient is notified and given an opportunity to conform to the approved action. This has happened rarely, but the right is reserved as a precaution against the possibility of approving a course of action that might work against the public interest.

THE FTC AS POLICEMAN

President Wilson and the others who originally conceived the Federal Trade Commission did not anticipate that it would have direct regulatory authority or quasi-judicial power. What they envisioned was a governess agency for business. Many believed that, when the Trade Commission had defined a particular business conduct as an unfair method of competition and had issued its prophylactic cease-and-desist order, the business community would welcome the codification. There would then only be occasional enforcement proceedings and, in rare instances in which there was deliberate failure to obey an order, application to a circuit court of appeals. Deterrence was to be achieved by civil process. Neither the FTC Act nor the Clayton Act, as they emerged in 1914, contained any concept of criminality.

By a series of amendments to the original FTC statute, however, the concept of the cease-and-desist order was changed. Originally conceived of as largely an admonition, convertible, if necessary, to a judicial injunctive demand, the cease-and-desist order is today a self-executing order, the violation of which can carry monetary civil penalties of potentially great proportions. Paradoxically, the possible fine for violation of an FTC order can be larger than Congress specified in 1955 as the criminal fine for hard-core violations of the Sherman Act ($50,000).

Twenty-four years after enactment of the 1914 legislation, Congress both expanded the substantive reach of Section 5 of the FTC Act and completely changed the method of enforcement. The Wheeler-Lea Act of 1938, in addition to giving the FTC increased authority over food, drug, and cosmetic advertising, made cease-and-desist orders automatically final if not appealed within sixty days. This eliminated the much-criticized "three bites at the apple" procedure under which the FTC had operated. Previously, a first violation was required to sustain a cease-and-desist order, a second to secure a judicial order of enforcement, and a third to warrant punishment for contempt. Without elaboration in hearings or debate, Congress introduced into the FTC Act a new concept of punishment by civil penalty action. Thereafter, violation of a Commission order resulted in "a civil penalty of not more than $5,000 for each violation" recoverable in a civil action brought by the U.S. Government. The Act provided for certification by the Commission to the Justice Department of any case in which an action for penalties is ordered by the Commission. (There have been differences on occasion between the two agencies as to whether an action should be brought.) This change involved a move from enforcement by contempt of an order of the reviewing court to enforcement by civil suit.

Congress also provided in 1938 that the reviewing court might issue a temporary injunction during review, if necessary to prevent public or competitor injury in cases involving food, drugs, and cosmetics. It also provided that violation of Section 5 through false advertisements, where the commodity advertised might be injurious to health, would also constitute a misdemeanor punishable by fine (up to $5,000 for a first offense and $10,000 for a second offense) and by imprisonment.

Another addendum to the enforcement powers of the FTC was slipped into the statute twelve years later. During the course of a two-year debate preceding passage of the Oleomargarine Act of 1950, Senator George D. Aiken, of Vermont, a butter-producing state, became concerned about the possible advertising of colored margarine that might suggest that it was a "dairy product." He feared that an order prohibiting such advertising might be violated with impunity for an entire year, and yet the penalty for the violation would be only a modest $5,000. As a result, he offered on the floor of the Senate an addition to the oleomargarine bill which read: "Each separate violation of such an order shall be a separate offense, except that in the case of a violation through continuing failure or neglect to obey a final order of the Commission each day of continuance of such failure or neglect shall be deemed a separate offense." This "sleeper" was adopted casually by the Senate, but aroused strong objection in the House because of the absence of any hearings on the proposal and the impropriety of its inclusion in the oleomargarine legislation. But the measure passed. Each violation of a Commission order under Section 5 of the FTC Act became a separate offense, with the addition that for continuing failure or neglect to obey, each day of continuance was also to be a separate basis for a $5,000 penalty. The largest single penalty exacted up to 1959 had been $38,000 for violation of an order in a price-fixing case, and relatively few penalties have exceeded $5,000. In 1960, a contempt proceeding nudged the record up to $60,000, and, in a recent case, a penalty of $200,000 was imposed for violation of a Commission order not to make additional mergers without FTC approval.

Although the Commission's law enforcement powers are now an integral part of its operations, they are essentially preventive in nature. The Commission has no power to punish for past violations; it can only issue cease-and-desist orders requiring a party to abandon a past unlawful practice.

The FTC, like the Justice Department, follows three basic steps in handling cases—investigation, issuance of a complaint, and enforcement. Unlike Justice's, however, the FTC's procedures make it both complainant and judge. The FTC also limits its cases to those clearly involving the public interest, an approach spelled out by the Supreme Court in a 1929 ruling in *FTC* v. *Klesner,* in which the FTC had charged the respondent with "passing off" his store as that of another man. The Court ruled:

Section 5 of the Federal Trade Commission Act does not provide private persons with an administrative remedy for private wrongs. The formal complaint is brought in the Commission's name; the prosecution is wholly that of the Government; and it bears the entire expense of the prosecution. A person who deems himself aggrieved by the use of an unfair method of competition is not given the right to institute before the Commission a complaint against the alleged wrongdoer. Nor may the Commission authorize him to do so. He may of course bring the matter to the Commission's attention and request it to file a complaint. But a denial of his request is final. And if the request is granted and a proceeding is instituted, he does not become a party to it or have any control over it. . . . While the Federal Trade Commission exercises under Section 5 the functions of both prosecutor and judge, the scope of its authority is strictly limited. A complaint may be filed only "if it shall appear to the Commission that a proceeding by it in respect thereof would be to the interest of the public."

How the FTC Gets Cases

When the Commission first opened its doors, businesses rushed in with hundreds of complaint applications. Business interests sought a reckoning with their competitors, knowing that, under a procedure adopted almost immediately by the Commission, the names of those making application would not be revealed. For the first twenty-five years of the FTC's existence, almost 95 per cent of all requests for complaints came from competitors. They still do to a great extent.

The procedure for lodging a complaint is simple. All that is necessary is a letter to the Commission detailing the facts of a practice believed to constitute a violation of law. Requests for action are received from consumers, business competitors, government agencies, Congress, and the President. The Commission may also take action on its own initiative.

During its first year, the FTC adopted a policy of "utmost circumspection" in instituting formal proceedings. No formal proceeding would be undertaken, it was decided, without a thorough preliminary investigation. That proved to be a wise approach, for the Commission found that a considerable number of the early complaints were groundless.

A case is docketed only if it satisfies all of three jurisdictional requirements: it must deal with interstate rather than intrastate matters; it must involve a violation of one of the laws enforced by the FTC; and, finally, it must affect the public interest.

The FTC's problem in sorting out applications for complaints was described by Chairman Dixon in a speech delivered on April 18, 1967, to the Washington Conference on Business-Government Relations:

> The FTC in the past has often been accused of following an "in-box" approach to antitrust enforcement. Because we receive numerous complaints concerning trade practices from consumers and business, there is always a danger that our resources will be entirely consumed in an attempt to investigate all the matters brought to our attention. As a result, we could conceivably end up spending as much time investigating the handkerchief industry as we do the entire department store industry.

The FTC has developed some criteria for selecting targets for action. The Commission gives high priority to deceptive advertising cases involving the safety or health of large numbers of consumers and to cases involving points of law that need clarification. The Commission also takes into account three other factors: (1) the importance of the industry in terms of gross national product originating from it, (2) the size of the firm within the industry and the degree of concentration of the industry, (3) the number of man-hours required to investigate and follow up the complaint. "Although these are the types of criteria we keep in mind in planning our enforcement activities, it must be remembered that we also have a responsibility to each citizen who writes to the Commission," Dixon told his business audience. "Although we cannot follow up on every complaint, we sometimes take action on seemingly unimportant complaints simply because we do not want any company to feel that it is guaranteed immunity from the antitrust laws because of small size or obscurity."

Powers of Investigation

The Supreme Court, in a 1950 decision in *U.S.* v. *Morton Salt Co.,* described the power to investigate as the one "without which all others would be in vain." That decision upheld authority that had originally been granted to the FTC by Congress but had been severely modified by subsequent court decisions. The Federal Trade Commission Act provided the Commission with investigative powers greater than those granted to either the Interstate Commerce Commission or the Bureau of Corporations, including the so-called visitation power, the authority to require annual and special reports from any firm, and the power of subpoena.

Visitation power—access to all of a company's records during an investigation—has been characterized as an atomic bomb that proved to be a dud. Congress conceived of it as the most significant and effective of the Commission's investigative powers. But soon after the FTC began operations, this provision was said to constitute an unreasonable search and seizure in violation of the Fourth Amendment to the Constitution. Twice the issue was brought to the Supreme Court. In *F.T.C.* v. *American Tobacco Co.* in 1924, in which the FTC was overruled, Justice Oliver Wendell Holmes contended that the right of access given by the FTC Act was limited to documents to be used as evidence. "Anyone who respects the spirit as well as the letter of the Fourth Amendment would be loath to believe that Congress intended to authorize one of its subordinate agencies to sweep all our traditions into the fire . . . and to direct fishing expeditions into private papers on the possibility that they may disclose evidence of crime," he wrote. The Court later upheld the FTC's stand in *American Tobacco,* but Holmes's fishing-expedition principle was not abolished until the 1950 *Morton Salt* case. The Court asserted in that decision that "sometimes, especially early in the history of the federal administrative tribunal, the courts were persuaded to engraft judicial limitations upon the administrative process. The courts could not go fishing, and so it followed that neither could anyone else."

In the *Morton Salt* case, in which the Commission had brought suit against Morton for refusing to heed its request for a report on the company's compliance with an FTC order against illegal price discrimination, the Court also upheld the Commission's authority to require special reports from corporations. "An administrative agency charged with seeing that the laws are enforced . . . has a power of inquisition . . . which is not derived from the judicial function," the Court said. "It is more analogous to the grand jury, which does not depend on a case or controversy for power to get evidence but can investigate merely on suspicion that the law is being violated, or even just because it wants assurance that it is not." The FTC had for many years been severely handicapped by adverse court decisions in exercise of its power to require corporations to file special reports in answer to specific questions. In the most limiting, the 1927 *Claire Furnace Co.* case, the Court had ruled that the Commission could not itself appeal for enforcement of requests for information but could only submit its requests to the Attorney General for whatever action he might choose to take. As a result, the Commission made little use of its report power until after World War II.

The power to require special corporation reports is vital for a number of Commission activities. Reports have been used to gather information for the *Quarterly Financial Report for Manufacturing Corporations,* prepared jointly by the FTC and the Securities and Exchange Commission, and for general economic surveys conducted by the Commission. Special reports have also been used to gather data in the trial of antimonopoly cases, particularly merger cases, as well as to investigate compliance with cease-and-desist orders. In recent years, the Commission has used its special report power to conduct general investigations of alleged violations of the antitrust laws and trade regulations throughout an entire industry.

The Commission's subpoena power, its third investigative weapon, was fairly clearly established in a series of Supreme Court decisions in the 1950's. Section 9 of the FTC Act confers the "power to require by subpoena the attendance and testimony of witnesses and the production of all such documentary evidence relating to any matter under investigation." Historically, the principal issue here was whether a party under investigation could be compelled to give evidence in the absence of a charge or allegation that he had violated some provision of existing law. On this issue, the Supreme Court held that the FTC was given subpoena power to aid investigation. "The very purpose of the subpoena and of the order, as of the authorized investigation, is to discover and procure evidence, not to prove a pending charge or complaint, but upon which to make one, if, in the Administrator's judgment, the facts thus discovered should justify doing so." The test—that the subpoena is good if "the investigation is authorized by Congress, is for a purpose Congress can order, and the documents are relevant to the inquiry"—remains the basic criterion of the law of administrative investigations. The FTC may request the Attorney General to enforce a subpoena by bringing action in a U.S. district court or to institute civil proceedings to compel the filing of a special or annual report. Disobedience of a court decree enforcing a Commission order or subpoena may be punished as a contempt of court.

Each of the FTC's investigative powers has teeth in it. For a refusal to "submit to the commission or to any of its authorized agents, for the purpose of inspection and taking copies, any documentary evidence of such corporation," the penalty is a fine of not less than $1,000 or more than $5,000, or imprisonment for not more than three years, or both fine and imprisonment. For a refusal to testify or to produce documents "in obedience to the subpoena" of the Commission, the penalty is $1,000 to $5,000 and not more than one year's imprisonment. Refusal to obey a Commission order to file a written report to provide answers to specific questions subjects the corporation to a forfeiture of $100 per day.

LIMITED INJUNCTIVE POWERS

Unlike Justice, the FTC lacks statutory authority to use the temporary injunction except in a few carefully circumscribed cases. In an effort to grant adequate protection to the public during the period pending issuance of and final action on a Commission complaint, the agency was authorized in 1938 to bring suit to enjoin the dissemination of false advertisements of food, drugs, devices, and cosmetics. Such temporary injunctions were to remain in effect until the order of the Commission to cease and desist became final, unless the complaint was dismissed by the Commission or the order was set aside by a court on review. Similar injunctive powers were included in the later specialty statutes giving the FTC jurisdiction over furs, textiles, and flammable fabrics.

The FTC has used its injunctive powers sparingly, and, despite an occasional setback in the courts, its record of success in these cases has been excellent. For a long time, the FTC limited the situations in which it sought temporary injunctions to those in which the product was dangerous to health or when there was likely to be irreparable and substantial financial loss to the public. In 1966, a Supreme Court ruling confirmed the FTC's right to seek an injunction from the appellate courts to prevent actions by respondents that would nullify a Commission order to cease and desist.

This limited injunctive power has been a crippling restriction on the FTC's authority. Beginning with Chairman Kintner in the 1950's, all FTC Chairmen have asked, in vain, that temporary injunctive powers be extended to cover all types of products. Chairman Dixon described the problem before the House Committee on Interstate and Foreign Commerce in March, 1967:

> By the time we finish the hearings and issue an order, the offender often has counted his money and even embarked on a different practice as illegal as the previous one we challenged. If temporary injunctive relief were available as soon as we had enough evidence to make out a *prima facie* case of law violation —and thereby protect the public while the litigation is going on—it would prevent many of the hit-and-run offenses that now defraud the public.

The Complaint Procedure

When letters of complaint come to the Commission, they are directed by the secretary's office to the appropriate bureau. The staff then investigates the matter and makes a recommendation either to close the case, issue a formal complaint, or settle the case with a respondent's assurance that he will discontinue the practice.

If it is decided that a legal proceeding is in the public interest, the staff draws up the complaint document. Theoretically, both the Commission and the General Counsel's Office pass on this document, not to decide on the merits of the case, but to determine whether it is based on sound legal theory, follows correct form, adheres to precedents, and so forth. If the Commission decides to issue the complaint, the party named as respondent is served with notice of the Commission's intention, sent a copy of the complaint, and given a chance to consent to a cease-and-desist order without admitting any violation of the law. If a consent agreement is not entered into, the Commission may then formally issue the complaint and set a hearing date.

A complaint is issued whenever the Commission has found "reason to believe" that the law has been violated and that a proceeding is in the public interest. The issuance of a complaint simply marks the initiation of a formal proceeding in which the charges will be ruled upon after a hearing. It does not indicate adjudication of the matters charged.

CONSENT SETTLEMENT

Before a complaint is formally issued, the Commission sends a copy of it to those charged with the alleged fair-trade violation. The proposed complaint, in addition to naming the party or parties accused and presenting the charges, affords an opportunity for reply. If the respondents do not file an answer, the complaint may be formally issued. If they are willing to promise compliance, without necessarily admitting guilt, the terms of a consent order are worked out with the Commission staff, and the order is issued, if approved by the Commission. Consent orders differ from orders in litigated cases in that they do not constitute a finding or an admission that respondents have violated the law. But they are fully as binding in forbidding respondents to engage in the practices prohibited by the order. Consent orders may not be appealed to the courts. Sixty days after issuance, they become enforceable by fines up to $5,000 per day per violation.

An antecedent to the consent order was a procedure known as stipulating, a practice thought to be a revolutionary departure in law enforcement when it was introduced in 1925. There were strong disagreements among the Commissioners before it was adopted, but the arguments of greater informality, less expense, and the ability to handle more cases while employing sanctions allegedly as satisfactory as those resulting from formal proceedings outweighed the arguments against it. Some 3,000 cases were disposed of in this manner during the FTC's first ten years, and the proceeding was widely used, with some modifications, until 1961.

Under the procedure, a prospective respondent cleared himself after a complaint had been served on him by signing a stipulation admitting the practices charged and agreeing to desist from them thereafter. When the paper was accepted, the case was closed without penalty. If the person violated the stipulation, a complaint would follow immediately and the facts set forth in the signed statement would be used against the violator in a formal hearing. Stipulating was used more often in cases involving relatively minor methods of unfair competition than in those related to monopoly problems.

In 1951, the Commission's consent order procedure took on the flexible form it now possesses when the Commission provided that a respondent need only admit the jurisdictional facts in the order. He was not required to admit to, although he could not deny, the alleged unlawful acts and practices. In 1954, the consent settlement procedure was further liberalized by the adoption of a rule dispensing with the requirement that consent settlements be based on findings of fact.

When Chairman Dixon took office, he became convinced that too much time and effort were going into negotiations to arrive at agreements that did little to interpret Commission policy or establish legal precedent. The Commission decided that a simple letter of assurance would accomplish the same result without tying up the staff in lengthy investigations and negotiations. The stipulation procedure was thus abandoned for voluntary assurance. This optimistic approach to industry regulation was, in fact, one of the points singled out for special criticism by Ralph Nader's student investigators.

FORMAL HEARINGS

If a complaint is contested, a public hearing is required. Two steps are involved: a preliminary hearing before a trial examiner, followed by an oral hearing before the Commission, if the case is appealed. At both stages, the respondent may be, and normally is, represented by an attorney. The proceeding followed before the hearing examiner is similar to a court action governed by the Federal Rules of Civil Procedure. The respondent is given the opportunity to cross-examine witnesses and to present evidence in rebuttal. After the hearings are completed and evidence has been received from both sides, the hearing examiner makes his decision.

Hearings rarely proceed as smoothly as this description suggests. Commissioner Elman outlined some of the problems before the Administrative Law Section of the American Bar Association on August 7, 1961: "A hearing will be held in various cities on the installment plan, moving along in spurts and jerks for years or even decades. In this Alice-in-Wonderland way of trying a case, it is not surprising that it took 16 years to enter a final order deleting the word 'liver' from the name of a brand of 'little pills.' " At the same time, he announced that the Commission had taken two steps to eliminate "these inexcusable delays." First, its administrative structure had been reorganized to centralize staff responsibility. Second, the Commission had "drastically" revised its Rules of Practice. As a result of these changes, Elman said:

> The hearing will not be a game of combat by surprise, but will be an inquiry for the ascertainment of facts, fairly, expeditiously and economically. . . . There will be mandatory prehearing procedures, to simplify the issues and expedite presentation of evidence. . . . The hearing examiner will see that a case is proved only once, not many times over. And, most important, the hearing will be held at one place and continue without suspension until finished, unless the Commission orders otherwise upon a certificate of necessity filed by the hearing examiner.

Prior to 1950, the hearing examiner's decision took the form of a recommendation; the issuance of orders was reserved to the Commission itself, which could adopt, modify, or reject the examiner's decision. The respondent was given sixty days more in which to file a report of compliance or appeal the decision to the courts. Under a procedure adopted in 1950, the trial examiner's decision achieves the status of a cease-and-desist order unless reviewed by the Commission on its own motion or appealed within thirty days by either side to the dispute. If the initial decision is appealed to the full Commission, it may modify the order. In appeal cases, a final hearing is held before the full Commission.

Hearings are held in a large wood-paneled room resembling a court. The five Commissioners sit at a raised bench in front of which are counsel tables, a small table for the official recorder, and a podium on which witnesses may place their notes. The staff and those taking part in the proceeding usually take the front seats in the spectator section.

Appeal of initial decisions to the full Commission is allowed as a matter of right, and it is common procedure for either the staff counsel supporting the complaint or the counsel for the respondent to make such an appeal. It is also not unusual for the Commission to decide that a complaint it has issued should be dismissed because the evidence or the legal theory on which the case is based does not stand up when all the facts have been presented by both sides.

It is unusual for the commissioners of a regulatory agency to preside at rule-making sessions. Normally, a member of the Commission staff hears testimony and then presents his report to the Commission, which may then adopt, reject, modify, or shelve the staff recommendations. After examining the record, the Commission can call a second set of hearings over which its members may preside individually or as a group.

In recent years, there has been a decrease in the number of cases handled by hearing examiners, a reflection of the Commission's emphasis on guidance rather than formal litigation. During fiscal 1966, there were 71 cases on the hearing examiners' docket; in fiscal 1965, there had been 100. The number of FTC hearing examiners has also been reduced from a high of about twenty-four in the mid-1960's to eleven in 1970.

CEASE-AND-DESIST ORDERS

If the Commission decides against a respondent, the next step is the issuance of a cease-and-desist order. The order is the culmination of a Commission proceeding and rests upon proof of a complaint related to the agency's underlying statutes. It sets forth findings and conclusions and forbids the respondent from engaging in the alleged illegal practice. The order acts as an injunction and remains in effect indefinitely. Within 60 days from the order's date of issuance, a respondent must file a report setting forth the manner of compliance.

The task of drafting orders to proscribe future violations of the turgid and imprecise statutes enforced by the FTC has led to two quite opposite tendencies. One is to prepare lengthy, intricate provisions that become accepted or required for all similar (and even some unrelated) proceedings. Thus, a phrase prohibiting concerted or planned concerted action might read "entering into, conducting, cooperating in, or carrying out any planned common course of action, understanding, agreement, combination, or conspiracy between or among any two or more of the said respondents, or between any one or more of said respondents and any others not parties hereto." An easier technique is to phrase the prohibition in the formal, but obscure, language of the statute. Often, at least in earlier days, the basic order was formulated to cover all violations of the fair trade statutes and then appended with a necessary series of provisos. When called upon to defend this dragnet approach in court, the Commission resorted to clichés such as "the Commission [could not] be required to confine its road block to the narrow lane the transgressor has traveled; it must be allowed effectively to close all roads to the prohibited goal."

In advertising cases, orders have been tailored to the claims made, although the contest between the copywriter's skill and the Commission's insistence that it alone can determine the implied message of words, pictures, or combinations of both in television advertising has created an expanding field for litigation. A battle rages within the Commission over the wording of orders against price discrimination, which are still entered in the words of the statute. The courts have frequently asked the Commission to redraft or modify orders, and, in many cases, reviewing courts have rewritten orders themselves.

Most Commission orders were not appealed until after 1938, when respondents found themselves under the threat of large penalties. Review is foreclosed for those who have entered consent orders.

During its first years, the Commission issued a full set of findings with its orders, but no opinions. It was believed that preparing opinions would absorb too much time and energy. Furthermore, the majority of the Commission, observing the enormous number of opinions that were coming forth from courts and other commissions, hesitated to write on economic questions when they knew lawyers would interpret the application of law to the facts in one case as a precedent for the application of law to similar facts in another. The Commission was also apparently reluctant to take action in its role as judge that might in some way embarrass it in the role of prosecutor.

During the early 1920's, several Commissioners wanted to express their views in written opinions. Those in the minority wanted to explain why they were taking a position contrary to the silent majority. The result was a series of informal minority expressions on the part of several members, including Commissioners Huston Thompson, John F. Nugent, and, later, the flamboyant Lowell Mason.

With the development of administrative law and the growing complexity of matters put before the Commission, however, the necessity for opinions grew. Throughout the early 1940's, the American Bar Association and other law experts recommended that the Commission give its reasons for issuing cease-and-desist orders. The practice of dismissing complaints without opinions had engendered confusion. Finally, in 1946, Congress passed Section 8 of the Administrative Procedure Act, which said, in part: "All decisions (including initial, recommended, or tentative decisions) shall become part of the record and include a statement of . . . findings and conclusions, as well as the reasons or basis therefor, upon all the material issues of fact, law, or discretion presented on the record." Since then, the FTC has issued opinions with its orders.

APPEAL TO THE COURTS

Respondents in FTC cases may appeal decisions to the courts, but the findings of the Commission as to the facts, if supported by evidence, are conclusive. This was one of the limits the FTC Act set on the interpretive role of the courts. It was later underlined when, in 1934, the Supreme Court upheld a Commission decision that had been overruled by a court of appeals.

The presumed expertise of the Commission, as well as the relative finality of its findings of fact, provides a losing party with a hard row to hoe. Appeals are normally made on points of law, although, under certain circumstances, suits challenging the Commission's jurisdiction or methods of procedure may be brought in a U.S. district court. The Commission's interests in these matters are presented and defended by the Justice Department through the local U.S. attorneys, who receive assistance from the office of the FTC general counsel.

The appeals court may enter a decree affirming and enforcing an FTC order, requiring its modification, or setting it aside. A copy of the petition is given to the FTC's General Counsel's Office, which represents the agency in the courts. A staff lawyer is then placed in charge of the case to see it through the appeals process, which can take up to three years.

If the respondent loses in the circuit court of appeals, he can request the Supreme Court to review the action of the lower court by filing for a writ of certiorari. Certiorari allows the Court to exercise discretion as to the cases over which it will take appellate jurisdiction. On the other hand, if the Commission loses before the appeals court, it can request the Solicitor General, who handles federal government cases brought before the Supreme Court, to file a petition of certiorari if he agrees that the FTC case should be taken to the high court. Briefs are prepared by staffs of the FTC and the Justice Department, and the case is argued in the Supreme Court by either the Solicitor General or one of the lawyers in his office.

COMPLIANCE AND PENALTIES

Every cease-and-desist order contains a compliance clause that requires the respondent to file a report, within 60 days of the effective date of the order, spelling out how he is complying. The Commission's authority to do this was upheld by the Supreme Court in the 1950 *Morton Salt* case, and defendants in that case were subsequently fined a total of $80,000 for refusal to report. Special sections within each FTC bureau check on these orders. If the respondent is not in compliance, the FTC can then go into federal district court to ask for civil penalties. Under some circumstances when enforcement efforts fail, it can also go to the circuit courts to seek criminal penalties against officers of the firm in question. Although the FTC monitors advertising and makes other checks on compliance, most compliance action results from complaints from competitors or disclosures or omissions in the compliance reports themselves.

During most of its life, the Commission made little effort to determine whether its orders had actually been observed. In 1947, a Compliance Division was set up within the FTC, but it was not until 1954, during the Eisenhower Administration, that the Commission made a concerted effort to check compliance with outstanding orders and to require regular compliance reports. At that time, the FTC inaugurated a comprehensive investigation of compliance with outstanding orders.

As a result of these systematic efforts to review compliance, many civil penalty suits for noncompliance have been filed since the 1950's. Prior to that time, the Commission rarely moved to punish violations unless outsiders brought renewed complaints. In case of noncompliance, the Commission applies to the appropriate federal appeals court to affirm and enforce its order. The 1914 FTC Act specified no penalty for violators of final orders, but the 1938 Wheeler-Lea Act provided, in addition to authority to institute actions to recover civil penalties, definite and substantial civil penalties through suits brought by the Attorney General for violation of cease-and-desist orders.

All the statutes enforced by the FTC carry criminal penalties for "willful" violations of cease-and-desist orders. These penalties may extend to a fine of $5,000 per day per violation or imprisonment for one year or both. Criminal prosecutions have been rare, but, in 1966, the Commission obtained from the Supreme Court confirmation of the criminal contempt jail sentence. The president of a respondent company was sentenced to a 6-month imprisonment for violation of a cease-and-desist order in the *Holland Furnace Co.* case.

V

The Role of the Economist

The creators of the Federal Trade Commission, impressed by the specter of vast economic power and market concentration at the end of the nineteenth century, gave a unique and important task to the FTC—that of developing reliable knowledge of the anatomy of the American economic system. The Wilsonian premise underlying this charge was that a democratic society must be adequately informed if it is to make sound public policy. As an outgrowth of the FTC's examination of business practices, Congress anticipated that the Commission, with expert knowledge of the functioning of the economy, would develop appropriate and particularized remedies, and, where necessary, make recommendations for needed legislation. The Commission's ability to carry out these tasks resides in its powers of investigation and economic inquiry. It is thus both natural and necessary that there be a marriage of legal and economic talents within the FTC.

ECONOMIC STUDIES

The FTC's economic reporting function is a direct outgrowth of the work of the Bureau of Corporations. Between

1905 and 1914, the Bureau published thirteen separate economic reports, many of them running to several volumes. These reports included, among others, analyses of the beef, petroleum, tobacco, and steel industries, a report on International Harvester Company, and a study of the economic effects of state taxation. The staff of the Bureau of Corporations was transferred almost intact to the FTC, and Dr. Francis Walker, assistant commissioner of Corporations, became the FTC's first chief economist. He retained that position until his retirement on December 31, 1940. In addition to the Bureau's pending economic investigations, the FTC inherited the knowledge of American industry gained by its predecessor and a fledgling economic reporting program.

Although Congress clearly had given the FTC the power to conduct wide-ranging economic investigations, the Commission began slowly. The great majority of the early economic inquiries were made at the request of Congress, other government agencies, or the President. Only a small number were undertaken on the motion of the Commission, although there has been an increased willingness on the part of the FTC to initiate investigations as congressional requests have declined.

The FTC's economic reports, which are published by the Government Printing Office, cover almost all important industries and a wide variety of business practices. They contain a comprehensive body of economic intelligence relating to the structure and operation of American industry, including information on resale price maintenance, international cartels, interlocking directorates, and mergers. They cover a wide spectrum of industries, such as cement, motor vehicles, tires, bread, installment credit, cotton, coal, canned food, farm implements, and millinery, as well as export trade associations. They encompass such diverse subjects as agricultural income, changes in the price of flags, profit margins in chain stores, advertising allowances, commercial bribery, cotton merchandising, public utilities, and livestock prices.

The value of the FTC's economic reports has been recognized by such vocal critics of the agency as the Hoover Commission, which said in 1949 that, of all FTC activities, the Commission's investigations have probably had "the most substantial impact and enduring value." The reports have also engendered controversy, and none more so than one of the agency's first—its investigation of the meat-packing industry.

THE MEAT-PACKING INVESTIGATION

At the beginning of World War I, President Wilson and Congress requested the Commission to make a number of special economic reports in connection with the nation's wartime needs. As a starter, on February 7, 1917, the President directed the Commission to conduct a comprehensive study of the entire food industry. Out of this effort grew what was to become a baptism by fire for the young agency—the meat-packing investigation. From the beginning, it was given the personal attention and direction of the Commissioners.

The Chicago meat packers had long been the object of attacks by farmers, merchants, and consumers as well as the subject of periodic investigation by the government after passage of the Sherman Act. It was well known that the major packers—the Swift, Armour, Wilson, Morris, and Cudahy companies—were in a position to control markets and prices. A preliminary report, issued by the FTC in 1917, stated that there was only an artificial show of competition among the Big Five packers: "Some independent packers exist by sufferance of the five, and a few hardy ones have survived in real competition. Around such few of these as remain the lines are drawing in." Further, the FTC said, the major packers had formed an unlawful combination to control the livestock market as well as prices and conditions in the sale of packing house products. And they were "using their enormous power and wealth to extend their control into many branches of the food business wholly unrelated to the business of meat and its by-products."

Two years later, the Commission sent its unpublished reports and basic evidence to the Justice Department and loaned six staff members to the Antitrust Division there to assist in contemplated grand jury proceedings. Meanwhile, the packers were becoming much concerned with adverse publicity, including Upton Sinclair's book *The Jungle,* and congressional threats of drastic regulatory legislation.

On August 24, 1919, the Commission submitted its report on the meat-packing industry to the Senate. Shortly thereafter, A. Mitchell Palmer, Wilson's Attorney General, announced that a criminal suit would be brought against the packers. There was an immediate uproar in Congress. Several members called for an investigation of the FTC, alleging that its report must have been inspired by Bolsheviks; others stoutly defended the agency's courage and zeal. A Senate resolution to investigate the Commission, strongly backed by Senator James E. Watson, an Indiana Republican, was introduced. The resolution was voted down by a substantial majority, but the charges against the agency and the ensuing discussion weakened the confidence of many in the fairness of the FTC and its report.

With the FTC on the firing line, Attorney General Palmer took over much of the responsibility for handling the government's case. The packers, hoping to put an end to public indignation and to ward off regulatory legislation, proposed a consent decree. Without consulting the FTC, Palmer negotiated a decree and, before it was entered, told a Senate committee that he saw no need for further legislation. The proposed decree attempted to divorce the packers from control of stockyard markets, market newspapers, and other facilities. Signed on February 27, 1920, the Packer's Consent Decree prohibited them from retailing meat, handling groceries, and loaning customers refrigerator cars and other equipment. The packers were also enjoined from owning or controlling any public stockyards and were required to divest themselves of any yards they owned. Pursuant to court orders, the packers submitted a proposal for disposing of their interests in fifteen principal public stockyards to F. H. Prince & Company. Following an investigation disclosing a close relationship between the Prince Company and the packers, the FTC informed the Attorney General that the plan not only would not carry out the separation decree but also would create a more serious infraction of the antimonopoly laws. The packers, undaunted, came back with another plan, proposing, among other things, that Armour & Company sell its interest in the Chicago stockyards to F. H. Prince. This plan was approved before the FTC could state its objections. After Attorney General Palmer was succeeded by Harry M. Daugherty with the advent of the Harding Administration, the packers and affiliated interests, by a series of legal maneuvers, managed to side-step the injunctions of the decree in whole or in part for more than twelve years.

Meanwhile, for its pains, the FTC had been left out in the cold. Congress passed the Packers and Stockyards Act in 1921, transferring jurisdiction over stockyards from the FTC to the Agriculture Department, despite widespread opposition from public leaders. The episode taught the FTC that pressure groups and their congressional supporters play a rough game. The agency thereafter became more cautious in taking on the giants of American industry.

Economic Studies and New Laws

A number of FTC industrial inquiries have played a role, sometimes a decisive role, in showing the need for new laws and new approaches to business regulation. The first to result in legislative proposals was the two-volume *Report on Co-operation in American Export Trade,* published in 1916. The report concluded that U.S. exporters were forced to compete with cartels in many foreign countries, some of which were backed by government subsidies. The Webb-Pomerene Export Trade Act was passed on April 10, 1918, in large part as a result of FTC findings. Firms forming or joining an export trade association were thus enabled to engage in many activities that would result in prosecution if undertaken in domestic trade.

The *Report of the FTC on the Radio Industry,* requested by the House of Representatives and completed in 1923, contributed materially to passage of the Radio Act of 1927 and the Federal Communications Act of 1934. A seven-part *Report on the Grain Trade,* prepared from 1924 to 1926, was an important factor in congressional enactment of the Grain Futures Act. The Commission staff also played a significant role in developing information on securities markets, which led to passage of the Securities Act of 1933.

One FTC achievement in a relatively inactive period during the Coolidge Administration was an extensive inquiry into the electric and gas utilities. The Commission, directed by the Senate in 1928 to conduct this monumental investigation, labored for four years on the financial and holding-company operations of public utilities. The final report was transmitted to the Senate on December 31, 1935. Nearly 100 printed volumes of hearings, summaries, and appendixes were published under the general title *Utility Corporations.* Almost every aspect of the operation of 29 major holding companies, 70 subholding companies, and 278 operating companies was covered. The FTC findings laid the foundations for the Public Utility Act of 1935, the Natural Gas Act of 1938, the Securties Act of 1933, and enlargement of the Federal Power Commission's powers through passage of the 1935 Federal Power Act.

In 1928, the Senate requested the Commission to make another landmark investigation, this time into the operations of chain stores. The FTC was directed to ascertain the extent to which consolidations had been effected in violation of the antitrust laws and to see whether there were evidences of unfair methods of competition in commerce or of agreements, conspiracies, or combinations in restraint of trade. It was to recommend what, if any, legislation should be enacted to regulate and control chain-store distribution. Results of the investigation were published in a series of thirty-three reports, the last of which was submitted to the Senate on December 14, 1934. The reports showed that special discounts and allowances were made available to chain stores with greater frequency and in larger amounts than to independent stores and contained recommendations for amending the Clayton Act to outlaw such discriminatory practices. Congress conducted another investigation. Bills were then introduced by Representative Wright Patman and Senator Joseph Robinson, out of which developed the Robinson-Patman Act, an amendment to Section 2 of the Clayton Act, barring certain types of price discrimination.

Perhaps the most significant legislation to grow out of FTC economic studies was the Celler-Kefauver Act of 1950, amending the antimerger section of the Clayton Act. In 1948, the Commission had published *The Merger Movement: A Summary Report* as part of a series of studies on corporate mergers. This report reviewed the legal history of the antimerger provisions of the Clayton Act and discussed individual mergers in detail, using maps, diagrams, charts, and tabular statistical materials to illustrate the effects of mergers. The subsequent legislation capped a twenty-four-year campaign by the Commission to convince Congress to close the loophole in the Clayton Act that permitted mergers through acquisition of assets.

New Deal Economics

FTC economists were deeply involved in the most dramatic and sweeping investigation of American industry ever undertaken—that of the Temporary National Economic Committee (TNEC) set up by Congress in 1938 at the request of President Roosevelt to study the concentration of economic power and its "detrimental consequences." In fact, the FTC's earlier studies on the basing-point system used in establishing prices in the cement and steel industries were instrumental in convincing the New Deal Administration of the need for a wide-ranging inquiry into the American economy. Fully one-third of the Commission's economic reports activity from 1938 to 1941 was devoted to the preparation of testimony, exhibits, and special reports for the TNEC investigations. The Commission also prepared monographs on the basing-point problem, the natural gas industry, and the relative efficiency of large, medium-sized, and small businesses.

Since World War II

In recent years, the FTC has conducted general inquiries into coffee prices, the baking industry, the frozen orange juice concentrate and vegetable industries, export trade associations, the cement and tire industries, and antibiotic drug manufacturing. Most of its emphasis, however, has been focused on two major economic problems—concentration in the domestic economy and international cartels.

In 1954, the FTC completed a comprehensive study of corporate mergers to determine those which tend to lessen competition. Since then, yearly statistical reports have been published on mergers in manufacturing and mining. A special report on conglomerate mergers was issued in 1969. The FTC has also published reports on general and specific industry concentration.

REPORTING ON CORPORATE FINANCES

The legislative history of the FTC Act shows that the Commission was expected to collect basic economic and financial statistics from corporations. This task, a carry-over from the work of the Bureau of Corporations, has not always proved easy.

In 1919, the House Appropriations Committee asked the FTC for its recommendations on ways of reducing the cost of living. In response, the Commission suggested the collection and publication of data regarding costs, prices, and profits of producers and distributors in coal, steel, and a number of other basic industries. It was believed that, if profits were large, the pressure of public opinion would bring about price reductions. Congress appropriated $150,000 specifically for that program, and, beginning in January, 1920, coal, coke, and steel producers were required to file detailed monthly reports showing quantities produced, value of shipments, production and marketing costs, and profits. Plans were made to expand these reports to other industries, but this program lasted less than six months. On June 12, 1920, Maynard Coal Company, and, shortly thereafter, the Claire Furnace Company were successful in obtaining injunctions preventing the Commission from requiring submission of the reports, on the grounds that the companies were not engaged in interstate commerce.

In 1938, the Commission revived its interest in the collection and publication of general financial statistics. Under the direction of the Central Statistical Board of the Bureau of the Budget, an interagency committee was set up to develop a program of collecting financial statistics. As finally determined, the Department of Commerce was designated to collect data on sales, orders booked, and inventories; the FTC was to collect complete profit-and-loss and balance sheet data.

In December, 1939, using its authority under Section 6 of the FTC Act, the Commission adopted a resolution requiring the submission of financial reports. During World War II, this program was transferred to the Office of Price Administration. After the war, it was handed over to the FTC and the Securities and Exchange Commission. Quarterly financial data for manufacturing corporations have been published jointly by the two agencies in the *Quarterly Financial Report for Manufacturing Corporations* since 1947. These financial summaries, used by the President's Council of Economic Advisers and others, present composite income statement and balance sheet data for all active manufacturing corporations by industry and asset size.

THE ECONOMIST AND LAW ENFORCEMENT

When it comes to law enforcement, the FTC economist plays only a small part. He does carry responsibility for developing the economic theory of a case and for mustering the facts to test its validity. He must therefore know his industry and be able to cut through a maze of industrial data. If the facts do not support the theory, then either the theory is no good or there is no case. The FTC tries to assign to each investigation an economist who already has considerable knowledge of the industry involved, but this is not always possible because there are simply not enough experienced industry economists on tap. Academic consultants are frequently used to fill in. Economists also often play a central role in determining the relevancy and validity of sources of data.

In hearings, evidence generally must be placed in the record by witnesses other than economists. Merger cases are the exception. Government economists may also be called as witnesses to comment on statistical procedures used by respondent witnesses.

In antitrust cases, it has been widely held that there is little need for economic expertise. The lawyers on each side have read the applicable legal precedents. Plaintiff's counsel (government or private) has found a number of cases in which, on facts quite similar to those he thinks he can establish in his case, the acts or practices of the defendant were held to be "unfair" or to constitute "restraints of trade." Counsel for the defense has been equally diligent in his search of the reported decisions and has found an equally large number of cases in which, as he sees it, the facts fit his case. Each lawyer argues that his own line of reported decisions represents the sounder view of the law.

A different approach to the monopoly problem is coming to the fore, however, and, in it, economists play a special role. Whereas the authors of the Sherman, Clayton, and FTC acts thought largely in terms of the small businessman caught in the grip of an industrial octopus, the authors of the Celler-Kefauver Antimerger Act had a different problem in mind. Their thinking was based less on the idea that monopoly is a wrong directed against the small businessman than on the concept that the consumer loses from the monopolist's reduced output and higher prices. Economic arguments employed in merger litigation have come to be used with increasing frequency in other antitrust cases as well. The economist thus has a conceptual framework of his own to offer those responsible for administering the antitrust laws, one that has been receiving increased acceptance in the case law in recent years.

Nevertheless, within the Commission, economic theory and the economist himself have served mainly to bolster the lawyer's and businessman's approach to industry regulation. In the opinion of Professor Jesse Markham, FTC chief economist from 1953 to 1955, economics at the FTC has played a more vital part in shaping and conditioning antitrust and regulatory legislation than in administering the laws after they have been passed. "When lawyers administer, they seem inevitably to rely on rules, especially simple *per se* rules," he wrote in an article in the March, 1964, issue of the *Columbia Law Review*. "As governance by rules increases, the need for economic analysis declines." This was, and to a large extent remains, the position of the FTC vis-à-vis its law enforcement function. There is a lawyers' adage at the Commission that one incriminating letter in the correspondent's files is worth the testimony of ten economists. This attitude is changing, but slowly.

VI

Unfair Trade in General

"I have been told by a great many men that . . . it is just free competition that has made it possible for the big to crush the little. I reply that it is not *free* competition which has done that; it is *illicit* competition." President Woodrow Wilson voiced the temper of the times in 1914 when he argued for creation of the Federal Trade Commission with these words. The insistence that there be rules of the game in the rivalry for trade was the impetus behind the agency's birth, but there was no uniformity of opinion inside or outside Congress concerning the acts and practices that were to be outlawed.

As a body of experts, the FTC was to render certainty where there had been none. That has been no easy task. Changes in the composition of the Commission, in judicial reasoning, and in political philosophy have led to varying interpretations of what constitutes unfair trade and how far the FTC can go in regulating business. From the broad but vague congressional mandate given the agency, the FTC's authority has been shaped and reshaped over the years.

IDENTIFYING THE STATUTES

The FTC administers a diverse collection of statutes, most of which do not provide clear economic guidelines and many of which actually conflict with one another. They include the Sherman, FTC, Clayton, and Robinson-Patman acts as well as numerous specialized laws that set forth specific prohibitions, regulations, and exemptions. Even as late as 1953, Justice Felix Frankfurter, in his dissenting opinion in *FTC* v. *Motion Picture Advertising Service Co.* pointed out that "the policies directed at maintaining effective competition . . . are difficult to formulate and not altogether harmonious . . . It is . . . incumbent upon us to seek to rationalize the four statutes directed toward a common end and make of them, to the extent that what Congress has written permits, a harmonious body of law."

For the FTC, the most important of these statutes is the Federal Trade Commission Act, basically, an expansion of the Sherman Antitrust Act. Section 5, the Act's substantive provision, contains a prohibition against "unfair methods of competition," which covers unreasonable trade restraints in interstate and foreign commerce, and another against "unfair or deceptive acts or practices," which reaches all unfair acts. Section 5 is presently viewed as applying to unfair conduct in commerce whether or not that conduct restricts competition or is used in competition. It therefore accords the Commission and the courts power to deal with most forms of trade restraints proscribed by the Sherman Act. Price-fixing, boycotts, and resale price maintenance, as well as misrepresentation and the utilization of lotteries in restraint of trade, are covered.

But the thrust of Section 5 goes deeper. Not only is the FTC authorized to proceed against Sherman Act violations; it may also proceed against *incipient* Sherman Act violations if they can be shown to be "unfair." The rationale for this extension of authority was put forth in 1920 by Justice Brandeis in his dissenting opinion in the Commission's first Supreme Court case, *FTC* v. *Gratz.* "What Section 5 declares unlawful," he wrote,

> is not unfair competition. That had been unlawful before. . . . What that section made unlawful were "unfair methods of competition," that is, the method or means by which an unfair end might be accomplished. . . . The purpose of Congress was to prevent any unfair method which may have been used by any concern in competition from becoming its general practice. It was only by stopping its use before it became a general practice, that the apprehended effect of an unfair method in suppressing competition by destroying rivals could be averted.

One of the basic legal concepts behind the FTC Act was that of "fairness," or equity. The traditional legal notion of commercial justice conceives of antitrust laws as a body of rules designed to see that the game of commerce is conducted fairly, that none of the participants—suppliers, competitors, or customers—are subjected to treatment that offends the community's sense of business morality or fair play. In the first cases tried by the FTC, relatively simple factual issues were presented to the courts on equally straightforward principles of equity. Did the defendant do the alleged acts and were they "unfair"? Later cases involved ideas of "efficiency," revolving around highly technical economic questions as to what course of conduct serves the public interest by preserving competition.

DEFINING UNFAIR TRADE

Early efforts on the part of the FTC to give a broad interpretation to its legislative authority were stopped cold in the courts. In the *Gratz* case, the Supreme Court ruled that the Commission was limited solely to proceeding against competitive conduct regarded as unlawful prior to 1914. Gratz sold steel ties and jute bagging used in baling cotton. The com-

e Federal Trade Commission is headed by five Commissioners, usually busismen or lawyers, who act as the final authority on all matters coming before FTC. The first Commission, appointed by President Woodrow Wilson in 5, is pictured here. Its members were, from left to right, George Rublee, liam J. Harris, Chairman Joseph E. Davies, Edward N. Hurley, and William Parry.

Commission in early 1969, under the chairmanship of Caspar W. Weinger, is pictured here in the FTC's formal hearing room. Its members were, n left to right, Everette MacIntyre, Paul Rand Dixon, Weinberger, Philip an, and Mary Gardiner Jones.

An FTC field inspector discusses labeling regulations for fur products wit
retail store owner. Although the Commission was intended to be primaril
guardian agency for business to ensure fair trade behavior among competit
it has increasingly become a guardian of the consumer as well. The Fur Produ
Labeling Act is only one of many consumer-protection statutes enforced by
FTC.

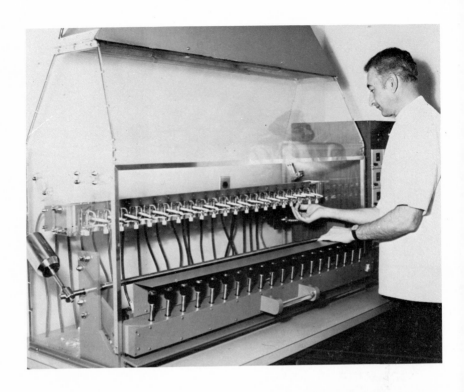

The FTC conducts laboratory tests to determine the safety of consumer products. Above, a cigarette machine puffs on a slew of cigarettes to measure their tar and nicotine contents. At right, a sweater fails a flammability test.

The Federal Trade Commission Building (above), a Washington landmark, was built in the 1930's, during the administration of President Franklin D. Roosevelt. Below: Standing with President Roosevelt after dedication ceremonies, on July 12, 1937, are FTC Commissioner Garland S. Ferguson (far left) and FTC Chairman William A. Ayres.

pany refused to sell the one without the other. The FTC found the practice of tying sales of the two products together an unfair method of competition and ordered it stopped. The Court reversed the order, saying, in effect, that the FTC was not free to interpret the wording of the 1914 legislation, that it was up to the courts to decide what constituted unfair methods of competition. Justice James C. McReynolds, writing for the Court, said that the FTC had no right to challenge "practices never heretofore regarded as opposed to good morals because characterized by deception, bad faith, fraud or oppression, or as against public policy because of their dangerous tendency unduly to hinder competition or create monopoly."

Justice Brandeis, in his dissent, argued that the Commission's expert knowledge should be given weight and should not be upset without substantial reason. "Instead of undertaking to define what practices should be deemed unfair, as had been done in earlier legislation," he wrote,

> the Act left the determination to the Commission. Experience with existing laws had taught that definition, being necessarily rigid, would prove embarrassing, and if rigorously applied, might involve great hardship. Methods of competition which would be unfair in one industry, under certain circumstances, might, when adopted in another industry, or even in the same industry under different circumstances, be entirely unobjectionable. . . . Recognizing that the question whether a method of competitive practices was unfair would ordinarily depend upon special facts, Congress imposed upon the Commission the duty of finding the facts, and it declared that findings of fact so made (if duly supported by evidence) were to be taken as final.

His stand laid the groundwork for future high court decisions and eventual Commission policy.

The FTC had been fortunate earlier in the first court test of the FTC Act as a whole. *FTC* v. *Sears, Roebuck & Co.* tested both the enabling statute and the Commission's power to prohibit false advertising, although the case presented a clearly anticompetitive situation. Sears ads claimed cheaper prices because of the company's great size. The FTC charged that Sears used a false advertisement and its superior size to injure competition. The appeals court could have rested its decision on the question of competitive effect, but it went further by indicating that the Commission had jurisdiction over deceptive practices regardless of their direct effect on competition. In a decision affirming the FTC's cease-and-desist order against Sears, the Seventh Circuit Court of Appeals said in April, 1919:

> The Commissioners, representing the government as *parens patriae,* are to exercise their common sense, as informed by their knowledge of the general idea of unfair trade at common law, and stop all those trade practices that have a capacity or tendency to injure competitors directly or *through deception of purchasers,* quite irrespective of whether the specific practices in question have yet been denounced in common-law cases.

The *Sears Roebuck* case was an exception; other early decisions of the appeals courts were restrictive. The Commission was repeatedly rebuffed in its efforts to adapt the concept of unfair competition to newer trading methods and to place the competitive process on a more stable and equitable foundation. To accommodate itself to the restrictions thus imposed, the Commission was forced to concentrate its energies within the narrow confines of the field of action set by the courts and to refrain from a more experimental and venturesome exercise of its powers.

But even in those early years, there were victories for the FTC and inklings of the broad meaning "unfair methods of competition" would assume. In the second case to reach the Supreme Court, *FTC* v. *Beech-Nut Packing Co.,* the practice at issue was not one that had "never heretofore" been regarded as unlawful. It involved resale price fixing, a technique that had been found to violate the Sherman Act. The Court agreed that the Commission had properly condemned as unfair the respondent's system of fixing and policing its resale prices. More significantly, it added: "What shall constitute unfair methods of competition denounced by the act, is left without specific definition. Congress deemed it better to leave the subject without precise definition, and to have each case determined upon its own facts, owing to the multifarious means by which it is sought to effectuate such schemes."

In 1934, the Commission won a significant point in a lottery case decided by the Supreme Court. A manufacturer of candy had argued that, because his company's lottery did not fall within any of the classes earlier held subject to the Commission's prohibition and was unlikely ultimately to result in a monopoly, the Commission lacked jurisdiction. The Court, finding neither of those arguments persuasive, observed that "it would not have been a difficult feat of draftsmanship to have restricted the operation of the Trade Commission Act to those methods of competition in interstate commerce which are forbidden at common law or which are likely to grow into violations of the Sherman Act, if that had been the purpose of the legislation." The Supreme Court thus overruled *Gratz* and explicitly stated that the FTC had not been intended to limit the unfair-methods-of-competition concept to fixed and legally established categories.

The courts, having warned the FTC to refrain from amateurish administrative interference in commerce, had finally given the agency the power to define unfair methods of competition and to draft orders to carry out the statutory prohibitions. Court decisions in succeeding decades reinforced the FTC's tenuously established authority over a broadly defined concept of free trade.

It took almost as much effort to establish the FTC's jurisdiction over false advertising and other deceptive practices as to determine how far it could go in outlawing what it deemed unfair competition. In *FTC* v. *Winsted Hosiery Company* (1922), Justice Brandeis upheld for the Court an FTC cease-

and-desist order concerning false advertising. Moreover, as in the *Sears Roebuck* case, the Court indicated that deception of the public was unfair and could be prohibited by the FTC. But, in 1931, the Commission's power to prohibit false advertising suffered a temporary setback. A unanimous Supreme Court in *FTC* v. *Raladam Co.*, notwithstanding the earlier decisions, held that the Commission could not issue an order prohibiting a false advertisement when there was no proof that the ad affected any competitors of the respondent, regardless of its deception of the public. Thus, the consumer could claim no protection under the FTC Act. The effect of the *Raladam* case, however, was less critical than was immediately anticipated, for, in almost every instance of false advertising, a harmful effect on a competitor could be shown. Its practical result was simply to require that the Commission establish in each instance a competitive effect. In 1938, with passage of the Wheeler-Lea Act, Congress legislatively overruled *Raladam* and gave the FTC power over "unfair or deceptive acts or practices" in addition to unfair methods of competition. Thereafter, the Commission could act under its legislative mandate whenever deception of the public was involved, regardless of the effect upon competition.

The courts' position as final arbiter in cases of unfair trade has made them the final authority on what constitutes unfair trade and on how far the FTC can go in regulating business practices. The process of judicial review has been gradual and sometimes frustrating to the agency. Generally, though, the courts have harmonized the commands of the many antitrust statutes in favor of competition. Over the past half-century, the Commission has labeled as unfair under the FTC Act numerous practices unknown or uncondemned when Congress drafted the law in 1914, and Section 5 of the FTC Act has now been established as a flexible prohibition capable of expansion to reach new and ingenious unethical practices.

VII

Restraints of Trade

"People of the same trade seldom meet together, even for merriment and diversion but the conversation ends in a conspiracy against the public or in some contrivance to raise prices." That pessimistic appraisal of human behavior was delivered by Adam Smith in *Wealth of Nations,* and it is as relevant today as when it was written in 1776. There continue to be individuals who seek to enhance their position or wealth by attempting to control the market for their product through the elimination or restriction of competition. Prohibiting such restraints of trade is the basis of antitrust activity.

No longer the popular movement it was throughout the first half of the twentieth century, antitrust has now become solidly institutionalized. That process began in earnest after 1935, when public policy turned from government-sponsored cartelization, as represented by the NRA, back to a policy relying primarily on competitive market forces. Under Assistant Attorney General Thurman Arnold, the staff of the Justice Department's Antitrust Division grew fivefold and took on real life. Although antitrust enforcement was partially demobilized during World War II, the Justice Department and the Federal

Trade Commission rebounded at the war's end and went forward with big cases. Politicians and government officials, schooled in the TNEC and influenced by revival of antitrust during the "golden era" of the New Deal, pushed for stronger antitrust laws, particularly for a new antimerger statute. Passage of the Celler-Kefauver Act in 1950 capped the antitrust revival and signaled the close of the movement's popular appeal. But in its wake came an essentially bipartisan consensus that antitrust enforcement was an indispensable instrument of public policy.

The line between free competition and illegal restraint of trade has always been difficult to draw. Some violations of the law are obvious and flagrant; others, hidden and discreet. In the early years of the Sherman Act, the nation's attention was focused on trusts, mergers, pools, and holding companies. Contemporary methods of monopolization tend to be more circumspect than the turn-of-the-century squeeze tactics involving predatory pricing or malicious interference with the operations of rivals. They are also more difficult to attack through the antitrust laws.

The variety of practices that can be used to destroy competition approaches infinity. Among those most commonly found today are price-fixing, the price squeeze, and mergers. Each is peculiarly suited to and can only be pursued extensively by the largest corporations.

In several areas of antitrust law, the Federal Trade Commission and the Justice Department exercise concurrent jurisdiction. Under the Clayton Act, both agencies supervise the legality of business mergers and are empowered to proceed against interlocking corporate directorates. The Commission can and does move against price-fixing under the Federal Trade Commission Act, but since price-fixing is generally considered a *per se* violation of the antitrust laws, and, therefore, a criminal offense, the Justice Department is the logical agency to bring price-fixing charges.

Broadly speaking, the Antitrust Division of the Justice Department enforces the Sherman Act, particularly the prosecution of serious and significant infringements of the Act. Normally, Justice takes action under the Robinson-Patman Act only when charges under it are a factor in a Sherman Act violation. When large corporations are involved in criminal wrongdoing, the Justice Department is the appropriate agency to bring action, for it can move more quickly than the FTC and can go directly to court to seek an injunction. The FTC enforces its enabling statute, the Federal Trade Commission Act, and the Robinson-Patman Act amendments covering price discriminations. In general, it holds itself aloof from the criminal aspects of Sherman Act enforcement.

Restraints of trade fall into three broad categories: mergers, the contemporary equivalent to the nineteenth century trust problem (discussed in Chapter VIII); conspiracies, such as price-fixing or allocation of territories; and restrictive practices between buyer and seller, such as exclusive contracts and reciprocal trading.

CONSPIRACIES

One area of antitrust in which the law is more or less firmly fixed and where the government's response is predictable involves conspiracies. Both the Sherman Act and the Federal Trade Commission Act outlaw them. Section 2 of the Sherman Act, among other things, specifically prohibits a conspiracy to monopolize, while Section 1 contains a general prohibition against restrictive contracts, combinations, or conspiracies. Section 5 of the FTC Act prohibits unfair methods of competition and unfair acts or practices in commerce. The heart of such violations is that competitors have given up independent action and are agreeing for an illegal purpose. When an agreement to eliminate competition is found, the violation is considered so serious that it constitutes a *per se* violation. No justifications are allowed, and the courts and the FTC give short shrift to arguments about the reasonableness of the conspiracy or its ineffectiveness.

For many years, the antitrust enforcement agencies proceeded against conspiratorial cases on the assumption that conspiracy to eliminate competition would be difficult to prove. With the traditional reticence of conspirators well known, the courts have allowed the crime to be established by indirect proof, especially demonstration of certain acts of the alleged conspirators.

The most obvious act which can be evidence of conspiracy is a discussion among competitors about prices to be charged, but even discussion is not really required. Conspiracy is inferred from certain facts—meetings, communications, discussions—and, above all, from what takes place afterward.

TRADE ASSOCIATIONS

Where traders are few in number, competition may be eliminated by simple agreement. Where they are numerous, it is more difficult to bring them together and keep them in line, and some sort of contractual arrangement or formal organization is usually required. In Western Europe, this need has long been satisfied by cartels; in the United States, it is met by trade associations, agencies through which the sellers of a like commodity unite to promote their common interests.

Trustbusters have always regarded trade associations with suspicion. In the view of some economists, they have had a greater influence on economic concentration and restraint of trade than the trusts did in their prime. An FTC official testified at TNEC hearings that, in most cases involving unlawful restraint then before the agency, a trade association was the prime mover or instrument.

The trade association is ideally suited to the carrying out of a price leadership program, one of the most common techniques for controlling prices. Everyone of importance in an industry belongs to the association, and all are disposed to cooperate to the fullest. A communication that came to light during the course of the TNEC hearings is revealing. "By this time you should be in a position to select your 'market leader' who has the courage and those qualities of leadership that others recognize and will follow," wrote one trade association to its members. "After he is selected, give him your whole-hearted support. Remember not to agree upon a price, but each individual has the right to determine what he wants to do and to announce it, thus avoiding any conspiracy. Your 'market leader' can set a price and the organizations can send out a notice." Whether the leader raises his price or lowers it, the others are expected to follow suit. The object of this device is to make it impossible for government investigators to prove a conspiracy.

In more than two hundred cases, trade associations have been found to have eliminated competition in a variety of ways. In one case, the Milk and Ice Cream Institute had standardized products and discounts, circulated daily reports, and administered a delivered pricing plan. In another, the Crepe Paper Association was shown to have operated a system of zone pricing. In the case of the Salt Producers Association, an exchange of statistics facilitated adherence to a system of voluntary quotas for production and sales. All these activities were held to violate the law.

Resale Prices and Fair Trade

Resale price maintenance is an arrangement whereby the seller, whether manufacturer or distributor, of a product identified by a brand name or a trade-mark sets a minimum retail price below which the item may not be sold. This technique is used to prevent retailers from competing in the prices charged for branded goods.

Before the 1930's, resale price maintenance was repeatedly condemned by the courts as a violation of the Sherman Act and an unfair method of competition under the FTC Act. That position has gradually been eroded. Although a large number of Commission orders preventing resale price maintenance have been affirmed by the courts, a jurisprudence developed in which fine distinctions were drawn between what was permissible and what was prohibited in the control of resale prices by the manufacturer.

Traditionally, the states had stood consistently with the federal government on antitrust policy. In fact, state antitrust laws anticipated the Sherman Act. But disillusionment with antitrust enforcement, the influence of the NRA, and the work of pressure groups chipped away at the structure of the antitrust laws. California was the first state to turn its back on its former antimonopoly position. In 1931, it passed a fair trade law approving a system by which a resale price may be maintained. Following the demise of the NRA, the snowball began to roll. By 1939, forty-three states had passed so-called fair trade statutes, although in several instances, these laws were later declared unconstitutional by state courts.

The policy of the fair trade laws was subsequently written into the federal antitrust laws by the 1937 Miller-Tydings amendment to the Sherman Act and the 1952 McGuire Act, which amended the FTC Act. This legislation, in effect, exempted from prosecution sellers abiding by the terms of the state fair trade laws. Without the sanction of a state fair trade statute, the Commission may, and does, take action under Section 5 of the FTC Act if a seller and his purchasers agree to fix resale prices.

RESTRICTIVE BUYER-SELLER RELATIONSHIPS

Restrictive buyer-seller relationships can be lumped together as another main category of anticompetitive practice.

If buyer and seller agree on long-term requirement contracts, or tie in the sale of one commodity with the sale of another, with the result that other sellers are foreclosed from competing for the buyer's business, the Commission may subject such arrangements to the tests of Section 3 of the Clayton Act, which declares such activity to be illegal if it substantially lessens competition or tends to create a monopoly. The Commission may also strike at this problem under Section 7 of the Clayton Act by challenging mergers that might lead to the concentration of an inordinate amount of buying or selling power in the hands of one company. And, of course, the Commission may apply the theory of Section 2 of the Sherman Act, which prohibits monopoly or attempts to monopolize, in proceedings brought under Section 5 of the FTC Act.

What happens when the Commission is faced with situations that do not come within the precise terms of these laws? The courts have long held, and have recently reaffirmed, the concept that the Commission, using Section 5 of the FTC Act, may declare that anticompetitive practices that apparently do not violate these antitrust statutes are, nevertheless, unfair methods of competition. For example, the Commission claimed that an arrangement in which Atlantic Refining Company "sponsored" the sale of Goodyear tires, batteries, and accessories to Atlantic's wholesale outlets and retail service station dealers was an unfair method of competition. In *Atlantic Refining Co.* v. *FTC,* decided by the Supreme Court in 1965, the Court upheld the Commission and, in so doing, reaffirmed the FTC's power to determine the legality of anticompetitive practices that do not fit snugly within the four corners of other antitrust statutes. The Court specifically recognized that, although the Goodyear-Atlantic arrangement was not a tying contract, it was nonetheless illegal because it was contrary to the declared policy objectives of the Clayton Act. The Court stated flatly that "when conduct bears the characteristics of recognized antitrust violations it becomes suspect, and the Commission may properly look to cases applying those laws for guidance."

TYING AND EXCLUSIVE CONTRACTS

Tying and exclusive contracts, two of the most common arrangements to restrict competition, were used by the early trusts to obtain and extend a position of monopoly. Several of the trusts persuaded the railroads to grant them substantial rebates. Standard Oil not only recovered 40 to 50 per cent of the sum it paid the railroads for carrying its own products, but also collected a similar share of the rates paid by rivals. The Aluminum Company of America, enjoying a patent monopoly in its early years, bought power with contracts that forbade suppliers to sell to other manufacturers of aluminum. The American Can Company prevented its competitors from obtaining up-to-date equipment by entering into exclusive contracts with the manufacturers of automatic can-making machinery.

Under the Sherman Act, tying contracts were, in most cases, canceled by consent decrees and enjoined by decisions of the lower courts. But in two cases, monopolies obtained through tying contracts involving patents were allowed to stand. In 1912, the Supreme Court, in a private suit brought against the A. B. Dick Company, permitted Dick to bind the purchasers of mimeograph machines to buy from Dick their stencils, paper, and ink, holding that a patentee could impose such restrictions. In the *United Shoe Machinery* case in 1913, the Court found leases tying one machine to others to be a lawful exercise of patent rights. These decisions prompted passage of Section 3 of the Clayton Act, which makes it illegal for any person to require exclusivity as a condition to his willingness to do business, whenever the effect of such dealing "may be to substantially lessen competition . . . in any line of commerce."

Tying and exclusive contracts have been attacked more often under the Clayton Act than under the FTC and Sherman acts, and the Court has consistently refused to permit a patentee to extend his monopoly to cover other goods. But the courts and the FTC have had considerable difficulty determining what market facts reliably demonstrate that an exclusive contract substantially lessens competition.

EXCLUSIVE DEALERSHIPS

Exclusive dealerships, outlawed under Section 3 of the Clayton Act, are another hard-to-pin-down restrictive practice that the FTC moves against. Three of the Commission's first orders against such arrangements were reversed by the courts in 1923. In the *Pearsall* case, it was found that a manufacturer marketing oleomargarine under exclusive contracts controlled only 1 per cent of the market, and it was therefore held that his contracts did not tend to give him a monopoly. In the *Curtis Publishing Co.* case, in which schoolboys delivering the Curtis publications were forbidden to carry other magazines, it was found that the company did not sell its publications to the boys but employed them as its agents. It was held that Section 3 did not preclude exclusive agencies. In the oil pump cases, the Commission had issued twenty-seven orders against refining companies who leased to retailers of gasoline, at nominal rentals, tanks and pumps marked with their brand names, prohibiting their use in storing and selling gasoline produced by their competitors. This arrangement, however, did not prevent dealers from installing other tanks and pumps to handle other brands. And, although the cost of financing such installations handicapped independent refiners, the Court held that exclusion of their products from equipment financed by their competitors did not substantially lessen competition or tend toward monopoly.

As a result of its early setbacks, the FTC has adopted a practical approach toward exclusive contracts. It does not hold such contracts to be illegal *per se,* but confines its orders to cases in which substantial injury or the probability of such injury to competition in a market as a whole can actually be shown.

Delivered Price

In many industries where the cost of transporting a product is high, sellers located at different places have worked out a system whereby their prices for delivered goods at any location are identical. This was once accomplished through the use of common basing points. A seller would refuse to quote a price for the sale of goods at his own mill. Rather, he quoted a delivered price, which included the cost of moving the goods to the buyer's place of business or to the dock or station nearest him. All sellers employed the same city or cities as base points from which the delivery charges were calculated. The charges were based on the cost of rail haul and were recorded in a common rate book. Since the aim of the arrangement was identical prices, the sellers' base prices had to be the same, too. This was achieved through agreement or general acceptance of price leadership. Such a system enabled sellers to eliminate competition without a formal organization or evidence of overt agreement.

Delivered prices were the basis for a controversy that raged for nearly thirty years.

The story begins in 1880, when three independent producers began quoting delivered prices for steel beams identical with those charged by the Carnegie Company. By 1900, the practice had been extended to every concern and to every product, with the exception of rails (which are picked up by the railways at the mills) in the steel industry. After the U.S. Steel Corporation was organized in 1901, the level of prices was effectively controlled, first through open agreements and finally through price leadership.

In 1919, immediately after the war, fabricators in the West and the South began to carry complaints to the FTC concerning the prices they were forced to pay for steel. In 1920, when the government returned the railways to their owners, a 40 per cent increase in freight rates pushed these prices even higher. Protests mounted. Resolutions condemning the basing-point system were passed by the legislatures of eleven states, and thirty-two states joined in organizing the Associated States Opposing Pittsburgh-Plus, Pittsburgh then being the basing point for all U.S. Steel products. In response to this pressure, the Commission issued an order in 1924 directing U.S. Steel to cease and desist "from quoting for sale or selling . . . rolled steel products upon any other basing point than where the products are manufactured or from which they are shipped." U.S. Steel promised to obey the order "insofar as it is practicable to do so" and proceeded to set up a multiple basing-point system by establishing bases at Chicago and Birmingham. U.S. Steel had plainly failed to obey the FTC order, but the Commission made no attempt to have it enforced.

In 1933, under the provisions of the National Industrial Recovery Act, the antitrust laws were suspended and codes of fair competition were approved for steel, as for other industries. The steel code required all producers to adhere to the multiple basing-point system (with the Code Authority picking the basing points), and to charge all-rail freight, the rates of which would be published in an official freight rate book. As a result, the steel industry could not obey the FTC's order without violating the NRA code, and it could not adhere to the code without disobeying the FTC. This situation persisted until the NRA was declared unconstitutional and the FTC order again came into force. The industry, however, continued to employ the multiple basing-point system throughout the following decade.

A 1943 cease-and-desist order against the Cement Institute and seventy-four cement producers was a major move in a general campaign against basing-point pricing conducted throughout the 1940's. The cement industry appealed the Commission's order, and in 1946 a court of appeals upheld it in part and reversed it in part. The government then appealed to the Supreme Court.

In 1947, the FTC issued a complaint against the American Iron and Steel Institute and more than 100 steel companies. They were charged with engaging in a conspiracy to fix prices, limit production, and otherwise violate Section 5 of the FTC Act. The case went to trial, but the larger steel companies sought a lenient settlement since the Commission had not had the full support of the courts in prohibiting the use of delivered prices.

The year 1948 marked a change in the delivered price controversy. In a sweeping decision in the *Cement Institute* case, the Supreme Court reversed the lower court, sustaining the Commission at every point. The Court ruled that uniform prices throughout the country resulting from the basing-point system overlook differences in transportation and other costs and are an illegal mask for monopoly and restraint of trade. In 1948, too, U.S. Steel signed a decree affirming and enforcing the 1924 FTC order.

Following the 1948 Supreme Court decision, charges were leveled against the FTC that the Commission had exceeded its authority, that it had usurped the prerogatives of Congress, that it was embracing alien ideologies. A rise in steel and cement prices, due to factors other than abandonment of the basing-point system, stirred a public outcry. Senator Homer Capehart of Indiana called congressional hearings, and a parade of business witnesses called for a reversal of the high court decision. Senator Joseph C. O'Mahoney of Wyoming introduced a bill to amend the FTC and Clayton acts to permit a seller "acting independently" to quote or sell at delivered prices or to absorb freight. The bill passed both houses of Congress, but was vetoed by President Truman on June 16, 1950. The delivered price controversy was nearing its end.

In 1951, the American Iron and Steel Institute and its members accepted an FTC order, based on the 1947 complaint, requiring them to sell steel products at their plants and accepting identity of delivered prices at any destination as proof of violation of the law. In 1953, when demand for steel dropped, U.S. Steel announced that it would again absorb freight. Other companies followed suit but the old basing-point system was not re-established.

FRANCHISING

Franchising poses restraints to trade if the parent company places unreasonable limitations on the right of a franchisee to make his own business decisions. This concern for the freedom of franchises was established in *FTC* v. *Brown Shoe,* decided by the Supreme Court on June 6, 1966.

The case actually began on October 13, 1959, when the Commission issued a complaint charging the Brown Shoe Company, one of the world's largest manufacturers of shoes, with unfair methods of competition in violation of Section 5 of the FTC Act in its Brown Franchise Stores Program. Under the franchise plan, held to be unfair and illegal by the FTC, independent dealers were given what was admittedly a valuable package of services—architectural plans, merchandising records, the help of a Brown field representative, and an option to participate in inexpensive group insurance—in return for a simple promise of the dealer-franchisee to concentrate on the Brown shoe line and not to handle competing lines.

The Eighth Circuit Court of Appeals set aside the FTC order on December 8, 1964. The Justice Department, acting on behalf of the FTC, filed for a writ of certiorari in the Supreme Court.

The high court, with Justice Hugo Black writing the unanimous opinion, reversed the decision of the appeals court. The record in this case, Black wrote, showed "beyond doubt" that Brown's program required shoe retailers, "unless faithless to their contractual obligations with Brown, substantially to limit their trade with Brown's competitors." Thus, the program "obviously conflicts with the central policy of both Section 1 of the Sherman Act and Section 3 of the Clayton Act against contracts which take away freedom of purchasers to buy in an open market." Brown had contended that the Commission had no power to declare the franchise program unfair without proof that it injured competition. But the Court held that it was not necessary to prove injury to competition since "the Commission has power under Section 5 to arrest trade restraints in their incipiency."

RECIPROCAL TRADING

Business reciprocity—an I-will-buy-from-you-if-you-will-buy-from-me or if-I-buy-from-you, -you-will-buy-from-me arrangement—is not new, but there has been a revival of interest in it in the last few years. Reciprocal buying arrangements involve an agreement between supplier and purchaser to fill some, perhaps all, of their needs for particular products by buying from each other.

As long ago as the 1930's, the FTC challenged reciprocity as an unfair method of competition under Section 5 of the FTC Act. It brought three cases, two of which involved firms using their freight volume to compel railroads to purchase supplies from them. Since these cases were not characterized by any particular subtlety, the FTC had no difficulty in finding that the use of coercion in the form of threats and promises in those circumstances an unfair method of competition.

Following these three cases, reciprocity, as an antitrust consideration, lay dormant for almost three decades. The issue was not revived until the *Consolidated Foods* case, which was argued before the Supreme Court and decided unanimously in favor of the FTC on April 28, 1965. *Consolidated Foods* differed from the earlier cases, even though reciprocity as an economic evil was the central consideration, in that it demonstrated the legal significance of reciprocity in a merger setting. But the case represents an authoritative comment of the Supreme Court on the question of reciprocity.

In 1951, Consolidated, a large Chicago-based, diversified food company owning several processing plants and a nation-wide network of wholesale and retail food stores, acquired Gentry, manufacturer of about one-third of the dehydrated onions and garlic sold in the United States. Gentry and one competitor accounted for almost 90 per cent of the industry's sales. Seven years after the merger, Gentry's share of the onion and garlic markets had gone up only slightly. Nevertheless, the Commission argued that the acquisition had given Consolidated, a corporation with assets of $99 million in 1956, an advantage denied its competitors. Processors seeking to win or retain Consolidated's patronage as a customer for their products were "likely to prefer Consolidated-Gentry as a source of supply for their onion and garlic requirements," the FTC said. It argued that reciprocity makes growth and success dependent not upon such competitive factors as price, quality, and service, but upon "the relative size and conglomeration of business." The Commission contended that a merger creating the danger of substantially lessening competition through reciprocal buying violates the antitrust laws.

In March, 1963, the Commission ordered Consolidated to divest itself of Gentry. A year later, however, the Seventh

Circuit Court of Appeals held that the Commission had failed to show that a probability of substantially lessened competition existed and set aside the order. Although the markets had rapidly expanded, the court found, Consolidated had increased its share of total onion sales by only about 7 per cent, while sustaining a 12 per cent decrease in the garlic market.

The government then appealed to the Supreme Court. In a significant victory for the FTC, the high court held that Section 7 of the Clayton Act had been violated. The case was the first in which the Court had dealt with reciprocity as a competitive weapon or determined its significance under the Clayton Act. The narrowly decided verdict called for Consolidated Foods to divest itself of Gentry. But the implications for the business community are far-reaching. In reversing the lower court, the high tribunal agreed with the FTC that the acquisition gave Consolidated the advantage of a combined threat and lure of reciprocal buying in competing for business. Reciprocity has become entangled in a thicket of merger facts and law from which the essential evil of reciprocity standing alone does not clearly emerge. But Consolidated established the proposition that potential reciprocity or reciprocity power provides a sufficient probability of lessening of competition to make an otherwise unobjectionable acquisition bad.

VIII.

Mergers

When a company secures a strong market position by internal growth, there is strong presumption that, unless it has used predatory tactics and the like, it has bested its rivals in a fair fight and is entitled to reap the rewards of victory. When it does so by merger, no such presumption is justified. Not all mergers are anticompetitive, however. A great many are either neutral in effect or contribute in various ways to maintaining a competitive framework for industry. Bringing in a new firm may introduce uncertainty in a complacent industry. Procompetitive effects may also flow from an efficiency-creating merger. Quite clearly, though, a great many mergers do restrict competition by decreasing the number of firms in a particular market. The effects of combination on competition must thus be judged case by case.

The historical development of corporate combination, usually referred to as the merger movement, has been characterized by three widely separated periods of heightened activity, the first around the turn of the century, the second following World War I, and the last dating from World War II. The first period was marked primarily by the use of holding companies to effect combinations in mining and manufacturing; the second, by an extension of the movement to public utilities, banking, and the distributive and personal service trades and by the emergence of many different patterns of combination. In both of these periods, mergers were facilitated by the existence of a ready market for corporate securities and stimulated by the prospect of quick profits through promotional and speculative activities. Some of the largest and best-known American corporations—General Motors, for example—began through a series of mergers.

The current merger movement far exceeds any of its predecessors. It began about 1948 and accelerated in 1954–55. Since 1948, food retailing mergers alone have involved concerns with combined sales of around $3 billion. This sum is about twice as great as the combined sales of all companies absorbed by the major turn-of-the-century trusts. Mergers rose to an all-time high in 1967, when the Commission reported 1,496 acquisitions in the manufacturing and mining industries, an increase of nearly one-third over the previous year. Large mergers, those over $10 million in assets, represented acquisitions of nearly $8 billion, almost double the previous year. Of the recorded mergers, 75 per cent were of the conglomerate type.

TYPES OF MERGERS

Mergers are commonly referred to as horizontal, market extension, vertical, or conglomerate. The type of merger is relevant in assessing the likelihood of anticompetitive consequences. If concerns selling the same product combine, for example, a resulting lessening of competition is more obvious than among other types of mergers.

A horizontal merger involves the acquisition by one company of all or part of the stock or assets of a competitor that offers the same goods or services in the same market area. A chain combination unites companies at the same stage of production selling the same product in different local markets. Chains of restaurants, hotels, retail stores, public utilities, and banking systems fall into this category.

Closely allied to the horizontal merger is a market extension merger. Such a merger involves the acquisition of a company whose general business is the same as that of the acquiring company but in a geographic area in which the acquiring company does not operate. Lateral combination brings together companies engaged in the production of goods that are related but not competitive. This kind of combine is also known as a product extension merger.

A vertical merger is one in which the acquiring company merges with a supplier or a customer. If the merger is with a supplier, it is regarded as backward integration. If merger is made with a customer, it is a forward integration. When corporations stand at different stages of the productive process, unified control may give them advantages over competitors in obtaining raw materials or in marketing. For instance, combined ownership of anthracite mines and railroad lines once made it possible for the companies concerned to withhold cars and to charge high transportation rates to other mining companies.

A conglomerate merger involves the acquisition of a company engaged in a business unrelated or distantly related to that of the acquiring company. The highly diversified Litton Industries, for example, is a conglomerate.

THE CLAYTON ACT

Section 7 of the Clayton Act is the Commission's fundamental authority for prohibiting anticompetitive mergers. It originally read, in part:

That no corporation engaged in commerce shall acquire, directly or indirectly, the whole or any part of the stock or other share of capital of another corporation engaged also in commerce, where the effect of such acquisition may be to substantially lessen competition between the corporation whose stock is so acquired and the corporation making the acquisition, or to restrain such commerce in any section or community, or tend to create a monopoly of any line of commerce.

Although it made direct reference to stock acquisition, the Act said nothing about the acquisition of assets, a loophole that was used for nearly forty years to effect mergers beyond the reach of the FTC or the Justice Department.

During the eleven years following passage of the Clayton Act, the FTC issued thirty-seven antimerger complaints. After such an auspicious start, a series of Supreme Court decisions from 1926 to 1934 rendered the Act almost totally ineffective. Although the Commission issued thirty-one complaints from 1926 to 1950, only four resulted in orders, and those four were issued before 1934. In cases against three meat-packing firms, decided in 1926, the Supreme Court decreed that the Commission could not order a company to divest itself of the assets of a competitor if the merger had been effected while the proceeding was pending, although the opinion expressly recognized that the acquisition of such assets had been effected in violation of Section 7.

Between 1929 and 1936, the FTC found that among the 547 mergers consummated, 54 per cent had been brought about through the acquisition of assets. This finding came out in a TNEC preliminary report. As a result of the assets loophole in the Clayton Act, enforcement of the original Section 7 had no appreciable impact on the merger movement that swept across many industries during the late 1920's.

The Commission's campaign, beginning in 1926, to persuade Congress to close this loophole was uniformly unsuccessful prior to World War II. In part, the lack of success was a reflection of the economic philosophy of the time, but it was also a reflection of the Commission's inability to convince the Congress of the size and economic significance of corporate mergers and to demonstrate the adverse competitive effects resulting from them.

The Celler-Kefauver Antimerger Act

In his message to Congress on April 29, 1938, calling for creation of the TNEC, President Roosevelt declared, "Private enterprise is ceasing to be private enterprise and is becoming a cluster of private collectivisms." Following the President's cue, the TNEC, in its final report issued in 1941, recommended that the Clayton Act be amended to forbid acquisition of assets as well as corporate stock where the effect may be to substantially lessen competition and that the authority to enforce the law be given to the FTC.

The Commission directed a substantial portion of its postwar economic reports program to an examination of concentration in American industry, including extensive analysis of the volume and competitive significance of post-1940 merger activity. In 1947, 1948, and 1949, the Commission published reports which, for the first time, presented current data on the volume of mergers consummated and the extent of concentration that prevailed in industry. An alarmed Congress saw the economy heading toward domination by a few holding companies on the way to becoming "collectivist" corporations, with the huge enterprises built up by conglomerate acquisitions driving out competition. The fear of accelerating industry concentration led to action.

On December 29, 1950, Congress approved a revised Section 7, the Celler-Kefauver Antimerger Act, named for Representative Emanuel Celler and Senator Estes Kefauver, chairmen of the antitrust subcommittees of the House and Senate respectively. It was assumed that primary responsibility for administering the new Section 7 would continue to reside, as it had since the original enactment of the statute, in the Federal

Trade Commission. The new Section 7 forbids acquisitions of assets as well as shares where the effect of such acquisitions not only tends to create a monopoly but also merely "substantially" lessens competition. At the same time, Congress amended Section II(b) of the Clayton Act to permit the Attorney General to intervene in proceedings brought by the Commission under the Act, an indication that enforcement of the Clayton Act was intended to be channeled primarily through administrative rather than judicial proceedings.

TEMPORARY INJUNCTIVE POWER

In June, 1966, the Supreme Court awarded the Federal Trade Commission a new weapon against consummation of business mergers considered anticompetitive by the agency. The Court, in a 5 to 4 decision, gave the FTC a power similar to that of the Justice Department. In an opinion by Justice Tom C. Clark, the Court said that the court of appeals must consider, and has power to grant, applications originated by the FTC for temporary injunctions against mergers alleged to violate the Clayton Act before holding an administrative hearing on a case. The Commission had long but unsuccessfully sought such authority from Congress on the ground that it is difficult if not impossible to unscramble assets after a merger has taken place. Nevertheless, the FTC has made almost no use of this preventive power, probably because it resulted from a court action rather than legislation.

A MARKET STRUCTURE APPROACH

Basic to the current enforcement of the merger statute is the general consensus among economists that it is the structure of a market that governs its economic performance. This approach is of particular importance in the case of a statute such as Section 7, which requires the enforcement agencies to engage in a kind of economic forecasting of the probable consequences of a merger. The two crucial market characteristics in evaluating an acquisition are concentration within the industry and the barriers to entry of new competition.

Beginning with the 1962 *Brown Shoe* decision in a case brought by the Justice Department, the Supreme Court has handed down an unbroken line of decisions supporting the market examination approach. "The shares of the market controlled by the industry leaders and the parties to the merger are, of course, the primary index of market power; but only a further examination of the particular market—its structure, history and probable future—can provide the appropriate setting for judging the probable anticompetitive effect of the merger." More recent decisions have reaffirmed the Court's reliance on market structure considerations, bringing the law close, perhaps, to the proposition that an industry which does not have a competitive structure will not have competitive behavior.

REMEDIES IN MERGER CASES

In the existing dual enforcement system, in which both the FTC and the Justice Department are empowered to move against anticompetitive mergers, remedial consequences vary greatly depending on which agency brings suit. Violation of Sections 1 or 2 of the Sherman Act, almost always handled by Justice, can result in the imposition of criminal penalties. The normal remedy for the violation of any of the other antimerger statutes is an order requiring divestiture of all the stock or assets acquired. If firms have already merged, a complete reorganization may be required, although partial divestiture can be ordered if that will cure the violation. In the event that the acquiring company has been involved in a number of mergers, an order preventing future acquisitions for a given period of time may be entered. Future acquisitions may also be conditioned on prior notification to or prior consent by one of the government agencies. Because these remedies, particularly divestiture, are extremely disruptive and costly, a small but steady stream of companies have been seeking pre-merger clearance from the FTC. The Commission has also issued guidelines for several industries.

The actual scope of the FTC's remedial powers has never been authoritatively determined, however, and doubts about how far the agency can go have limited its selection of cases. Although the Commission has ordered divestiture in some merger cases, it has handled remedial problems in a rather gingerly fashion on the whole.

THE PATTERN OF ENFORCEMENT

The contrast between enforcement of the original Section 7 of the Clayton Act and the amended Section 7 is striking. Between January 1, 1951, and June 30, 1967, the Federal Trade Commission and the Department of Justice issued a total of 205 merger complaints. Three-fourths of them (153) challenged acquisitions by manufacturing and mining corporations. The stepped-up enforcement activity began in response to the increasing tempo of over-all merger activity in the mid-1950's. Prior to 1954, there had been relatively few large mergers. After 1954, however, the pace quickened, reaching high points for the decade in terms of acquired assets in 1955 and 1956.

The antitrust agencies have issued merger complaints against a sizable percentage of the largest industrial corporations. Thirty-two of the fifty-two industrial corporations with assets in excess of $1 billion in 1965 have had one or more of their acquisitions challenged. Large mergers, too, have been scrutinized, with the FTC and the Justice Department questioning the legality of about 10 per cent of all large mergers since 1950. Over half of those challenged involved a horizontal relationship between the merging companies. Another 27 per cent involved vertical relationships. The remainder were conglomerate mergers.

The effect of the FTC's successful blocking of a large proportion of horizontal mergers has led to a virtual horizontal merger ban. From 1951 to 1954, following passage of the new Section 7, horizontal mergers comprised about 37 per cent of all mergers and 40 per cent of the assets of all large acquisitions in manufacturing and mining. After 1956, the peak year for horizontal mergers, the trend changed dramatically. From 1959 to 1962, horizontal mergers comprised only about 17 per cent of all mergers and 19 per cent of the assets of large acquisitions. By 1966, they represented only 8 per cent of the assets of all acquisitions.

MERGER GUIDELINES

In recent years, the FTC has made use of its particular abilities to formulate merger rules on the basis of industry-by-industry analysis. In the spring of 1965, it set forth guidelines for mergers in the dairy products industry in an opinion in a proceeding against Beatrice Foods Company, one of the leading firms in the business. Since then, it has issued statements of enforcement policy with regard to the food distribution industry, the cement industry, automotive tire producers, and textile mill products. The FTC's guideline program has not put the Justice Department nor the courts out of business. In fact, the Department of Justice, in May, 1968, released some broad merger guidelines of its own, rules of more general applicability than those issued by the FTC.

To expedite execution of enforcement policies with respect to food distribution and cement, the Commission in each case established a requirement that it be notified, in advance, of certain types of mergers. The Commission undertook annual notification of the affected firms as long as the enforcement policy should remain in effect, and those affected are required to file special reports with the Commission.

INTERLOCKING DIRECTORATES

Competition may well be impaired when normally independent corporations are brought under some form of common control short of merger. To prevent such indirect consolidation, Section 8 of the Clayton Act forbids interlocking directorates between competing corporations. Surprisingly little use has been made of this provision. In its annual report for 1927, the FTC said that "the few cases arising under this part of the statute are probably due to the fact that its requirements can readily be met and desired results obtained by other means." Violation of Section 8 has been among the charges brought by the Justice Department in antitrust suits and the Commission in its complaints, but, in most cases, threat of action has been sufficient. The directors in question have resigned before the issue came to trial.

An FTC report, issued in 1950, examined interlocking relationships among the one thousand largest manufacturing corporations, and between these corporations and some 330 financial, railroad, public utility, wholesale, and retail companies. Although a few of these interlocks appeared to be in violation of Section 8, most fell outside the prohibitions of the Act as limited by Congress and restricted by the courts. For example, there is no legal barrier to interlocks between potential competitors. Members of the same family or partners in the same banking house can serve as directors of competing concerns. Directors of two competitive corporations may sit with each other on the board of a third. Many interlocks are lawful because the interlocked concerns are related to each other as actual or potential suppliers and customers rather than as competitors or because the individuals through whom the relations are maintained are officers or stockholders rather than directors. In other words, the prohibition in Section 8 is so narrow that it has had little practical effect on one of the principal methods by which economic power is concentrated.

THE CONGLOMERATE MOVEMENT

On a single day in August, 1968, the *Wall Street Journal* published a number of want ads that clearly indicate the current direction of the merger movement. One carried the arresting caption, "Let's Conglomerate Together." In that ad, a "successful, imaginative profit-and-growth oriented" electronics manufacturer was publicizing his desire to meet with top management of other firms for an evaluation of combined potential for "synergistic growth." Others ads proclaimed, "Available for Acquisition," or "$1,000,000 Available. Type of Business Not Important."

This form of corporate consolidation derived primarily from an accumulation of capital by U.S. corporations during World War II and a resulting desire to diversify. Many of today's conglomerates are not giants surfeited with cash, though, but growing boys who aspire to giantism. In the horse-and-buggy era, firms diversified to lessen risks of failure and more fully utilize their resources, like the coal-yard operator who delivered ice in the summertime. But today, synergism is the byword. In its corporate context, synergism implies that the total capabilities of a large organization far exceed those of the sum of its divisions taken separately. Roughly speaking, it is the proposition that two plus two equal five.

That business today is clearly bent on diversifying is confirmed by FTC statistics. Conglomerate acquisitions are now the most significant category of corporate amalgamation. In 1967, conglomerate acquisitions accounted for 83 per cent of the number of large mergers and 80 per cent of the acquired assets. The FTC figures also show that from 1963 to 1967 the importance of conglomerate combinations measured either in terms of assets or number of mergers increased substantially. Figures for the first half of 1968 show that in that 6-month period conglomerate mergers accounted for 79.3 per cent of the number of acquisitions and 89.8 per cent of the merged assets. In terms of the contributions of all mergers to the total asset growth of the two hundred largest manufacturing corporations in a recent six-year period, conglomerate acquisitions contributed three times more to the companies' growth than did horizontal and vertical mergers combined.

CONGLOMERATES AND COMPETITION

Conglomerate mergers may be procompetitive at times by providing a beachhead from which an outsider may enter an industry, thus providing a challenge to the industry's dominant firms. On the other hand, those industries most highly concentrated are generally protected from competition by barriers that prevent new entrants from coming in and sharing attractive returns. The barriers are frequently so high that new firms simply cannot climb over them. The conglomerate merger movement has radically changed the contours of the economy and altered many of those barriers. Significant for antitrust is the fact that certain firms have become more important than the industries in which they operate. As a result, the danger arises that some companies may no longer be subject to the normal competitive discipline of the markets in which they do business.

The Commission classifies conglomerates as product extension, market extension, or other. Market extension mergers are those in which the two parties to a merger are engaged in the same general line of business activity but operate in different geographical markets. Product extension mergers represent an extension of a firm's activity into another product line, but one that may be related functionally either in production, distribution, or sales of products. The "other" category includes mergers in which there is very little discernible relationship between the acquiring and acquired firms.

Although entry into an industry by "building-in" rather than "buying in" tends toward deconcentration and is more consistent with antitrust policy than entry via the merger route, Congress did not intend to foreclose entry by merger completely. But the Clayton Act was clearly meant to apply to anticompetitive conglomerate mergers as well as to monopolistic holding companies. In the words of the Supreme Court's decision in the *Brown Shoe* case, "by the deletion of the 'acquiring-acquired' language in the original text, [Congress] hoped to make plain that Section 7 applied not only to mergers between actual competitors, but also to vertical and conglomerate mergers whose effect may tend to lessen competition in any line of commerce in any section of the country."

Although relatively few conglomerate mergers have been challenged, the FTC has led the way. For once, the Commission has paced the courts.

PROCTER & GAMBLE–CLOROX

The federal government's first formal challenge of a conglomerate merger involved a product extension merger by Procter & Gamble Company. The FTC in 1957 issued a complaint attacking P & G's acquisition of Clorox Chemical Company. Clorox, the nation's leading manufacturer of household liquid bleach, clearly dominated its highly concentrated industry. It was the only national seller, with 49 per cent of total bleach sales and much more in some important regions of the country. Yet Clorox was a relatively small firm, with total sales of only $40 million a year, almost all in bleach. Although chemically identical to the other brands, Clorox bleach sold at a premium price, attesting to the manufacturer's capacity to "presell" its product to consumers by means of extensive advertising.

Procter, a resourceful and feared competitor, was much larger than Clorox or any other bleach producer. Its advertising budget alone was twice Clorox's total sales. By reason of its size and diversification, P & G enjoyed substantial strategic advantages in advertising and promotions, in particular, large discounts in television and magazine advertising.

In 1961, the Commission re-examined the case after Procter appealed the first decision of the hearing examiner, who had held the merger illegal. The Commission's subsequent opinion intimated that there could be no standard for determining the legality of a conglomerate merger in advance of its consummation; all would depend on what happened afterward. Accordingly, the Commission remanded the case to the examiner to consider developments in the bleach industry in the four post-merger years. By the time the Commission was ready to decide the case on Procter's appeal from the examiner's second decision, in December, 1963, the Supreme Court's decisions in *Brown Shoe* and *Philadelphia Bank* had come down, stressing an approach to mergers based on market structure and indicating the economic studies on which an analysis of the relevant market in a particular case could be based.

Thus guided, the Commission placed the facts of the *Clorox* case in a framework of economic theory based on the adverse effect of the merger on a determination of the behavior of oligopoly markets, the impact of potential competition, and the ease with which new firms could enter the market. The FTC found, in a decision written by Commissioner Elman, that the amended Section 7 of the Clayton Act had been violated by the entrance of Procter & Gamble into the liquid bleach industry through the acquisition of Clorox. In the Commission's opinion, injurious consequences to competition could be expected to flow from several circumstances, including the large advertising discounts now available to Clorox.

The case ended its tenth year with a Supreme Court decision in April, 1967, requiring P & G to divest itself of Clorox. Both the FTC and the Supreme Court ruled without dissent in finding the merger illegal. Central to the Commission's theory, and supported by the Court, was the notion that P & G's established marketing and advertising power would open the way to its dominance in the bleach field. "The substitution of Procter with its huge assets and advertising advantages for the already dominant Clorox would dissuade new entrants and discourage active competition from the firms already in the industry," the FTC declared.

ADVERTISING AND CONCENTRATION

The FTC's second major case in the grocery products industry demonstrated the validity of the findings in P & G. In 1957, General Foods had acquired S.O.S., the nation's third largest manufacturer of household steel wool. Shortly thereafter, S.O.S. captured the dominant share of the household steel wool market, aided by the availability of pooled discounts on General Foods products and the company's saturation marketing efforts. The effect on smaller competitors was predictably dramatic. While General Foods substantially increased its share of the market, the second largest competitor, Brillo, faced a rapidly deteriorating position. The Third Circuit Court of Appeals, upholding an FTC decision, held that the merger raised entry barriers in the steel wool market since consumer preference for the dominant brands had been generated by extensive advertising.

In further recognition of the importance of product extension mergers and the role of advertising as a competitive tool, the FTC on May 15, 1968, issued a statement of enforcement policy with respect to product extension mergers in grocery products manufacturing. The Commission's statement indicated that although acquisitions by the largest firms would be suspect, amalgamations of smaller firms to achieve advertising efficiency would not necessarily be opposed. This statement rested on the findings of an FTC survey of grocery products manufacturing in which it was noted that large-scale promotional activity and heavy advertising expenses resulted from and contributed to a trend of increased conglomeration and concentration in the industry.

WHAT NEXT FOR CONGLOMERATES?

The Supreme Court's decision in *Procter & Gamble* immediately stirred speculation in the business press that the conglomerate-issue doves on the Commission were becoming slightly more hawkish. At the same time, according to *Business Week* (May 6, 1967), a series of consent settlements negotiated at the FTC created friction inside the agency. The controversial agreements prohibited the companies involved from making future acquisitions for a period of time but required only limited divestiture. In one case, Commissioner John R. Reilly commented that the Commission had "thundered in the complaint and cheeped in the order." Commissioners Reilly and Mary Gardiner Jones both contended that more conglomerate cases needed to be litigated to clarify the law. "If we just settle everything," Commissioner Reilly told *Business Week,* "where the hell will we be 10 years from now as far as conglomerate mergers are concerned?"

In July of 1968, prodded by the Senate Antimonopoly Subcommittee and its chairman, Senator Philip A. Hart, the FTC announced that it was undertaking an in-depth investigation of the conglomerate merger movement, encompassing its causes, effects, and implications. Noting that merger activity had reached the highest levels in American industrial history with no signs of abatement, the FTC said there was "growing concern on the part of the Commission, as well as Congressional committees, including the Senate and House Antitrust

Subcommittee and the Joint Economic Committee, as to the long-run dangers of the continuation of the conglomerate merger movement."

The FTC staff report was sent to Congress in November, 1969. It warned that the conglomerate movement threatened consolidation of corporate assets and decision-making into an exclusive "industrial elite." The study contended that only more stringent public policies could slow down merger activity. "In 1968 the merger movement reached such a magnitude that in a single year nearly 10 per cent of all independent manufacturing corporations worth over $10 million were acquired," the report said, adding that a more vigorous antitrust enforcement policy might have forestalled much of the rush for acquisitions.

The report went to Congress without official Commission endorsement because of disagreement among the Commissioners over its conclusions. Commissioner Jones claimed that the findings rested essentially "on hypothesis and theorization" rather than real, conclusive evidence. Chairman Dixon called the study "useful background," but noted that neither the Commission as a whole nor the individual Commissioners "necessarily endorse or adopt the report or its recommendations."

Like the "trust problem" that preceded it, the "conglomerate problem" is being examined, debated, and, in theory at least, remedied. It is clear, however, that the FTC has only begun to work out a policy that will permit it to deal with the spiraling movement effectively.

IX

Price Discrimination

The Robinson-Patman Act outlawing price discrimination has been variously described as the Magna Carta of small business and the Typhoid Mary of antitrust. The Act is "sometimes praised, sometimes abused, much interpreted, little understood, and capable of producing instant arguments," Earl W. Kintner wrote in his book, *An Antitrust Primer*. The Supreme Court even observed that the law is a "singularly opaque and illusive statute."

Although its provisions are complex, controversial, and sometimes difficult to apply to given situations, the Act has one alleged purpose—to correct discriminatory abuses that might result from the concentration of selling or buying power in a few companies. Robinson-Patman is intended to act as a footbrake on large buyers and sellers, thereby giving small buyers and sellers a chance. It broadened price-discrimination law to cover the seller's customers as well as his competitors and to stop large purchasers from inducing lower-than-normal prices. The statute also covers indirect price discrimination in which large buyers are favored with services not granted competing purchasers or are guaranteed sums of money in the form of promotional allowances or brokerage not available to their competitors.

Robinson-Patman was not the first federal act to deal with price discrimination. Congress, in writing Section 2 of the Clayton Act, sought to outlaw the vicious price-cutting used by some of the big trusts as a weapon against competitors they wanted to eliminate. With their enormous resources, the trusts could comfortably face a period of selling below cost in a selected area where, for example, an obstinate independent was refusing to sell out or a new entrant was making inroads. A great many small concerns were put out of business by such predatory price-cutting. The competition which Congress thus regarded as threatened by price discrimination was that between a supplier and his competitors.

Yet Congress realized that not every difference in price was discriminatory, and its members did not wish to penalize the small firm that found it necessary to lower its price in a particular area or to a particular customer to meet a price offered by a powerful competitor. The lawmakers of 1914 therefore tried to meet these points in the Clayton Act with a general prohibition that made it "unlawful for any person engaged in commerce . . . to discriminate in price between different purchasers of commodities, which commodities are sold for use, consumption, or resale . . . where the effect of such discrimination may be to substantially lessen competition or tend to create a monopoly in any line of commerce." But they left open a wide escape route when they added: "*Provided,* that nothing herein contained shall prevent discrimination in price between purchasers of commodities on account of differences in the grade, quality, or quantity of the commodity sold." Differences in quantities sold could nearly always be adduced as an explanation of different prices, and the courts were not disposed to question too closely whether the difference in quantity could really be said to account for or to justify the whole of the difference in price. Before 1936, when the Robinson-Patman Act was passed to amend this provision of the Clayton Act, the FTC was successful in very few outright price-discrimination cases.

The deficiencies of the Clayton Act were brought to public attention by the FTC's 1934 report on chain stores. The report concluded that the growth of the chains and other large concentrations, with their ability to buy cheaply, endangered the survival of small businessmen. It also showed that the lower prices accorded to chains, particularly food chains, were rarely related to the actual quantities purchased, the quality of the goods, or the cost of selling. Moreover, the report indicated that preferential prices were exacted by the chain grocery stores in various concealed forms, such as brokerage commissions and advertising and promotional allowances. The family grocery store was finding it hard going and its future was in question. The report engendered broad public support for legislation that would compel suppliers to treat all buyers on a fair and equal basis.

At the time, the United States was in the grip of a depression that had already given rise to regulation of security transactions, labor and banking, and other aspects of the economy. The time was ripe for additional regulatory legislation that would extend protection to those businessmen hit hardest in hard times, the small businessmen. On June 19, 1936, the Robinson-Patman Act was passed as an amendment to the original Clayton Act, entirely replacing Section 2. Congressman Wright Patman, co-author of the Act and chairman of the Antitrust Subcommittee of the House Committee on the Judiciary, stated that the amendment was "designed to accomplish what so far the Clayton Act has only weakly attempted, namely, to protect the independent merchant, the public whom he serves, and the manufacturer from whom he buys, from exploitation by his chain competitor."

Summary of the Law

The Robinson-Patman Act, for which the FTC was given primary enforcement responsibilities, has six parts. Section 2, with its five subdivisions, is considered an antitrust law. It imposes civil prohibitions, and treble damage suits may be sustained in the federal courts for violations. Section 3, which the Supreme Court has held not to be an antitrust statute, declares that it is an offense punishable by fines or imprisonment to be a party to discriminatory transactions or to engage in local price-cutting or to sell goods at "unreasonably low prices for the purpose of destroying competition or eliminating a competitor." With its criminal prohibitions, Section 3 falls primarily under the jurisdiction of the Justice Department, but it is rarely used. In nearly twenty years, Justice has not litigated a single case under this section.

The heart of the Act, Section 2, contains the following provisions: Section 2(a), the substantive and most frequently cited provision, prohibits sellers from discriminating in price among competing buyers except under certain circumstances; Section 2(b) sets forth burdens of proof in defending violations of Section 2(a) and provides that a price discrimination may be justified if it is made in good faith to meet competition; Section 2(c) prohibits the seller from paying any brokerage fee, commission, or an equivalent to a buyer or an agent of the buyer and prohibits the buyer from accepting any such brokerage fee or commission; Sections 2(d) and 2(e) prohibit a seller from granting discriminatory allowances, services, or facilities to a buyer unless such assistance is made available to other competing buyers on proportionally equal terms.

Interpreting Robinson-Patman

The law's full meaning was first established in the first *Morton Salt* case, decided by the Supreme Court in 1948.

Morton Salt, one of the largest manufacturers of branded table salt in the United States, sells directly to large retailers such as the chain stores as well as to wholesalers, who supply the greater part of the retail trade. The FTC showed that only five companies—five large chain stores—had ever bought enough salt in one year to get Morton's top discount rate of nearly 15 per cent. As a result of this concession, the five chains could sell the salt over the counter at a price below that at which small retailers could buy it from wholesalers, let alone sell it. Small retailers had suffered damage, according to testimony. The Supreme Court ruled in favor of the FTC. More importantly, the *Morton Salt* decision made Robinson-Patman a sweeping prohibition against price differentials. Justice Hugo Black, who spoke for the Court in the case, said all that need be shown to demonstrate illegal price discrimination was a "reasonable possibility" that competition had been substantially lessened. For years after the *Morton Salt* decision, the FTC condemned virtually any sizeable price differential among competing resale customers regardless of the competitive situation.

In recent years, however, the courts and the Commission have retreated from the rule of *Morton Salt*. In 1951, a court of appeals reversed a Commission order against the discount structure of the Minneapolis-Honeywell Company, finding insufficient evidence of injury to competition. The Seventh Circuit Court of Appeals nullified the FTC's ruling in light of virile competition from the respondent's rivals in the oil burner thermostat business and their successful inroads into the respondent's business. Cautioning that the Act "must be read in conformity with the public policy of preserving competition," the same court also reversed another FTC order in *Anheuser-Busch* a decade later, declining to condemn vigorous but non-predatory pricing by a large competitor that "forthrightly met its robust competition" in "conformity with the principle that competition is the decisive force in the market place."

PRICE WARS AND THE OIL INDUSTRY

Most of the case law that has developed under Robinson-Patman focuses on the harm that price discrimination may do to competition between buyers. But price discrimination was first recognized as a danger to free trade when it was applied by a supplier as a weapon against his own competitors. It was the ruthless price-cutting by the giants of the oil industry at the turn of the century that raised the protest which eventually led to Robinson-Patman. Most of the recent cases illustrating this aspect of the law are a far cry from the predatory competition of the trusts, although they serve as a reminder that price-cutting campaigns are still used as a means of disposing of inconvenient competitors.

The retail distribution of gasoline has been marked by more price wars than any other distributive trade in the nation. The factors that caused the wars are difficult to assess, and generalizations are impossible. In some cases, over-supply of refined gasoline weakened the market price. In others, the opening of a new gas station caused a general price reduction by others in the area. Probably there are cases in which the argumentative disposition of a single person touched off a conflict. But because of the serious legal problems involved, particularly those of price discrimination, and because of the potential adverse effects on competition, this industry-wide practice of granting selective price assistance has been attacked by the FTC again and again.

During the 1950's, the FTC took on the major oil companies with a series of complaints involving price wars, dealer aid, alleged price discrimination, vertical integration, unfair competition, and alleged restraint of trade. The Commission's campaign began on September 26, 1956, when the FTC issued a complaint against Pure Oil Company, charging violations of Section 5 of the FTC Act and Section 2(a) of the Robinson-Patman Act. The price discrimination count was based on

Pure's charging a lower price to favored dealers in Jefferson County, Alabama, than it charged to nonfavored dealers elsewhere in Alabama and in other states where Pure operated. The Section 5 count was based on an alleged conspiracy between Pure and its retail dealers to permit Pure to set the retail prices.

The same month, the FTC also lodged a complaint against Sun Oil Company. Sun sold gasoline to thirty-eight independent retail dealers in Duval County, Florida. In June of 1955, the Super Test Oil Company, a nonmajor, opened a competing station at the same intersection as a Sun station operated by Gilbert V. McLean. Initially, Super Test posted its price at two cents below McLean's, but in August it began a series of sporadic reductions, dropping as much as eight cents below the Sun price. McLean's volume of business decreased substantially. Other majors entered the skirmish by reducing their prices to all of their dealers in the area, but, despite this action, McLean went out of business. The FTC charged that Sun had violated the Robinson-Patman Act by charging a lower price to McLean than to the other Sun dealers in Duval County.

Three years later, on April 13, 1959, the Commission issued a complaint against the Atlantic Refining Company. And on November 23, 1960, the FTC issued a complaint against the American Oil Company. The Commission had thus adopted a case-by-case approach to the price-war problem. Relying primarily on Section 2(a) of the Robinson-Patman Act, but using Section 5 of the FTC Act as a potential catch-all provision, the Commission issued complaints alleging price discrimination violations as well as the use of unfair methods of competition in price-war situations. Although this approach permitted the agency a great deal of flexibility in meeting varying situations, it did not offer much guidance to the petroleum industry.

In September of 1964, the District of Columbia Circuit Court of Appeals suddenly disqualified FTC Chairman Dixon from participating in the oil cases pending before the agency. The court ruled that, in a speech before the National Congress of Petroleum Retailers, Dixon had prejudged the illegality of certain practices. The court's ruling, plus heavy pressure from gasoline dealers and smaller suppliers who felt threatened by the major oil companies, combined to spur re-examination by the FTC of its oil industry policies. The Commission's first action, taken in late 1964, was to dismiss its complaints against the four major oil companies. Although Commissioner Everette MacIntyre dissented and accused the FTC of abdicating its responsibilities, the immediate reason for the dismissal was administrative. A quorum of three Commissioners is needed to decide cases. The disqualification of Dixon left only MacIntyre and Elman, since Commissioners Reilly and Jones had been appointed after hearings had been held on the cases. If the Commission had decided to pursue the cases, new hearings would have been required.

There were other reasons why the FTC decided to wipe the slate clean. The Commission, with the exception of MacIntyre, felt that the pending cases only partially covered the complex picture of gasoline marketing. Since most alleged abuses involved the entire industry, lawsuits against three or four companies based on practices of ten years before seemed unfair and inefficient. Finally, in response to the clear need to develop standards of conduct for businessmen desiring to comply with the law, the FTC requested its Bureau of Economics to come up with a report on industry practices. Public hearings were held.

The Commission's report, issued in June, 1967, reviewed in detail what appeared to be the most important causes of gasoline price wars and then attempted to point out how each of these causes affected competition in the various segments of the industry. Its conclusions were: (1) that price competition in gasoline marketing primarily placed the larger sellers against their smaller rivals, (2) that such competition under certain circumstances may take the form of discriminatory or unfair practices, and (3) that continuation of these practices may result in the elimination of important independent factors and thus damage, if not destroy, free and open competition in the industry. In sum, it reflected a desire to protect the independent segment of the industry.

Although the indistinct guidelines offered in the report satisfied few, the inquiry itself seemed to act as a caution light to the oil industry, and few cutthroat practices, including the once-common price wars, have been reported to the FTC. Commissioner Elman, in a dissent in an unrelated case in March, 1969, summed up the situation. "Thanks to the Commission, gasoline price wars seem to have disappeared, as well as price competition at the retail level. The price of gasoline has gone up 'only a few pennies' per gallon, and there is plenty of 'competition' in the form of game promotions, trading stamps, etc. Everybody is happy except the consumers."

Inducing Illegal Discrimination

Although Congress was exercised about the coercive use of buying power, the main provisions of the Robinson-Patman Act strike against the supplier who grants the discrimination rather than against the buyer who benefits from it. But Congress also included in the Act a provision aimed at the big buyer who presses his suppliers to grant discriminatory price concessions. Subsection 2(f) makes it unlawful for any person "knowingly to induce or receive a discrimination in price which is prohibited in this Section."

Automatic Canteen Company of America v. *FTC*, decided by the Supreme Court in 1953, is the leading case on this point. Automatic Canteen not only leases vending machines for sweets but supplies, wholesale, sweets that go in them and is, therefore, a large buyer of sweets from manufacturers. The

FTC alleged that the company put great pressure on candy manufacturers to give it price concessions by quoting prices, often substantially lower than other wholesalers were getting, that it thought the manufacturers should be able to meet. The manufacturer was told of savings he might enjoy in supplying such a large buyer as Automatic Canteen.

The FTC based its case on a demonstration of the price difference and the ensuing threat to competition. In effect, the Commission's approach placed on the customer the onus of showing that the discrimination involved was not prohibited. Speaking for a majority of six Justices against three, Justice Felix Frankfurter rejected the Commission's case.

After the decision in *Automatic Canteen*, it was believed that Section 2(f) was seriously impaired and would be little used, for Commission counsel had been given the onerous burden of proving that the buyer knew or should have known that the favored prices received could not be justified by savings in cost on the part of the seller by their dealings. In addition, staff counsel had to prove that the buyer either knew or should have known that the preferential price received had the requisite effect of injury to competition.

In spite of the apparent heavy burden of proof imposed on the Commission, most of the eighteen FTC 2(f) complaints issued since *Automatic Canteen* have been directed against buyer groups since they were believed to be the real instigators of discriminatory concessions from hapless sellers.

ILLEGAL BROKERAGE

No provision of the Robinson-Patman Act has been subjected to more attack than the illegal brokerage section, Section 2(c), and none has created such deep divisions within the FTC. Subsection 2(c) makes it unlawful for a buyer of goods (or any agent or representative of a buyer) to receive from or to be paid by the supplier any brokerage or commission "except for services rendered in connection with the sale or purchase of goods." This provision closed a loophole through which large buyers might have received favors without breach of subsection 2(a). Illegality may be established without showing of injury or any of the other defenses associated with the more flexible price prohibitions of subsection 2(a).

The illegal brokerage section was aimed at specific practices that existed in the food retailing industry at the time the Act was passed. To avoid the prohibition on price concessions in Section 2 of the original Clayton Act, large chain buyers used a number of devices for obtaining indirect price concessions. One technique was to set up a dummy broker who, in fact, performed no brokerage services but was merely an agent of the buyer. The buyer would then demand that the seller pay "brokerage" to the dummy. In other circumstances, the chain would simply demand that the seller pay it an allowance "in lieu of brokerage" on the pretext that it had saved the seller part or all of its brokerage costs. The purpose of the brokerage section was to force these disguised transactions out into the open by imposing an absolute prohibition on them.

One of the first orders issued by the FTC under Robinson-Patman tested Section 2(c). The case involved the Atlantic and Pacific Tea Company (A & P), a gigantic holding company with retail subsidiaries, which had been demanding a broker's discount when it bought directly from suppliers. The Supreme Court upheld the brokerage section of the law and enjoined the A & P from accepting the unearned discount. The A & P then asked that the prices it paid be cut by an amount equal to the brokerage payments. When this was forbidden, the A & P announced that it would buy only from suppliers who would sell directly to it. This and similar practices were challenged in a 1949 civil suit brought by the Justice Department, which was seeking to break up the huge chain. The suit was settled by consent decree in January, 1954. The A & P was not broken up, but it was enjoined from engaging in certain restrictive and discriminatory practices.

One question that has frequently arisen in brokerage cases is whether the words "except for services rendered in connection with the sale or purchase of goods, wares, or merchandise" permit a buyer to receive (and a seller to grant) brokerage or any allowance or discount in place of brokerage on his purchases. For years, appellate adjudications unanimously held that Section 2(c) expresses an absolute prohibition against a buyer receiving brokerage, or other compensation in lieu thereof—either directly or through someone acting as his agent—from a seller on the buyer's own purchases. To interpret the "services rendered" provision as a general exception allowing buyers to receive brokerage was regarded as contrary to the purpose of the law. Consistent with this interpretation, early cases prohibited payments of any brokerage savings by the seller to cooperative buying organizations, since such organizations were considered under the direct or indirect control of the buyers.

From 1936 until 1961, the FTC issued 588 cease-and-desist orders under Robinson-Patman, of which 246 were for illegal brokerage. Most of these were in the food industry. Since then, however, few complaints have been lodged under Section 2(c), in large part because of an abrupt shift in emphasis.

Section 2(c) is now being re-examined as a result of a long fight waged by Commissioner Philip Elman. Elman contended that the Commission's strict interpretation of Section 2(c) tends to protect the vested interests of the food brokers. According to the Elman thesis, the distortion of Section 2(c) came about through the early devitalization of the proscribed exception for cases in which legitimate services are rendered and through the erection of the dogmas that a "true broker" cannot serve two masters and that a buyer's agent cannot perform legitimate services for the seller for which he is entitled to compensation. Recent FTC and court decisions have tended to confirm Elman's opinion that past enforcement of the section has penalized small independent wholesalers and cooperative distributing organizations—the very people the Act was passed to protect.

DIFFERENTIAL FUNCTIONAL DISCOUNTS

There are some other applications of the Robinson-Patman Act which its sponsors probably never envisaged. One of them is its application to functional discounts. The most common type of trade discount is that which a manufacturer grants to a wholesaler. No one is surprised that a wholesaler buys goods more cheaply than a retailer and a retailer more cheaply than a housewife. But when a supplier sells a product to customers at different discount levels, he is selling goods of like grade and quality to different customers at different prices and may well become snarled up in the provisions of the Robinson-Patman Act. Normally, there is no problem because a wholesaler and a retailer perform different functions in different markets and are not in competition with each other. But trouble can arise when a single concern straddles two or more trade functions. The wholesaler-cum-retailer, for example, is nonetheless a retailer and in competition with other retailers. If he is given the wholesale discount on goods he sells by retail, he will, in effect, be getting a preferential price as against his competitors. Goods of like grade and quality will be reaching like purchasers at different prices.

That is what happened in the *Standard of Indiana* case. Standard's jobber customers got a higher discount than its direct retailer customers, with the result that the wholesalers were supplying rival retailers more cheaply than Standard was supplying its own retailers. On that ground, Standard's operations were found to threaten competition. The Commission solution, spelled out in its cease-and-desist order, was to remedy this threat by prohibiting Standard from selling gasoline to retailers at higher prices than known to be the prices at which wholesalers buying from Standard were selling gasoline to retail competitors. The effect of this order was to impose a rigid system of resale price maintenance on Standard's wholesalers, a contradiction since the FTC has opposed legislation legalizing resale price maintenance. If the federal and state laws allowing resale price maintenance were repealed, Standard might find itself in the dock for destroying competition between its wholesalers by maintaining prices pursuant to a Commission order.

PROMOTIONAL ALLOWANCES AND SERVICES

Congress was well aware when the Robinson-Patman Act was passed of the many ways in which a supplier can favor one customer over another. In addition to price concessions, he can offer advertising and promotional allowances, displays, demonstrators and demonstrations, warehouse facilities, and other merchandising assistance. Discriminations by suppliers in two of these areas were covered in Sections 2(d) and 2(e) of the Act. In the case of pricing, Section 2(f), a corollary to Section 2(a), was added, making it illegal for the buyer knowingly to induce and receive price discriminations prohibited by Section 2(a).

But the Robinson-Patman Act contained no prohibition against the inducement and receipt of discriminatory advertising and promotional allowances by large buyers. This apparent legislative omission has been remedied by simply applying the familiar, long-established principle that it is an unfair trade practice in violation of Section 5 of the FTC Act to procure, participate in, or aid and abet the use by another of a trade practice that is illegal and against public policy.

The courts have thus upheld the Commission in requiring that services provided to any buyer must be made effectively available to all.

But how is "on proportionally equal terms" to be measured? Here, the Commission has adopted no clear rule. Proportionality could be measured on the dollar volume of the sales or on the buyer's cost of his services to the seller. For a time, it appeared that legality could be assured only by conformity to the first of these tests. But a Commission decision involving the big soap companies shows this to be untrue. These concerns made one allowance in their price per case to buyers who advertised the product in handbills and a still smaller allowance to those who featured it in store displays. These allowances were not proportionate to the quantities of soap sold to buyers in each group. But they were given for services actually rendered, and on this basis the Commission found them to be within the law.

Commissioner Elman has voiced criticism of the FTC's enforcement of the promotional and advertising allowance section of Robinson-Patman. In a speech delivered at the University of Washington Law School on August 2, 1966, he compared the background of this section to that of the illegal brokerage section. "Section 2(d) had its origin in the view that promotional and advertising allowances were forms for disguising price rebates," he said. "By making the prohibitions of 2(d) absolute, it was hoped to force such disguised rebates out into the open as price concessions where they could be dealt with under the price discrimination sections. However, to treat all promotional allowances as disguised price rebates obviously conflicts with commercial realities."

In 1966, Elman dissented in a case involving a key agency program to ban cooperative advertising in the clothing industry. Several years before, the FTC had conducted an investigation of the apparel industry and found what it alleged to be a widespread practice of granting certain retailers allowances without providing equal allowances to other retailers. Some 300 firms signed consent decrees to avoid protracted litigation. During fiscal 1967, a total of fifty Robinson-Patman cases were settled informally, but several firms held out. Among them was House of Lord's, a New York dressmaker. The FTC ruled, after lengthy hearings, that House of Lords had violated the law by paying half the advertising costs of certain retailers of its Viyella dresses without giving equal allowances to competitors. An FTC examiner then ruled that the company's practice did not violate the law because the payments to retailers were not based on a customer's purchases, and the customer determined the costs of the advertising. A majority of the 5-man Commission overruled its examiner and said the testimony showed that all retailers were not informed that they were eligible for the promotional program.

Divergent views among Commission members over this case in particular, and how to deal with discriminatory allowances in general, led to a public squabble among the Commissioners and considerable confusion over how to regulate special allowances under Robinson-Patman. It may take new legislation to resolve this and a number of other price-discrimination issues not clearly dealt with in the existing laws.

X

The Tetracycline Case

The tetracycline case is the FTC's wonder case. It involves an antibiotic of vital importance and several giants of the American drug industry who exploited a fraudulently obtained patent to exercise monopoly rights and maintain artificially high prices.

In July, 1958, the FTC lodged a complaint charging that the patent for tetracycline had been obtained through deception by Charles Pfizer & Company and American Cyanamid Company, two leading firms in an industry with sales of more than $330 million a year. Ten years and several go-arounds later, in spite of the odds against the underdog agency, the FTC won a striking victory in the courts. The drug companies were forced to give up their monopoly of the important antibiotic, make a public accounting of their actions, and pay out millions of dollars in damages.

The case is remarkable in a variety of ways. It put the FTC into the patent field. It defined a new unfair trade practice—the exploitation of a patent fraudulently obtained. And it fulfilled what, in the opinion of many, constitutes the primary goal of antitrust—it brought consumer prices down. For drama, including a wiretap incident, it goes unsurpassed in the annals of the FTC.

The story begins with a parent drug of tetracycline, Aureomycin.

On September 13, 1949, American Cyanamid Company obtained a (Duggar) patent on Aureomycin and, on September 2, 1952, it obtained an improvement (Niedercorn) patent on the Duggar process for producing Aureomycin. On July 19, 1950, Pfizer & Company obtained a (Sobin) patent on Terramycin. Cyanamid and Pfizer therefore had a legal monopoly on the production and sale of Aureomycin and Terramycin respectively, which put them in a position to establish a monopoly on a derivative drug known as tetracycline.

Pfizer filed application for a patent on tetracycline on October 23, 1952. It was followed by a similar application by Cyanamid on March 16, 1953. On October 29, 1953, H. J. Lidoff, the patent examiner who handled the Pfizer application, declared an interference for the purpose of determining priority of invention between these two applications.

A month earlier, Heyden Chemical Company had announced that it, too, had discovered tetracycline and subsequently filed its (Minieri) application for a patent. Within five weeks of this announcement, Cyanamid acquired the antibiotic division of Heyden, including the rights to the Minieri patent application, for $12.5 million, some $6 million more than its book value. Thereupon, Pfizer and Cyanamid began negotiations for a cross-licensing agreement, which was formally executed on January 11, 1954. Under this agreement, the two companies were assured of sharing a monopoly on tetracycline if the Patent Office could be persuaded to grant a patent to either of them. Cyanamid then ceded priority of invention to Pfizer and withdrew its patent application. The result was termination of the first interference on February 9, 1954, and removal of the first obstacle from the pathway to obtaining a patent.

A second obstacle soon arose, however—a patent application for tetracycline filed by Bristol-Myers Company. Lidoff declared a second interference. Bristol's patent application was the opening gun in its battle against Pfizer and Cyanamid to secure a place for itself in the tetracycline market.

In May, 1954, while these rival claims were being fought out, Bristol began to sell tetracycline in bulk to E. R. Squibb and, later, to the Upjohn Company and to make tetracycline agreements with foreign firms.

On November 14, 1954, Lidoff dissolved the second interference, ruling that tetracycline was not patentable because it appeared to lack novelty. In an earlier ruling on the Minieri application, dated September 28, 1953, Lidoff had concluded that the production of tetracycline appeared to be inherent in the Duggar process used to make Aureomycin.

On November 29, 1954, Pfizer's patent representatives met with examiner Lidoff at his office to contest the rejection of their application. A summary of the interview, prepared by Pfizer's representatives and filed with the Patent Office, reveals that Pfizer argued that there was no reasonable basis for Lidoff's speculation "as to the coproduction of tetracycline in the prior art processes." Pfizer also argued that Cyanamid, which had manufactured literally tons of Aureomycin under its Duggar and Niedercorn patents, had failed to discover *any* tetracycline in its large-scale manufacture, although Cyanamid had devoted extensive research to the recovery, purification, and properties of Aureomycin. It was argued that the experience of Cyanamid "should conclusively refute the tenuous basis for the Examiner's unwarranted assumption." The summary shows that Lidoff adhered to his position that he would not withdraw his rejection unless the applicant would submit evidence overcoming the speculated basis for rejection.

Pfizer thereupon embarked on a program to convince Lidoff that his finding of inherent coproduction was erroneous. The details of this campaign, the basis of the FTC case, came out later.

Under patent law, the Patent Office must grant a patent for a product or process that is new, but a patent cannot be granted for something that is not new. With neither laboratories nor scientific resources to carry out experimental work itself, the Patent Office relies on a requirement of full disclosure by an applicant. If the applicant does not supply full and accurate information, he is liable to prosecution.

Pfizer, asked to repeat the process outlined in the Aureomycin patent, reported that it was unable to find any tetracycline in the drug produced by the process, and that, therefore, none was made. Having no alternative, Lidoff granted Pfizer a patent on January 11, 1955.

On the same day that Pfizer received its patent, it brought infringement suits against Bristol, Squibb, and Upjohn, seeking damages and a restraining order preventing them from marketing tetracycline. Bristol responded with a countersuit against Pfizer. Counter actions were also taken by Olin Mathieson Chemical Corporation and Upjohn.

"In these otherwise discouraging circumstances," said Bristol in 1967, "a startling development took place." In September, 1955, John G. Broady, a private detective retained by Pfizer, was indicted for tapping telephone lines, including those of Bristol and Squibb. Broady was convicted of the wiretap charges on December 8, 1955. For eavesdropping on the two rival drug makers and their lawyers, Broady had been paid $60,000 by a Pfizer official, who met the detective at the entrance to the Holland Tunnel in New York City to hand over the cash. Testifying later in a Justice Department suit, John E. McKeen, board chairman of Pfizer, denied any personal responsibility for the 1955 wiretap episode. He blamed the phone monitoring on Robert C. Porter, then Pfizer's general counsel.

The same month that Broady testified and was convicted

in the wiretap trial, Charles H. Walker, a lawyer for Bristol, served notice that Broady's testimony would be used by Bristol in its patent suit. According to McKeen's later testimony, Pfizer had experienced a "bath of bad publicity" in the wiretap trial. To avoid a second one, he had decided to do what he had firmly refused to do earlier—to settle the dispute with Bristol. A few days later, an agreement was reached under which Bristol was licensed to produce, use, and sell tetracycline, and to sell it in bulk to only two customers, Olin, and Upjohn. The three countersuits were then dismissed.

The evidence in the record of these lawsuits was known to the FTC, as were several other developments. There was the FTC's own study of antibiotics, undertaken at the request of the Senate Commerce Committee, which revealed tetracycline's high price. In the meantime, the Defense Department and the Veterans Administration, as they are required to do in the case of identical bids, had informed the Justice Department and the FTC that they had been quoted identical prices for purchases of large quantities of tetracycline. Investigators at the FTC, putting two and two together, began to surmise that the anticompetitive prices were being kept artificially high. The next step was to look at the records of the U.S. Patent Office. The interferences in Pfizer's patent application suggested the possibility that the patent had been fraudulently obtained.

On July 28, 1958, the FTC issued a complaint charging Charles Pfizer & Company with making false, misleading, and incorrect statements to, and withholding material information from, the U.S. Patent Office for the purpose of inducing issuance of a patent on tetracycline. The complaint also alleged that Bristol-Myers Company and American Cyanamid Company had withheld from the Patent Office material information in the course of the prosecution of patent applications, as a result of which Pfizer was aided in obtaining its tetracycline patent. Furthermore, it was alleged that Cyanamid, Bristol,

Olin Mathieson, and the Upjohn Company had solicited and accepted licenses from Pfizer under the tetracycline patent, knowing that material information had been withheld from the Patent Office by one or more of the respondents. The complaint further alleged that all five respondents had fixed and maintained prices of a number of antibiotics, including tetracycline, through conspiracy and combination.

But on October 31, 1961, FTC Hearing Examiner Robert L. Piper filed an initial decision holding that the evidence failed to establish that the respondents had engaged in any of the unlawful practices alleged in the complaint. Piper was apparently convinced that Pfizer had settled its private suit because the company was embarrassed over the well-publicized wiretap incident.

Examiner Piper's initial decision was appealed to the full Commission, which, on August 8, 1963, set aside the decision and issued a cease-and-desist order against the respondents. The Commission found that Pfizer, in securing its tetracycline patent, had deliberately misled and withheld information from the Patent Office. It concluded that the whole business had been conducted with "unclean hands," "inequitableness," and "bad faith." The Commission further found that Pfizer asserted monopoly rights under its patent to prevent competition in the tetracycline market and that the effects of those acts had been to restrain competition, to foreclose a substantial market, and to create a monopoly in the manufacture and sale of tetracycline in violation of Section 5 of the FTC Act.

It also found that Cyanamid had made erroneous representations to the Patent Office concerning matters bearing on the patentability of tetracycline, and that, although Cyanamid had discovered that these representations were inaccurate, it had not disclosed this fact to the Patent Office until after the tetracycline patent had been granted to Pfizer, thereby aiding the latter in its efforts to obtain a patent. The Commission ruled that Cyanamid's acceptance of a license from Pfizer to make and sell tetracycline with knowledge that it had made false statements of fact to the Patent Office constituted an illegal attempt on its part to share in a monopoly on tetracycline and amounted to a combination in restraint of trade. Similar charges against Bristol, Squibb, and Upjohn were dismissed.

On the issue of price-fixing, the Commission held that the record as a whole sustained the charge that all five respondents fixed and maintained the price of tetracycline in substantial markets through conspiracy and combination.

The respondents appealed from the Commission's decision, taking their case to the Sixth Circuit Court of Appeals. They challenged the FTC's findings, conclusions, and cease-and-desist order on both the patent and price-fixing phases of the case. They also claimed that they had been deprived of a fair hearing by reason of Chairman Dixon's participation. The appeals court, in an opinion filed on June 16, 1966, held that Dixon was disqualified to sit on the case because he had made prejudicial statements during the drug price investigation of the Senate Anti-Monopoly Subcommittee of which he had earlier been staff director and counsel. The appeals court remanded the proceeding for reconsideration without the Chairman's participation.

The Commission was forced to reopen the proceeding, and the case was assigned to Hearing Examiner Abner E. Lipscomb. Under normal procedure, the same examiner would have reheard testimony, but Robert L. Piper was no longer in the employ of the FTC. By order of August 1, 1966, the Commission directed that a hearing examiner begin expeditious hearings to determine if Lidoff had been deceived into granting a patent which otherwise never would have been approved.

After two days of hearings, the new examiner ruled that official representatives of both Pfizer and Cyanamid had made "false and misleading statements to officials of the United

States Patent Office and suppressed and withheld information from them, all of which was relevant and material" to their consideration of the application for the tetracycline patent. With the Chairman not participating, the Commission, on September 29, 1967, adopted the findings and conclusions contained in the decision of Hearing Examiner Lipscomb, concluding that as a result of its dishonest behavior, Pfizer had been able to exercise monopoly rights over an important antibiotic with sales that exceeded $100 million per year.

The Commission ordered Pfizer to grant any domestic applicant a license to make, use, and sell tetracycline. No limits were imposed on the use of such licenses, but Pfizer was permitted to collect royalties of not more than 2.5 per cent of the net sales of tetracycline manufactured or sold under them. At the request of Pfizer, the Commission also authorized the drug maker to require that applicants pay an amount of $2,500 upon acceptance of a license, which would be applied against future royalty payments.

Commissioner Jones objected to the royalty feature of the Commission order. "I vigorously dissent from that portion of the order entered by the Commission which expressly permits these respondents to collect royalties under the patents which the Commission found were wrongfully procured and exploited by them," she said in a dissenting statement. "Under the Commission's order these competitors of respondents who have been wrongfully excluded from the market all these years must now come to respondents for a license for which they must pay a substantial royalty and thus the order in essence permits respondents to maintain competitive advantages unlawfully achieved."

The drug companies appealed again to the Sixth Circuit Court of Appeals, and the case was re-argued in June, 1968. On September 30, 1968, the court upheld the FTC order.

In the meantime, the prices of tetracycline had declined substantially subsequent to the Commission's 1963 order directing Pfizer and Cyanamid to license any qualified applicant under their respective patents for the manufacture or sale of tetracycline. New firms not licensed by Pfizer or Cyanamid had also entered the field. According to its own brief, Pfizer's bid prices to hospitals had moved downward to levels of less than one-fourth of the 1958 bid prices, and list prices in the prescription market had also fallen. The price to the retailer of one bottle of 100 capsules (250 mg.), which the record shows was $30.60 in 1958, was subsequently listed by Cyanamid at $11.22. The lowered prices were not due solely to the FTC order. Tetracycline users, including the Defense Department and the Veterans Administration, had been ordering tetracycline for 3 cents a capsule from an Italian firm because of the 50-cents-a-capsule price of the domestically produced antibiotic. When the FTC case finally ended in 1968, the Justice Department charged three of the companies with price-fixing, using much of the evidence in the FTC record. Pfizer, Cyanamid, and Bristol were named individually as defendants in the case, said to be the biggest case in three decades to go to trial under the criminal antimonopoly provision of the Sherman Act. All three companies were found guilty of conspiring from 1953 through 1961 to monopolize and fix the prices of tetracycline and two chemically related antibiotics.

A number of treble damage suits grew out of this conviction. Some sixteen states and two cities sued for themselves and their political subdivisions. The Washington law firm representing some of the plaintiffs estimated that triple-damage suits based on direct purchases of tetracycline could aggregate between $240 million and $300 million. Claims of states and their subdivisions on reimbursements for purchases of the antibiotics made at retail by welfare patients could come to an additional $240 million.

On February 15, 1969, *Business Week* reported that the five drug companies had agreed to pay $120 million in final claims to cities, states, and others. Of the $120 million settlement, Cyanamid would pay $48.4 million; Pfizer, $40.9 million; Bristol-Myers, $19.3 million; Upjohn, $6.2 million, and Squibb, $5.2 million.

The repercussions were not over. In July, 1969, the Justice Department charged Pfizer and Cyanamid with fraud in obtaining the tetracycline patent and sued them for $25 million in damages.

In the tetracycline case, the FTC was up against the well-armed and well-heeled giants of the drug industry. The respondent companies were represented by some of the highest paid lawyers from some of the most prestigious law firms in America. Four top Wall Street firms, a number of leading patent firms, and Washington's largest and best-known law firm, Covington & Burling, went to bat for the drug companies. One of the lawyers in the case later became a U.S. district court judge in New York State, and another became a district court judge in Washington, D.C. Appearing in the FTC hearings and in court at any one time during the lengthy trial, there were as many as fifty representatives of the respondent companies, including the companies' general counsel as well as a front-line lawyer, two assistants from each of the law firms, patent counsel, and scientific advisers. Such was the caliber and quantity of the legal talent employed by the drug companies.

On the government side, at most, three or four lawyers, none of whom was paid more than $15,000 a year, were on hand at any one time. One FTC attorney estimated that over the ten-year period from 1957 to 1967, he devoted about five years of his working time to the tetracycline case. It was sheer perseverance on the part of the Commission that brought the giants down.

XI

Deceptive Practices

The FTC, in addition to its antitrust activities, seeks to curb a whole galaxy of business frauds and misrepresentations and, by so doing, affords protection to the consumer and honest businessman alike. A fraud, a false pricing claim, a deceptive advertisement not only victimizes the misled consumer, it unfairly diverts trade from reputable sellers. Had the question of misbranding been taken up on its merits in 1914, the result would probably have been a law similar to the Food and Drug Act with its enforcement procedures. But the original FTC Act dealt only with unfair methods of competition, and that is where the Commission's regulatory efforts were concentrated. It soon became apparent, however, that situations occurred in which the public was victimized by false claims for a product or service that did not involve an adverse effect on competition. Under the existing law, the FTC was prevented from stopping such practices unless it could show anticompetitive effect. That changed in 1938 with passage of the Wheeler-Lea Act, which gave the Commission a mandate to act whenever deception of the public was involved. After Wheeler-Lea, the Commission began to move consistently against such deceptive practices as false advertising, payola, medical quackery, and unethical door-to-door sales techniques. In the 1940's and 1950's, the Commission assumed specialized consumer-protection duties under the Wool Products Labeling Act, the Fur Products Labeling Act, the Flammable Fabrics Act, and the Textile Fiber Products Identification Act. Additional authority and consumer-protection responsibilities came with the passage of the Fair Packaging and Labeling Act of 1966 and the truth-in-lending legislation of 1968.

How Much Can the FTC Do?

The Commission acts to protect a multitude of individuals who might be misled by deceptive business practices, but there are limits to what it, and state consumer-protection agencies, can do. The FTC has no authority to make a merchant redress injury a consumer has suffered. If a consumer was falsely induced to enter a contest or to buy goods that did not meet his legitimate expectations, the Commission cannot secure a refund of his money or compel the merchant to deliver the goods as originally bargained for or to take back ones which were, in fact, delivered. If consumers purchase goods believing they are fully guaranteed when the guarantee is shot through with undisclosed limiting conditions, or if consumers purchase drugs believing they will cure an ailment when they are only temporary palliatives for symptoms of the condition, the Commission can only act to require that, in the future, the advertiser or seller make full disclosure of the guarantee terms or the exact effect of the drug. Similarly, if consumers who execute retail installment contracts in blank or fail to keep a copy of the contract did not understand that the contract would be assigned to a third party or stopped paying upon discovering that the goods purchased were not as represented, the Commission can only proceed against the merchant or finance company to prevent such things from happening again. In sum, the FTC can only act in the public interest. To lodge a complaint, it must show that a given practice is likely to mislead or deceive appreciable numbers of people. And in determining whether deception has taken place, or is likely to take place, the FTC takes into account the educational level and economic status of the consumer to whom the sales pitch is made. The aged, the sick, and the poor are particularly vulnerable groups.

DECEPTION BY NONDISCLOSURE

The Commission has interpreted its mandate to include moving against deception by nondisclosure as well as by fraudulent practice. It asserted this principle first in 1942 by requiring disclosure of the true composition of paper food-serving trays that had been treated to simulate the appearance of wood. The principle was further established in a case brought by the Commission in 1945 involving imitation pearls. The FTC found that, because of consumer preference for domestic products, failure to disclose the foreign origin of imitation pearls constituted an unfair and deceptive act. Its order of August, 1950, required that products not be offered for sale without clearly disclosing the country of origin. The Seventh Circuit Court of Appeals, affirming this order in 1951, said:

> The Commission may require affirmative disclosures where necessary to prevent deception, and that failure to disclose by mark or label material facts concerning merchandise, which, if known to prospective purchasers, would influence their decisions of whether or not to purchase, is an unfair trade practice violative of Section 5 of the FTC Act.

The cases in this area cover almost every variety of nondisclosure, many of them, instances in which an individual's health or safety might be endangered. The Commission has ordered manufacturers and distributors of certain electrical products to cease advertising without a warning against possible electric shock. It has often required information on flammability. Danger of radioactivity prompted the Commission to order disclosure, warning, and advice on a product designed to eliminate static electricity from phonograph records. The most outstanding example of this kind of protection is the health warning (proposed by the FTC and then adopted by Congress) required on all cigarette packages.

COMMON DECEPTIVE PRACTICES

The Justice Department has played a major role in prosecuting hard-core consumer frauds involving use of the mails or the crossing of state lines. Although its record is spotty where hard-core frauds are concerned, the FTC moves against many fraudulent practices.

Section 5 of the FTC Act can be used to cover the procuring of business or trade secrets of competitors by means of espionage, including the use of paid spies posing as customers. Stealing trade secrets or enticing an employee to induce breach of an employment contract can run afoul of Section 5, too. The Commission has also proceeded in a few instances where inducements were made by means of fraudulent statements, usually disparaging to the original employer. False claims to be the agent or employee of a business concern, concealment of business identity, misrepresentation of the seller to others, attempts to pass off goods as the product of a competitor, use of a misleading name to enhance the value of a product—all these practices fall under the strictures of the law.

The fictitious bargain is another common form of deception. Many devices are used to lure buyers into believing they are getting something for nothing or an unusual value for their money. Prices may be advertised as "greatly reduced," "cut in half," "formerly sold for," or otherwise touted as exceptional when, in truth, the merchandise is being sold at the sellers' regular prices. The Commission insists that the "former" or "regular" price from which the reduction is claimed must be the usual price of the product and not a fictitious one.

Claims that the consumer has been specially selected are another device often involving deception. Advertisers may use a telephone survey to tell a consumer that his household has been chosen to display the product of the advertiser at a low, discount price or that the advertiser offers a special scholarship rate for students who have a talent in art or music or writing.

"You can earn up to $———— a week" is a lure which often turns out to be deceptive. False representations of earnings account for a sizeable number of FTC actions each year. Particularly vicious because the so-called opportunities not only cost the buyer money but also his time and effort, the schemes involve gross exaggeration of potential earnings and hollow assurances of help from the seller in obtaining a market for the product when, in fact, the sole motive is to sell the product or vending equipment.

Deceitful methods for debt collection are outlawed, also. "To receive this money, you must fill out the enclosed form, giving your name and address and place of employment" is a timeworn but continuing method of locating persons for the purpose of collecting debts. Frequently, the request for this information is mailed in an official-looking envelope from Washington, D.C., and the return address carries the name of a fictitious bureau or department. A variation of the money-due-you theme is that the federal government is making a legitimate demand for the information. The Commission does not permit such false or misleading means of collecting debts.

PAYOLA

The FTC has condemned, with varying success, certain practices that may be categorized as bad business morals. It has attempted to wipe out both the cruder and more subtle forms of commercial bribery, described by the Commission as "bribing buyers or other employees of customers and prospective customers without the employers' knowledge or consent to obtain or hold patronage." But some FTC orders in these cases have been set aside by the courts either because they related to transactions regarded by the courts as intrastate in character or because the courts were not prepared to go as far as the Commission in condemning the bestowing of gifts or favors of a nonmonetary nature on actual and potential customers. Generally speaking, if payment of what is sometimes called "push money" is made known to the recipient's employer, the cases indicate no violation. Deception enters with the element of secrecy.

Secrecy was the key in the well-known "payola" cases that exploded onto the public scene in the late 1950's. The television quiz show scandals, which revealed that allegedly unrehearsed programs were actually rigged, shattered many illusions about public idols. They also led to the disclosure that phonograph records were being promoted by disc jockeys for value received. Disc jockeys were taking under-the-table payments to falsely represent that records were being played because of their popularity. The idea was, of course, to develop a market for purchase of the recordings produced by the firms giving the payola. The Commission issued nearly one hundred complaints attacking this practice. Fifty-seven respondents—including some well-known firms—consented to the orders and agreed to terminate all forms of payola.

DOOR-TO-DOOR SALESMANSHIP

The FTC contends that corporations that send out salesmen to promote their products from door to door are responsible for the representations the salesmen make. In the 1940 *International Art Company* case, the Seventh Circuit Court of Appeals rejected the argument that the company had no power to control its agents, stating: "Here, the agent was clothed with apparent, and, we think, real authority to speak and act for and on behalf of the principal, and the latter is bound thereby."

The *Holland Furnace* case far outweighs all other door-to-door cases in importance. It is the only FTC action that has resulted in a company official going to jail.

For thirty years, Holland salesmen used "tear and scare" tactics which they were taught by company officials. Salesmen were encouraged to prey on old people. The trick was to go into a home in winter, posing as a safety inspector, and look over the existing furnace. Later in the evening, a different salesman would return to try to convince the home-owner to sign up for a new furnace, something three times as expensive as he could have bought elsewhere. In the 1950's, Holland was peddling obsolete 1920's-type coal burners. The company sold nine furnaces consecutively in six years to one woman in her seventies for a total of $18,000.

The FTC at first secured a stipulation that Holland stop these practices on the basis that they were misleading. This had little effect. It then entered a cease-and-desist order. Between 1954, when the original complaint was issued, and 1958, when the order was issued, the FTC compiled 10,000 pages of testimony from all over the country. The company appealed, but the Seventh Circuit Court of Appeals affirmed the Commission's order. When the company failed to comply, the FTC, in 1962, filed a petition to cite for criminal contempt of court. In 1965, the appeals court sentenced the company to a fine of $100,000 and two former sales managers to fines of $500 each. The president of the company, Paul T. Cheff, was given a 6-month jail sentence.

The company and the president petitioned the Supreme Court for certiorari. Review was denied in the case of the company, but granted in the case of the president, who argued that he had been unjustly denied a jury trial. The Supreme Court, on June 6, 1966, affirmed the conviction of the appeals court on grounds that the conviction was for not more than six months. At that point, the company decided to file a petition for bankruptcy, and Cheff went to jail. He was paroled on the first day of eligibility after serving two months. Holland was taken over by a New York firm as a tax loss, its name was changed, and its headquarters moved to New York. The deceptive practices were halted, but, as Chairman of the Senate Commerce Committee Warren G. Magnuson later observed, "Holland Furnace at the height of its business cost the American public $30 million a year."

LOTTERIES AND GAMES OF CHANCE

The exploitation of children led to the downfall of lotteries as a sales promotion device. The Commission, in the famous *Keppel* case of 1934, successfully brought proceedings against the use of so-called break-and-take candy packages in the penny candy trade. Use of lotteries to promote sales was not treated as an unfair competitive practice under common law. Nevertheless, the FTC has devoted much energy to prohibiting this kind of sales stimulation. If a consumer can participate in a lottery or contest without the expenditure of money or personal effort, the practice is not considered illegal. But the FTC has virtually eliminated the use of merchandising schemes based on lot or chance where some consideration is present, and the courts have consistently upheld the Commission on this.

Lottery schemes have not been limited to the area of children's candy. In recent years, the FTC has found many deceptions in the use of games and contests in food and gasoline retailing. An FTC investigation in 1966–67 disclosed that in many cases the stated number of prizes did not correspond to the number awarded and that the advertiser continued to inform the public that customers could win big prizes when winning slips were no longer in the cards. One grocery chain went so far as to advertise that the chances of winning were 1 in 3, when, according to information furnished the FTC by the promoter of the game, the actual chances of winning in a single store visit were 1 in 33 and the chances of winning a cash prize were 1 in 15,373.

Increases in gross margins of profit indicated that grocery chains absorbed some of the costs of promotional games and passed the rest along to the consumer. The FTC did not come up with any estimate of price increases resulting from the games, but the FTC staff found that introduction of games by a chain store had an almost immediate impact on business. Safeway grocery stores, for example, saw their sales rise almost twice as fast as usual in the first three months after Bonus Bingo was introduced. Stores of the Giant chain in the Washington, D.C., area reversed a 3–8 per cent annual sales loss to a 3–4 per cent gain in the months following its adoption of Win at the Races.

MEDICAL QUACKERY

The FTC has consistently moved against false advertising of alleged cures, whose claims range from the absurd to the frightening. A principal deception, aimed primarily at the elderly, is a cure for arthritis and rheumatism. Testimony before the Senate Subcommittee on Frauds and Misrepresentations Affecting the Elderly revealed that businessmen were pushing such ineffective treatments for arthritis as drinking alfalfa tea, plunging hands into hot and cold water, talking over the telephone, applying salves, and obtaining a box containing "numerous little bottles with lavender caps" over which a transparent crystal ball was swung. The subcommittee, a unit of the Senate's Special Committee on Aging, produced evidence that the cost to Americans of medical quackery runs into the hundreds of millions of dollars each year.

HOME IMPROVEMENTS

The FTC receives more consumer complaints about practices in the home improvements industry than in any other single industry, according to unofficial estimates. For years, the Commission has been aware of widespread fraud and deception in this industry, in which Americans spend an estimated $15 billion a year or more. The FTC has lodged numerous complaints, but has scattered its shots rather widely. In 1967, at the request of Senator Magnuson, the FTC made a report detailing findings of a somewhat cursory study. Some of the techniques used by firms the FTC had investigated included phony bargain prices, false claims and guarantees, and promises of prizes or refunds for referrals of friends to the contractor. Other abuses involved misrepresentations of interest and finance charges when the customer agreed to pay the debt in installments, obtaining signatures on blank completion certificates before the work was done, and adding unauthorized charges to signed contracts. Homeowners were also enticed into executing second mortgage notes without their knowledge.

In 1967, Senator Magnuson asked Congress to provide for a special $500,000 appropriation for the FTC to carry forward its home improvement industry investigations. The bill passed the Senate but died in the House. It was introduced again in 1969. The money, if appropriated, will enable the FTC to carry out a structural study of the home improvements industry as well as step up its case-by-case enforcement and, possibly, spell out some industry-wide rules and regulations.

GUARANTEES AND WARRANTIES

When foreign and domestic manufacturers of consumer electronic products were displaying their wares at the Americana and New York Hilton hotels in mid-June of 1969, FTC Chairman Dixon warned that the industry had not done enough to curb unfair and deceptive practices. He told the opening session of the annual Consumer Electronics Show that, particularly in the matter of guarantees, the public is upset and "the interest of the Congress has been aroused." Legislation had already been introduced in Congress to require that products be sold, according to Dixon, "with both express and implied warranties and with provisions of the former proscribed by Government regulation." Fines, punitive damages, and other penalties would be imposed on violators.

In February of that same year, Dixon had spoken against automobile warranties, claiming that car manufacturers had been using warranties more as sales gimmicks than as guarantees of service. At the time Dixon made his remarks, his agency had been looking into the problem of automobile warranties for almost five years and had just completed eight days of hearings on the subject. Robert J. Klein, economic editor of *Consumers Union,* told the FTC during the course of the hearings that 1969 model automobiles tested by the magazine had an average of thirty-six defects per car—twice as many as the models tested in 1967. Pressures exerted on the auto makers by the FTC had apparently failed either to reduce the number of defects or to improve the repair situation. Meanwhile, a public outcry had been building, with the FTC receiving a torrent of complaints from auto purchasers. Consumer advocate Ralph Nader had clearly contributed to this groundswell of consumer indignation with his running criticism of General Motors and the automobile industry as a whole.

The growing public concern finally led to action. In a surprise move, the Nixon Administration, on March 11, 1970, proposed legislation for federal regulation of warranties covering automobiles, appliances, and other consumer goods.

TEXTILES AND FURS

In addition to its general authority to prevent deceptive practices and false advertising under the FTC Act, special laws give the FTC responsibility for requiring truthful labels on wool, fur, and textile products and for preventing the sale of dangerously flammable fabrics. Through field representatives, the FTC counsels the textile and fur industries on the requirements of four statutes—the Wool Products Labeling Act, the Fur Products Labeling Act, the Flammable Fabrics Act, and the Textile Fiber Products Identification Act.

FTC inspectors assigned to field offices and field stations spot-check mills, manufacturers, wholesalers, importers, and retailers to see if goods are properly labeled. They look at records and inspect raw materials. Inspectors arrive unannounced on the premises of firms to be inspected, present their credentials, and explain their mission. If they find misbranding or question fiber content, they send samples to the FTC for tests. In department stores, inspectors record the style number and the manufacturer's number of a product in question, make a facsimile of the label, get the manufacturer's invoice, and send the information on to the FTC for inspection of the particular garment. These inspectors also obtain evidence to sustain the Commission complaint if serious violations are established. Although the FTC generally relies on complaints from the outside for the bulk of its cases, in the fields of textiles and furs, 95 per cent of the Commission's cases are developed through inspection. The Commission has injunctive power under all four textile and fur statutes, and it is used when necessary. Some 1,800 outstanding orders covering textile and fur regulations are policed by the Commission's compliance staff. In 1970, there were forty-three specialists engaged in fur and textile inspection work. In searching out misbranded textiles and dangerously flammable fabrics, cooperation of the U.S. Customs Bureau is also involved. Many highly flammable or otherwise illegal products destined for U.S. markets have been detected and seized at port of entry.

Wool Products

The Wool Products Labeling Act, as its name implies, is strictly a labeling act. Although it is now considered a consumer-protection statute, it was not so much the purpose of the law to protect consumers against misrepresentation as to protect wool growers against competition from nonwool fibers and weavers of woolens against competition from nonwool fabrics. The law does have the effect, however, of protecting consumers against the concealment of substitutes for wool in products claimed to be made wholly or partially of wool.

The law requires that labels be affixed to products containing 5 per cent or more of wool (with certain exceptions, such as carpets, rugs, and upholstery) showing the percentage of new wool, reused or reprocessed wool, and other fibers or fillers in the products. These labels must set forth the generic names of all fibers present. Fiber content labels must be attached to the product when the goods are shipped from one manufacturer to another. At no time along the way may the product be falsely labeled as to fiber content or other material fact.

The Textile Revolution

The development of many new fibers, blends, weaves, finishes, and processes has created a revolution in the textile field. The first regulatory response to the changes came in 1958 with passage of the Textile Fiber Products Identification Act, which, together with the Wool Act, provides virtually complete coverage of labeling in the entire textile field. The later Act also fixed standards for proper advertising of the fiber content of textile fiber products. Manufacturers, distributors, and sellers of all textiles, both natural and man-made, were given a year and a half to become acquainted with the new law and to comply with it before it became effective on March 3, 1960.

In preparing the legislation, Congress directed the FTC to establish generic names for manufactured, man-made fibers. Rule 7 under the Act originally set forth sixteen such names. Some of them—rubber, glass, rayon, acetate, nylon—are familiar. Three have been used frequently in conjunction with trademarks or trade names—acrylic, polyester, and saran. In 1969, a seventeenth name, anidex, was added. Manufacturers are permitted to use their trade name if the generic name of the fiber is used along with it. For example, Orlon, a Dupont trade name, must be labeled Orlon-Acrylic.

The Act was amended in 1965 to provide for disclosure of fibers constituting 5 per cent or less of a product if that fiber has a definite functional significance. A problem arose when spandex, which provides elasticity with a content of 3 or 4 per cent, was used in making stretch fabrics. Under the law, as previously written, spandex under 5 per cent was lumped under the category "other fibers."

In 1965, too, President Johnson's Committee on Consumer Interests announced creation of a committee to study information needs of consumers in buying textiles. Esther Peterson, the President's special assistant for consumer affairs, said in October, 1965, that in many cases retailers and dry cleaners as well as consumers had difficulty evaluating performance and care requirements of the new fibers. Although the federal laws require disclosure of fiber content, there was widespread feeling among government experts that the labeling laws should be broadened to include information on care, shrinkage, and color fastness. Care labeling had been discussed in the textile industry for thirty years. In 1967, a volunteer committee from the textile and apparel industry worked with the President's assistant for consumer affairs to produce a voluntary guide for care labeling. Reports of that code's effectiveness vary, but the FTC apparently thought it was not doing the job. In November, 1969, the Commission initiated a proceeding to establish trade regulation rules to require care labeling of textile products.

Fur Labeling

The avowed purpose of the Fur Products Labeling Act, passed in 1951, was to protect consumers against deception resulting from misbranding, false or deceptive advertising, or false invoicing of fur products and furs. In short, the law was designed to stamp out the old racket of giving cheap furs high-sounding names in order to sell them at inflated prices. Rabbit and muskrat have been sold under scores of different names, including "Baltic Lion" and "Hudson Seal."

The law places an affirmative burden on a fur seller to state the truth about the furs he offers for sale. Under the 1951 law, the FTC was directed to hold public hearings to determine the true English names of furs and to issue a Fur Products Name Guide by February, 1952. Sellers were required to use these names on labels attached to fur products after August, 1952, and also to state whether the furs contained in such products were new or used, what country they originally came from, what part of the animal they came from, and whether they had been dyed or bleached. Labels must also show the name or registered identification number of the manufacturer or distributor of the product. The law also requires invoicing information similar to that on the labels to enable the FTC to check the product to its source. In addition, each fur product must carry an item number. Surveillance of furriers is carried out on all levels of manufacturing and distribution, with Commission emphasis on false and deceptive pricing and record-keeping.

The FTC has also directed its attention at the deception in calling a dyed, tip-dyed, or bleached fur "natural." There is nothing improper about dyeing or bleaching furs, but they must be labeled as such. To uncover this deceptive practice, FTC investigators call on the processors and dyers of the skins and obtain the names of furriers to whom artifically colored or dyed skins are being sent. Subsequent calls on the furriers establish whether the dyed furs have been upgraded to "natural." More than twenty such cases were opened in fiscal 1968, and fourteen cease-and-desist agreements were sent by field inspectors to the Commission.

FLAMMABLE FABRICS

It sometimes takes a series of disasters to arouse the public and prod Congress into taking preventive measures. Such was the case with the Flammable Fabrics Act. In 1945, several small boys wearing cowboy suits with chaps made of a highly flammable rayon pile were fatally burned. Several years later, a wave of severe burns and deaths was caused by "torch sweaters," flimsy knitwear of similarly combustible yarns. These tragedies spurred action: in 1953, Congress passed the Flammable Fabrics Act. The Commerce Department had previously taken some action to protect the public from dangerous fabrics by setting commercial standards for flammability of clothing textiles and general purpose vinyl plastic film. These standards were made part of the basic law.

The Act makes it illegal to sell garments that do not pass a prescribed flammability test devised by industry in cooperation with the National Bureau of Standards and enforced by the FTC. The Commission may institute proceedings to enjoin the manufacture or sale of such articles and to confiscate existing stocks. Willful violation of the law is made punishable by fine and imprisonment. Producers and distributors may not be prosecuted criminally if the manufacturer has provided them with a guarantee that a product passes the flammability test. To aid in enforcement, producers of flammable fabrics are required to keep swatches of each class of fabric sold and to maintain full records of their sales.

The FTC maintains a laboratory to test for flammability and to analyze the contents of fabrics. When testing for flammability, technicians take five samples of the fabric and clock the length of time it takes each sample to burn from one end to the other. In the case of plain surface fabrics, such as scarves, if the average burning time for the five samples is 3.5 seconds or less, the fabric is considered dangerously flammable. The standard is stiffer for pile, raised, or brushed fabrics. If the average burning time of the samples is 4 seconds or less, the fabric is considered dangerous. Before they are put to the test, the fabrics are placed in an oven to be dried out. Frames containing the samples are then put into a dessicator and subsequently allowed to cool to room temperature. They are tested when they are bone dry.

Although the 1953 law provided some protection against the most dangerous fabrics, many experts felt that it was not adequate. With consumer interest in more thorough protection growing, legislation to tighten the requirements of the law was proposed. At the instigation of Senator Magnuson, the FTC agreed to study the flammability problem anew, and, on December 14, 1967, an amendment to the law was passed extending coverage from wearing apparel to all fabrics, related materials, and products used in homes, offices, or other places of assembly or accommodation. Under the new law, the Department of Health, Education, and Welfare investigates the cause of fires and then makes the information it uncovers public. The Secretary of Commerce designates which fabrics or products are hazardous and establishes testing procedures.

This process was designed to keep the law up-to-date as new or different products appear, but it has been slow to be carried out. In February, 1968, Senator Magnuson prodded the Commerce Department. After the Nixon Administration came into office, he was assured by Commerce Secretary Maurice H. Stans that there would be no delays in completing a study expected to lead to tighter standards for flammability of clothing, especially that of children. Another year went by, however, before the Department, in the spring of 1970, held its first public hearing on the need for higher standards of flammability. That hearing covered standards for carpets and rugs. The resulting regulations were certified and will go into effect in April, 1971. The Department is now considering proposed specifications for children's clothing and for bedding.

XII

False Advertising

Since the creation of the FTC, advertising has grown from an infant business with a small dollar volume into a large and influential industry. It involves every company that has ever attempted to substitute for personal salesmen a written, spoken, or visual message. Concern over false advertising did not begin with the FTC, however. Two years before the Commission was established, the Advertising Federation of America spearheaded a Crusade for Truth in Advertising, a drive for the adoption by both federal and state legislatures of a model truth-in-advertising statute. *Printers' Ink* magazine also sponsored such legislation. The campaign was motivated less by an interest in protecting consumers than in building greater public confidence in advertising, for advertising dollars were being devalued by the growing public distrust of all ads. Reputable advertisers were fed up with the phony claims of unprincipled competitors.

The Federation followed its Crusade with a program to establish self-regulatory machinery through which business could police the truthfulness of its advertising claims. This program resulted in the formation of vigilance committees, which later developed into the Better Business Bureaus. But although pressure could be brought to improve the credibility of local ads, the problem of nationwide advertising remained. Support was therefore forthcoming from these advertisers for creation of a federal agency that would halt such unfair methods of competition.

In more than fifty years of defining the limits of legality by which proper advertising can be measured, the Commission has come in for considerable criticism. Critics have challenged whether the FTC has contributed to the improvement of the general level of advertising. Often, however, the agency has been taken to task for faults outside the scope of its regulatory authority. The FTC is not empowered to weigh the assertion that advertising merely adds to the price consumers pay. Nor is it concerned with matters of taste in advertising nor with disputes over whether advertising promotes the right or wrong social values. It is concerned with the honesty of advertising claims and promises.

How the FTC Hits False Advertising

In fair advertising enforcement, the FTC has followed a case-by-case approach coupled with industry guidance and has built up a great body of law. Although the Commission's precedential arsenal is well equipped to catch the miscreant, it has tried to ensure that no businessman will be handicapped by an order while his competitors remain free to conduct business as usual.

The Commission is empowered to issue cease-and-desist orders against all who are responsible for deceptive advertising, individuals as well as companies, their advertising agencies, and even the media. Commission orders try to draw a line between responsible programing, effective advertising, and good showmanship and a show that cheats and deceives its audience. The FTC recognizes, however, that both the printed and broadcast media would be hard put to investigate the truth of all advertising they carry. Consequently, the Commission's fire is directed almost entirely at the advertiser, although in a number of television cases, the Commission has named advertising agencies. The FTC enjoins an ad agency only when it is clearly involved in perpetrating the deception. If the agency does everything in its power to keep its hands clean, it is not named as a respondent.

INTERSTATE JURISDICTION

FTC standards regarding the matter of interstate jurisdiction have been somewhat ambiguous. As far as food, drug, and cosmetic advertising is concerned, the Wheeler-Lea amendments to the FTC Act give the FTC specific statutory authority to act when an advertisement is "in commerce" regardless of whether the product is sold in interstate commerce. Special statutes also cover furs and fabrics. But for the first forty-six years of its existence, the FTC did not attempt to assert jurisdiction over false advertising where the dissemination was interstate but the sale of the product was limited to one state. In 1960, the Commission broke this precedent. It lodged a complaint against S. Klein Stores of New York, charging violation of Section 5 of the FTC Act by an "interstate dissemination" of false advertising. The ads in question had appeared in New York, New Jersey, and Connecticut; the products were sold only in New York. After a lengthy proceeding, the FTC hearing examiner issued a cease-and-desist order. Klein challenged the legal basis for the order, and then the Commission, with two Commissioners dissenting, dismissed the action without explanation. The Commission contends that it has jurisdiction in such instances, but, evidently, with its limited resources, it did not feel equipped to move into this field.

Monitoring Advertising

The task of policing advertising boggles the mind. The FTC has been accused of a somewhat haphazard, catch-as-catch-can approach to it. Nevertheless, thousands of pages of magazine and newspaper copy and thousands of radio and TV continuities are scanned yearly. The Commission has, at times, found it necessary to utilize the services of medical men as consultants in the field of medicinal ads. When advertising over radio became extensive in the 1930's, the FTC established a Radio and Periodical Division, which took over the duties previously handled by the Commission's Special Board of Investigation. At the same time, the new division's authority was extended to cover mail-order catalogues and foreign-language newspapers.

The fall of 1959 marked a milestone in the history of advertising in America. Two events took place that created a nationwide stir and cast a dark shadow over the advertising industry. First, there were the revelations of rigged TV quiz shows. Then came the so-called payola scandals in the record industry. When the 1959 crisis arose, the FTC intensified its monitoring program and doubled the staff assigned to handle it. Attorneys were transferred from other areas of the Commission to monitor and investigate radio and television advertising claims. Seven trial attorneys were assigned to assist in the investigation and preparation of cases for trial. All commercial advertising on network stations was monitored throughout the broadcasting day. In December of 1959, the monitoring unit referred 510 advertisements to various other bureaus and divisions within the Commission for possible action. In fiscal 1968, the Commission monitored 570,142 radio, television, newspaper, and magazine advertisements, of which 16,491 were passed on to the legal staff for action of one sort or another and 566 were passed on to other federal agencies.

In 1969, the FTC announced plans to intensify its program for monitoring advertising on national television networks. To supplement a stepped-up schedule of visual auditing, the Commission directed its staff to obtain, on a systematic basis, copies of all network commercials used during a specified period each month. "Questionable network advertising will be given high investigative priority," the FTC said. The Commission also said it was concerned with the necessity of responding promptly to deceptive or misleading advertising on network television. As one step in meeting this problem, the Commission announced that any complaints it issued alleging false and misleading advertising on the television networks would be given immediate publicity. "It is hoped that this procedure will alert the advertising profession to the position taken by the Commission," an announcement said. "Advertisers may then reconsider their current campaigns in light of the announced position of the Commission." The Commission monitors both radio and TV by requiring submission of scripts on a sampling basis. It also monitors "live" programs as the occasion requires. In addition, a regular survey is made of newspaper and magazine advertising, not only to detect new ads that are questionable but to check on compliance with existing FTC orders.

Whose Intelligence?

The key question in any advertising case is: What is the meaning of the promise made? Before the FTC can determine the meaning, however, it must select the level of consumer intelligence against which to consider the promise. In early cases, the standard commonly articulated was whether the ad would be likely to deceive the "average purchaser." In 1937, however, the Supreme Court in *FTC* v. *Standard Education Society,* reversed a decision of the Second Circuit Court of Appeals in which Judge Learned Hand had been critical of the FTC for proceeding against "will-o'-the-wisps, which divert attention from substantial evils." The high court stated that "laws are made to protect the trusting as well as the suspicious." After that decision, the Commission lowered its intelligence standard.

A case in which the Commission adopted a minimal standard was *Charles of the Ritz Distributors Corp.* v. *FTC,* in which the Commission found that the trade-mark Rejuvenescense was being used in relation to a foundation make-up cream in a manner that promised the restoration of a youthful complexion. "While the wise and worldly may well realize the falsity of any representations that the present product can roll back the years," the reviewing Second Circuit said,

> there remains "that vast multitude" of others who, like Ponce de Leon, still seek a perpetual fountain of youth. . . . It is for this reason that the Commission may "insist upon the most literal truthfulness" in advertisements . . . and should have the discretion, undisturbed by the courts, to insist if it chooses upon a form of advertising clear enough so that, in the words of the prophet Isaiah, "wayfaring men, though fools, shall not err therein."

In the 1963 *Heinz W. Kirchner* case, the Commission moved to the position that advertisers are not held responsible to the lowest intelligence level. In that case, the respondent claimed that a swimming aid to be worn underneath a bathing suit was "thin and invisible." Commissioner Elman, writing for the Commission, declared: " 'Swim-Ezy' is not invisible or impalpable or dimensionless, and to anyone who so understood the representation, it would be false. It is not likely, however, that many prospective purchasers would take the representation thus in its literal sense."

WHAT CONSTITUTES DECEPTION?

Advertisements are considered, not in the abstract or in isolation, but in their actual context and in terms of the effect they may be expected to have on the general public. It is not a defense that an advertisement under question is literally true. Under certain circumstances, an ad may, though literally true, have the capacity to deceive. The Fifth Circuit said in *P. Lorillard Co.* v. *FTC* in 1950: "To tell less than the whole truth is a well known method of deception; and he who deceives by resorting to such methods cannot excuse the deception by relying on the truthfulness per se of the partial truth by which it has been accomplished." In this connection, the Ninth Circuit Court of Appeals held, in 1960, that "the shrewd use of exaggeration, innuendo, ambiguity and half-truth is more efficacious from the advertiser's standpoint than factual assertions. Facts are dull and dangerous, exaggerations are vivid, attractive and privileged." Advertising statements that could have two meanings, one of which is false, are also considered misleading. In one case, the Commission held that, because the statement that a toothpaste "fights decay" could be interpreted as a promise of complete protection, it was deceptive.

If nontruthfulness alone were grounds enough for the Commission to take action, however, it would be buried under its own complaints. The additional standard applied to all ads is public safety, and the courts more than the FTC have developed the meaning of this criteria.

In general, the courts have been critical of Commission decisions when an ad, although deceptive, does not appear likely to result in injury to the public. Public injury does not mean that a consumer must actually suffer damage but that the result of the advertisement has a tendency to induce action detrimental to the consumer. An ad must be misleading in a material respect to be actionable. This issue came up in two cases remanded to the Commission by the courts, both of which involved the use of displays, or mock-ups, on television. The Commission has now adopted a policy to prohibit only those advertisements that have a tendency or capacity to deceive. Simple falsity in the mock-ups is not enough. The representation must be such as to induce the public to act.

BAIT-AND-SWITCH ADVERTISING

A form of deception frequently used by disreputable merchandisers is bait advertising. The scheme involves advertising a popular article at a ridiculously low price simply for the purpose of luring customers into the store. The deception becomes apparent when the bargain bait cannot be purchased, for one pretext or another, and salesmen, after disparaging the advertised product, attempt to switch customers to higher priced substitutes. This practice has been under steady fire by the FTC. Bait-and-switch schemes are particularly prevalent with commodities such as used automobiles, combination storm windows, furs, furniture, home appliances, jewelry, pianos, radio and television sets, sewing machines, upholstery, and vacuum cleaners.

DECEPTIVE TELEVISION ADVERTISING

Probably the most publicized antideceptive cases brought by the FTC are those concerning false advertising on television. The Commission uses the same standards to determine whether an ad is false and misleading regardless of how it is disseminated. If a TV picture gives credulous people the impression that a product has virtues it lacks or falsely disparages a competing product, the FTC will take action. But television does present special problems, largely as a result of the techniques used to carry off the ads.

In 1959, the FTC issued complaints against the manufacturers of nine nationally advertised products alleging that either camera trickery had been used or essential facts had been omitted from the television portrayal of their products. One of these complaints challenged a TV commercial for a certain brand of oleomargarine. In the commercial, drops of moisture were shown on the advertised oleo and on butter. A competing margarine was shown without any such drops. An FTC complaint contended that the drops had no relevance to the flavor and quality of the particular brand of oleo, contrary to the assertions of the television announcer. Furthermore, the drops had been applied for the purpose of the demonstration. This action resulted in an agreement to discontinue the alleged deception.

The FTC has acted upon many other deceptive television commercials. One case involved the familiar white-coat theme, wherein a man in a white coat, called "doctor," recommended a certain digestive aid. The "doctor" was, of course, not a physician at all. The order in that case required that the advertiser stop representing "by the use of a white coat or any other object, device or words indicative of the medical profession, that doctors or the medical profession recommended [the product], unless the representation is limited to numbers of doctors not greater than had been ascertained to be the fact."

Mock-ups and the Rapid Shave Sandpaper Case

Mock-ups are frequently used in TV demonstrations to represent the product or some other object, and the FTC has had to consider, in a number of cases, whether these mock-ups were unfair and deceptive. The definitive mock-up case involves the so-called Rapid Shave sandpaper commercial.

Among the TV commercials challenged by the Commission in 1960 were three 60-second ads of Colgate-Palmolive Company's Rapid Shave cream. The FTC issued a complaint against the company and its advertising agency, Ted Bates and Company, charging that the representations in the commercials were deceptive. The advertiser claimed that its shaving cream possessed a "supermoisturizing" power so great that it could shave sandpaper. The commercials demonstrated the effective shaving of sandpaper with a single stroke of the razor after application of Rapid Shave. In reality, what the viewer saw was not sandpaper but loose sand spread over plexiglass. The advertiser and the ad agency argued that the mock-up was necessary because sandpaper appears on the TV screen as nothing more than plain, colored paper: therefore, unless a mock-up was used, the texture of the grain would not show, and it would appear to the viewer that only plain paper was being shaved. The Commission found that sandpaper could not be shaved within 1 to 3 minutes after application of Rapid Shave, even with numerous heavy strokes. Indeed, its tests showed that soaking for an hour in the shaving cream would not complete the test. It concluded that the shaving cream did not have the properties indicated by the demonstration and the ads were thus false, misleading, and deceptive. A cease-and-desist order was issued.

In his opinion for the Commission in the Rapid Shave case, Commissioner Elman concluded that the use of props in television commercials was not illegal as such. For example, he said, there was nothing objectionable in showing a person drinking colored water that appears to be iced tea as long as the liquid is not presented as proof of the fine color or appearance of an advertiser's tea. But, he added that further use of representations "by picture, depictions, or demonstrations, either alone or accompanied by oral or written statements" would be prohibited if "they do not genuinely represent what they purport to represent and do not prove what they purport to prove about the quality or merits of a product."

Colgate-Palmolive contended that since it had withdrawn the Rapid Shave commercial upon the issuance of the complaint, the proceeding served no useful purpose. Abandonment of a forbidden practice even before filing of the complaint, however, is no defense. The First Circuit Court of

Appeals upheld the Commission's finding that the sandpaper claim was false, but it said that the order was so broad as to make all mock-ups illegal. It remanded the case to the Commission for a new order. On February 18, 1963, the Commission issued a second order holding that the practice of using a sham demonstration with misleading effect is illegal. The second *Colgate* opinion was also reversed, but the FTC appealed and won in the Supreme Court.

The Commission's opinion in the *Colgate* case spelled out a philosophy about TV commercials and set down guidelines. As a result, many gimmicks previously used in television advertising have been dropped. The before-and-after demonstrations for detergents are one example. Previously, two garments, one soiled and the other unsoiled but unlaundered, were used to show the superior qualities of a certain detergent. The soiled garment is now laundered and used in the second photograph. In March, 1969, the FTC announced its acceptance of an assurance of voluntary compliance from Lever Brothers Company assuring the Commission that it would forthwith discontinue the use of certain television commercials advertising laundry detergent 3B All. The commercials show water rising across the breadth of the television screen to the level of an actor's chin and then receding. At the beginning of each commercial, the actor is shown wearing a stained garment which, in the final sequence of the commercial, is shown free of stain. During the commercial, the actor comments on the cleaning ability of 3B All as he pours it into the rising water. Upon inquiry, the Commission said it learned that the stain on the actor's garment had not been removed by the immersion depicted on the television screen, but in the normal fashion by washing machine. "The Commission's decision to accept the assurance of voluntary compliance rather than proceeding formally was based on its recognition that this commercial was probably intended to be one of a class of currently prevalent 'spoofing' or 'fanciful' presentations calculated to startle or amuse the television viewer," the FTC said. "Nevertheless, even humorous commercials have actionable capacity to deceive where, as here, they depict the product in use and exaggerate the results ostensibly achieved from such use."

Food, Drug, and Cosmetic Cases

The FTC shares broad responsibility with the U.S. Food and Drug Administration (FDA) in protecting the public against deception involving food, drugs, therapeutic devices, and cosmetics. The FTC's jurisdiction extends over advertising of nonprescription drugs as well as foods, devices, and cosmetics, while the FDA is charged with preventing deception in the labeling of all these commodities and the advertising of prescription drugs.

There are significant differences in procedure between the two agencies and in the nature of the sanctions imposed on violators. When the surveillance and investigative work of the FDA disclose a violation of the federal Food, Drug and Cosmetic Act, the facts are reported to the Justice Department with a recommendation for seizure, criminal prosecution, or injunction actions in the federal courts.

Under the Wheeler-Lea amendments to the FTC Act, the Commission is authorized to obtain temporary injunctions while cease-and-desist proceedings are in progress. Finally, when the use of such advertised items "may be injurious to health," criminal penalties attach. It is a criminal offense to advertise these goods "with intent to defraud or mislead." The maximum sentences that may be imposed for violations of the food and drug portions of the FTC Act extend to a fine of $5,000 and six months' imprisonment for the first offense and a $10,000 fine and one year's imprisonment for each future offense.

FTC physicians review and evaluate the advertising claims made for foods, drugs, and cosmetics, analyzing the scientific problems involved and reporting on the adequacy of available evidence to support regulatory action where the advertising is deemed to be false and misleading. When necessary, staff physicians consult with experts in medical schools, hospitals, and research institutions. Depending on the nature of the scientific problems raised by the advertising, the staff of scientific advisers arranges for, and monitors, clinical studies of products. These medical officers also appraise reports of clinical studies submitted by drug and food companies in support of advertising claims and participate in conferences with company representatives.

The standard of lawfulness under the food and drug sections of the FTC Act specifies circumstances in which nondisclosure may render an advertisement false and, hence, unlawful. The first circumstance is that in which the undisclosed facts are material by virtue of representations made in the advertisement. This is simply the principle of the deceptive half-truth, which was already a part of Section 5 liability. The 1963 FTC decision in *American Home Products* exemplifies the operation of this principle. Respondent's product, Outgro, a treatment for ingrown toenail, did in fact, as claimed in respondent's advertising, afford "relief and protection" for the condition, but the relief was temporary, and the protection nonexistent once infection set in. The use of Outgro after the onset of infection might actually aggravate the danger from such infection and make it more difficult to cure. Without explicit disclosure of these facts, which qualified and explained the claim of "relief and protection," the chance was great that purchasers of the product would misunderstand the limits of its effectiveness and forego necessary medical attention.

The second circumstance under which nondisclosure may render an advertisement false also relates to hazardous commodities. If the actual consequences of normal use of an advertised product are different from the expected consequences, actual consequences must be disclosed to avoid creating a false impression. If, for example, a food is advertised without disclosure of dangers of which the consumer is unaware, there is palpable—and very harmful—deception. In the case of dangerous products, the Commission not only may, but must, according to the decision in *Moretrenth Corp. v. FTC,* "insist upon the most literal truthfulness" and resolve all ambiguities and interpretive uncertainties against the seller. There are obvious reasons for this. First, the stakes are great. Second, although consumers may perhaps discount a certain amount of exaggerated and distorted advertising in the case of ordinary products, they do not expect loose advertising practices for goods that bear on health and safety.

CARTER'S LITTLE LIVER PILLS

One of the most famous cases in the annals of the FTC involves Carter's Little Liver Pills. The case is often cited as a classic example of the FTC's preoccupation with trivia and the delays that can accompany the enforcement of consumer-protection laws, especially if respondents are willing to keep up a fight and have resourceful legal talent at their disposal. It took sixteen years to get the "liver" out of Carter's Little Liver Pills.

It all began in 1943, when the Commission issued a complaint challenging the word "liver" in the product's name on the charge that the pills contained no ingredient of any therapeutic value to the liver. The Commission further charged that Carter was deceiving the public in its promise that the pills would "clear away the dark clouds of listlessness" and "keep one smiling and happy." Why the FTC chose that moment to take action against a product that had been a household laxative for seventy years is unknown.

Hearings before an examiner did not begin for another six months, and they ran for two years. By the time the examiner closed the case for the first time in November, 1945, after 149 sessions, the hearing record covered 15,000 pages, exclusive of the 2,209 exhibits. The examiner took seven months to write his decision. He concluded, in 267 pages, that Carter's should be found guilty of misleading the public. The examiner's decision remained pending until the Commission affirmed it on March 28, 1951. The case then went to court. After innumerable proceedings, the Ninth Circuit Court of Appeals upheld the Commission decision in 1959, stating that the FTC position "finds strong support in the records." One of the most labored cases in all of administrative law, the *Carter's Little Liver Pills* case finally came to end when the Supreme Court turned down a company appeal.

ASPIRIN BY ANY NAME

Since 1961, the FTC has repeatedly informed the public that aspirin by any name is aspirin and that none of the aspirins or aspirin-based products (analgesics), for which the public spent $500 million in 1966, appears to be any more or less effective than any other. In 1961, the FTC issued complaints against the four major analgesics producers—American Home Products Corporation (Anacin), Bristol-Myers Company (Bufferin and Excedrin), Plough (St. Joseph Aspirin) and Sterling Drug (Bayer Aspirin and Bayer Aspirin for Children). The competition between manufacturers and distributors of analgesic drugs largely had taken the form of comparative relief claims: "Bufferin gives pain relief twice as fast as aspirin"; Anacin contains "not one pain relieving element but three"; or "when you have a headache, cold fever or muscle pain, and you want relief—fast—St. Joseph Aspirin is ready to go to work faster to ease your pain and distress than all three other leading relief tablets."

FTC complaints charged that "in truth and in fact, there is no significant difference between the rate of speed with which other analgesic preparations available and offered for sale to consumers provide relief of pain." The complaints were not brought up for hearing, however, not even before a hearing examiner. The Commission apparently thought it did not have enough medical evidence to push charges or that it would be unfair to single out four manufacturers. The complaints were dropped pending an industry-wide investigation, but the plans to take a sweeping look at the aspirin market were abandoned in 1964 for lack of scientific personnel.

The Commission had, however, already authorized and financed a study of the five proprietary analgesic compounds by two Johns Hopkins Medical School doctors, Louis Lasagna and Thomas J. deKornfeld, who found that there was no significant difference in analgesics. When the report was completed, the Commission refused to allow its publication, although the findings supported those detailed in the suspended complaints. After considerable urging by Lasagna and deKornfeld that their report be issued in the public interest, the Commission authorized them to publish their findings without FTC endorsement. Their report appeared in the journal of the American Medical Association on December 29, 1962.

Resolution of the analgesics problem remained far from sight, though. In fact, trouble was just beginning. Sterling Drug, producers of Bayer Aspirin, decided that it benefitted from the findings of the Hopkins report. It began a strong advertising campaign to inform the public of the report's contents. The Commission objected to the interpretation placed on the study by Sterling and other companies and issued a new complaint. Neither the FTC nor the AMA, it was alleged, endorsed the published study. Moreover, the report did not conclude that respondent's Bayer Aspirin was more gentle to the stomach than compounded analgesics, nor that Bayer Aspirin afforded greater relief than other products at the end of 15 minutes. The enforcement problem that the scientific report was designed to simplify assumed new dimensions of complexity. Acting under Section 13 of the FTC Act, the agency attempted to obtain a temporary restraining order against the maker of Bayer Aspirin. This, as well as an application for a preliminary injunction, was denied the Commission by the District of Columbia court, which reasoned: "If the report of the experts employed by the Commission is accurate, then, the public has a right to know those facts. If the report of the experts employed by the Commission is inaccurate, the Commission itself is guilty of promoting false advertising."

On July 5, 1967, the FTC moved to halt deceptive advertising claims of analgesics by proposing new standards barring claims of special effectiveness. "Each of the various analgesic products now offered to the consuming public is effective to essentially the same degree as all other competing products supplying an equivalent quantity of an analgesic ingredient or combination of ingredients," the FTC said. The Commission coordinated its action against painkiller advertising with a drive by the Food and Drug Administration to police the labeling of analgesics.

CIGARETTE ADVERTISING

Scientific investigation linking use of tobacco with various diseases began at least as early as 1900, but relatively little research was done until 1939, when the first controlled retrospective study of smoking and lung cancer was conducted. The results of similar work were published in 1943, 1945, and 1948. In 1950, the investigatory pace quickened, with the year 1954 marking a watershed in the history of smoking research. In that year, the first results of a series of extensive studies were published, and the accumulated evidence linking smoking with lung cancer made a sharp impact on the scientific community and the public at large.

But even before then, the FTC had taken a number of formal actions involving cigarette advertising claims. These contained a variety of charges and were settled in various ways. A 1945 complaint lodged against R. L. Swain Tobacco prohibited representations that respondent's cigarettes were endorsed or approved by the medical profession; that they would soothe the nose, throat, or mouth; that they contained no irritating properties; and that they produced little or no stain on fingers and teeth. In 1950, the FTC moved successfully to curb R. J. Reynolds Tobacco Company from claiming that Camels aided digestion; did not impair the wind or physical condition of athletes; would never harm or irritate the throat or leave an aftertaste; were soothing, restful, and comforting to the nerves, and contained less nicotine than any of the four other largest selling brands. A 1942 complaint against Brown & Williamson Tobacco Company prohibited claims that Kools would keep the head clear in winter and give extra protection against or cure colds.

On September 15, 1955, the Commission promulgated the *Cigarette Advertising Guides.* They were never formally adopted by the Commission, but many questionable cigarette claims were voluntarily discontinued or revised. In 1960, as a result of FTC action, seven major manufacturers agreed to abandon tar and nicotine claims. The so-called Tar Derby had started in 1957 with the introduction of a filter-tip Kent following publication of a quantity of cigarette research, most of which tended to show that cigarette smoking is a cause of lung cancer and other diseases. Although some dissent was voiced, evidence of the harmful effects of cigarette smoking continued to mount. In 1962, the Surgeon General created a committee to study the problem. The FTC was called upon to contribute its expertise to this advisory committee. The committee report, issued in January, 1964, claimed that, in the judgment of its members, "cigarette smoking is a health hazard of sufficient importance in the United States to warrant appropriate remedial action."

The FTC was ready for action. On the very day the report came out, the Commission announced that it would move "to determine the remedial action which it should take in the public interest." Seven days later, it issued a notice of proposed rule-making, including a set of proposed trade rules calling for a health warning on cigarette packages and in advertising. The story of what happened then is well known. The tobacco industry moved to shift the scene of action to Congress, which promptly took over. Bills were drafted and countless hearings were held. Finally, in 1965, Congress passed a law requiring a mild health warning on cigarette packages. No warning was required in advertising, and a three-year moratorium was placed on FTC and state regulatory action. Opinion in the FTC was divided as to who "won" the 1965 battle. Chairman Dixon claimed credit for prodding the government into action while Commissioner Elman considered the moratorium a slap in the face for the Commission. The 1965 law, however, was generally considered a victory for the tobacco industry and proof once again that real policy-making power resides in Congress, not the regulatory agencies.

In 1966, the FTC rescinded its prohibition against mention of tar-nicotine content in advertising. At least one tobacco company had complained that competitors were using the earlier injunction as a protective device against adverse publicity while actually increasing tar and nicotine content.

The agency has made annual reports to Congress on the effectiveness of the new labeling law. In 1967, it said, "There is virtually no evidence that the warning statement on cigarette packages has had any significant effect . . . mainly because few people seem to pay any attention to it." At the same time, the Commission reported, scientific evidence of the dangers of cigarette smoking continued to pile up. "Cigarette smoking today poses a very great but preventable public health menace," the report concluded.

In separate recommendations in July, 1968, the FTC and the Department of Health, Education, and Welfare urged Congress to take far tougher steps to curb cigarette advertising. On May 20, 1969, the FTC issued formal notice of a proposed regulation to require a stronger warning in advertising as well as on packages. After another go-around on Capitol Hill, Congress acted to ban cigarette advertising on radio and television as of January 2, 1971. A health warning for packages was adopted, but the industry was still not required to include a warning in ads. It was another partial victory for the FTC.

XIII

Consumerism Comes to the FTC

The consumer movement is largely a phenomenon of the post-World War II era, when a fast-developing American technology poured a growing and confusing multiplicity of consumer goods onto the market. *Consumers Union* reports that its subscribers increased from less than 100,000 in 1945 to more than 1 million in 1966, with an estimated readership of some 5 million persons. The Government Printing Office reported that in 1965 alone it received 150,000 requests for the pamphlet *Consumers Quick Credit Guide,* some 30,000 requests for *Be a Good Shopper,* and an average of about 1,000 requests each for various pamphlets listed in its Consumer Information booklet covering such subjects as family finances, appliances, recreation, gardening, health and safety, house and home, child care, and fabrics. Behind this increased interest in consumer matters has been a growing frustration with the quantity and diversity of products offered in the market place and the lack of standard measures and significant information accompanying them.

As a result of this burgeoning concern over what the American consumer is getting for his dollars, American businesses and many offices of government have been inundated by a tide of questions and criticisms from those who see themselves as defenders of consumer interests. Ralph Nader, self-appointed consumer advocate, has led the movement. And, increasingly, there has been a growing willingness to see merit in Nader's argument that consumers are being manipulated, defrauded, and injured, not just by marginal businesses or fly-by-night hucksters, but by the U.S. blue-chip business firms whose practices are unchecked by the older regulatory agencies. Increasingly, too, the consumer movement has been infused by a growing number of restless youths and housewives. The youthful reformers and others have brought to the consumer movement a moralistic approach that does not consider it sufficient for a corporation to conduct its affairs legally if its business ethics are open to question. It is not an accident that much new consumer legislation has been labeled "truth-in...."

FEDERAL GOVERNMENT TAKES NOTE OF CONSUMERS

The existence of a consumer constituency was recognized in 1959, when Senator Estes Kefauver introduced a bill proposing creation of a federal Department of Consumers. In 1962, President Kennedy, in a special consumer message to Congress, enunciated a charter of consumer rights, including the right to safety, to be informed, to choose, and to be heard. Many consumer matters were already being attended to before President Kennedy focused national attention on the problem. Housing acts had been passed in 1961 and 1962. The tragedies arising from the use of thalidomide by pregnant women had awakened Congress to the need for greater protection in the area of drugs, and a truth-in-lending bill had already been introduced in the Senate. With the President's message, though, the executive departments began to get into the act. Twenty-three government agencies established consumer-protection offices, including all ten Cabinet-level departments, some of which, like the Department of Health, Education and Welfare, had been built around protecting the public. In 1964, President Johnson appointed the first Presidential special assistant for consumer affairs and created the first President's Committee on Consumer Interests. Recommendations for legislation specifically directed to consumer problems had become a prominent feature of the President's 1968 State of the Union message. By 1969, politicians of both parties were climbing aboard the "consumerism" bandwagon. There were some 120 consumer-protection bills pending in Congress, and, according to Mrs. Virginia H. Knauer, President Nixon's special assistant for consumer affairs, no less than 413 units of the federal government were engaged in some form of consumer-related activity. The FTC was one of them, of course. Although the FTC began as a watchdog agency for business, its consumer-protection role has expanded until, in recent years, Congress has looked to it to enforce one new specific consumer-protection statute after another.

THE FTC's FIRST CONSUMER CONFERENCE

The FTC became increasingly aware of the emergence of the consumer as a new weapon in the war against trickery in the market place in the late 1950's. In December, 1959, it called its first Conference on Public Deception. This conference was held in Washington with full publicity and Chairman Earl W. Kintner officiating. More than fifty conferees took part, representing consumer and public service organizations from all over the nation. The conference considered such topics as food and drug advertising, direct selling practices, fictitious pricing, and bait advertising.

The 1959 conference stimulated some activity on state and local levels. Several state attorneys general, recognizing the need for an exchange of views between law enforcement, consumer groups, and the media, called similar conferences. In 1960, the FTC held a series of conferences in various cities to discuss the FTC's deceptive advertising guides and to stimulate self-regulation. The most notable of these was held in Cincinnati with the cooperation of the local Better Business Bureau. Representatives of about 2,000 business concerns attended. The conference was followed by a community-wide informal compliance drive.

CONSUMER HEARINGS AND NADER'S RAIDERS

In November, 1968, the FTC held a nine-day series of hearings on consumer problems with a view to "reaching a more informed decision as to what further action the Commission may take" in the consumer-protection field. At the outset, Chairman Dixon and Commissioner MacIntyre took exception to a warning in the *Kiplinger News Letter* to businessmen to "get ready for the biggest antibusiness show in many years." Dixon said that none of the five Commissioners had any antibusiness ideas in mind and told prospective witnesses he would "hammer" them out of order if they named names or identified products in their testimony.

By the end of the first day, he repeated his threat to wield the gavel in a lecture to John Schultz, twenty-nine-year-old assistant law professor at the University of Southern California. Schultz had headed a 6-man team of law students sponsored by Ralph Nader, the first such team of Nader's Raiders to be set loose on the federal government. The team had just completed its examination of the FTC. Schultz outlined the highly critical findings, which were later published in book form, and wound up his testimony, after several clashes with Chairman Dixon and Commissioner MacIntyre, by calling on the agency to start "attracting the finest talent in the land" and to purge itself of "the continuing and devastating impact of political patronage, cronyism and that 'tired blood' which infects the Commission's staff with a general malaise of apathy, non-responsiveness and limited vision." Dixon deplored Schultz's "audacity" and contended that he should help the Commission obtain good staff members and adequate congressional appropriations. "You ought to be ashamed of yourself, or else you ought to come down here yourself and try to do something other than to try to tear down," Dixon said. In a broad indictment, Schultz accused the Commission of deliberately restricting its consumer-protection activities, paying inadequate attention to deceptive practices, and relying mainly on "sanctionless, informal and voluntary enforcement methods" that had "little deterrent value."

The Commissioners also got an earful from private citizens, representatives of business and industry, law professors, social workers, retailers, and others who poured out their likes and dislikes at the conference. The participants made recommendations ranging from better consumer education to licensing of auto mechanics. There were calls for passage of a deceptive-sales act and a home-improvement investigation act, for laws with stronger deterrents and penalties, for the creation of state consumer commissions. Witness after witness recommended consumer education and counseling. Dixon himself said this was perhaps the most effective means of eliminating deception. "False advertising and merchandising becomes futile in the face of the well-informed consumer," he said. "The consumer has found out that it pays to complain . . . and he isn't going to go away."

PROTECTING THE POOR

The new consumer movement has to a large extent been directed at protecting the poor and most defenseless elements in the population. Less than a year after passage of the Economic Opportunity Act of 1964, which marked the beginning of the federal government's war on poverty, Senator Magnuson, in his capacity as Chairman of the Senate Committee on Commerce, wrote to the FTC Chairman to suggest that the agency "develop a model program for policing those unfair and deceptive practices to which the poor are particularly susceptible." The Commission, urged on by consumer-oriented Commissioner Jones, responded promptly to Senator Magnuson's letter and announced a series of steps to comply with his suggestion, including a pilot program in the District of Columbia to investigate, among other things, "the misrepresentation of credit or finance charges or arrangements." During the poverty program's gestation period, the Office of Economic Opportunity had become increasingly aware of the waste and futility of trying to increase the incomes of the poor, only to have them drained away by unconscionable marketing and credit practices.

The District of Columbia pilot program developed in several directions and involved four kinds of activities—an economic study of actual conditions in low-income area stores, creation of an Office of Consumer Complaints, proposals for credit guides, and case-by-case litigation.

A staff study conducted by the FTC's Bureau of Economics revealed that the poor pay nearly twice as much for appliances and furniture sold in Washington's low-income-area stores. For example, a portable television set with a wholesale price of about $109 could be bought at any local department store for $129.95, but a poor resident of the inner city was charged $219.95 for the same television set at the store serving the low-income market in his neighborhood. The people paying these higher prices were mostly waitresses, janitors, truck drivers, domestics, and other low-income laborers as well as welfare and Social Security recipients.

The Office of Consumer Complaints set up in the District receives and records consumer complaints and offers assistance by referring the complainant to the nearest local office of Neighborhood Legal Services when the complaining person needs legal aid and cannot afford private counsel. The office has received hundreds of complaints about sales and credit practices, ranging from misrepresentation of a sales contract as a mere delivery receipt to outright refusals to return deposits made on goods that were never delivered.

In planning its program of law enforcement, the FTC soon realized that it could not confine its efforts exclusively to the practices and persons involved in the 400 complaints that came to its Consumer Complaints Office. It could not be assumed that those complaints were typical nor that they necessarily encompassed the most vicious practices requiring action, nor that they even involved the most frequent offenders in the market place. The great majority of those victimized do not register their complaints with government agencies. Accordingly, the FTC staff turned to the court records of garnishment and replevin proceedings to pinpoint the most persistent plaintiffs, to get leads on possible instances of fraud and deception, and to identify potential informants respecting the credit and marketing practices current in the District. The basic need to find a time and place of interview of the garnishee posed a problem of real seriousness. In some instances, employers permitted FTC investigators to talk with their employees at work. More often, such permission was refused. Evenings or weekends thus became the only time when the FTC staff could even contact its most important source of information—the poor themselves. Fifteen of the twenty-two formal cases in the FTC's pilot program in D.C. included charges of some form or variation of bait advertising. The D.C. program, still going on under the aegis of the Washington field office, served as a precedent for Chairman Weinberger's plan to set up local consumer-protection coordinating committees throughout the country.

TRUTH-IN-PACKAGING

On November 3, 1966, Congress passed the Fair Packaging and Labeling Act to provide consumers with accurate information on packages and labels to facilitate price comparisons. Passage came six years after Senator Philip Hart, of Michigan, opened his first series of congressional hearings on the subject. At that time, consumer complaints poured into his Antitrust and Monopoly Subcommittee. They painted a picture of confusion and deception over such terms as "giant," "king," and "jumbo." There was the riddle of the "cents-off" promotions and the enigma of the undefined and unmeasurable "serving," the puzzle of how to find the obscure statement of net contents amid the razzle-dazzle on the box. Finally, there was the problem of calculating the price. When Senator Hart first took his truth-in-packaging bill to Congress, he warned that such practices were undermining free enterprise. The Senator asked in his proposed legislation that the Food and Drug Administration and the FTC be empowered to set standards for the net contents of packages. Cookies and crackers, for example, which were then crowding the shelves of supermarkets in more than seventy different sizes, could be restricted to, say, half-pound and 2-pound packages. The price per pound could then be determined quickly by the least mathematical of shoppers.

But Congress side-stepped that issue and passed a greatly watered-down law that provided, in the most general terms, for consistent and uniform disclosures on packaging. Under the Act, the FTC and the Food and Drug Administration share authority over packaging with the Department of Commerce, which may act to curb "undue proliferation" of package sizes by asking industry to set standards for itself. The FTC was given authority to draw up requirements for package disclosures on nonfood and nondrug supermarket items. The

Commission and the Secretary of Health, Education and Welfare are also empowered to issue rules exempting certain consumer commodities from full compliance with the requirements of the Act where their application would either be impracticable or not necessary for the adequate protection of consumers. Certain items covered by other laws and regulations are specifically exempted, including tobacco, alcoholic beverages, meat, and poultry.

In 1969, the FTC finally moved out of the administrative and interpretive stage into the compliance phase of enforcement. It made 450 spot checks of those commodities about which consumers had registered the largest number of complaints and sent off 100 letters to various manufacturers advising them of labeling irregularities. This activity continues with the help of consumer aides in FTC field offices.

RACIAL DISCRIMINATION IN HOUSING HIT

As part of its consumer-protection program, the FTC in late 1968 made a controversial move in the area of racial discrimination in housing. It charged the owners of nine Arlington, Virginia, apartment houses with deceptive advertising that made their apartments appear open to everybody when actually they were closed to Negroes. The unprecedented action, taken over the objection of two Commission members, marked the first, and only, time the FTC has entered the civil rights field through the door of interstate advertising. Massachusetts Senator Edward M. Kennedy, who had promoted the FTC action, hailed the move as "the start of what could be an important new direction in the national effort to erase the last vestige of slavery in the United States." But Chairman Dixon, who voted against the action, expressed alarm at the Commission's willingness to venture into this sensitive area. "Before the FTC may proceed against unfair or deceptive acts or practices," he said, "the act or practice must be 'in commerce.' Historically the Commission has restricted itself, wisely, in my opinion, to proceeding only against acts or practices which resulted in the movement of goods or a sale in commerce." Dixon suggested that the problem of housing discrimination be resolved by Congress. The Commission finally dismissed its complaints after receiving assurances from the respondents that they had discontinued, and would not resume, a policy of restricting the availability of their apartments on the basis of race, color, or national origin. The FTC has since avoided this hot issue, leaving the burden of ensuring equal access to housing to the Department of Housing and Urban Development.

TRUTH-IN-LENDING

Efforts to protect consumers, especially low-income consumers, by requiring full disclosure of credit charges go back a long way. Senator Paul Douglas, the Illinois Democrat, pioneered in this field. He introduced the first truth-in-lending bill on January 7, 1960. After eight years of bitter controversy, the Consumer Credit Protection Act was passed, and, on May 29, 1968, President Johnson signed it into law.

From the original bill offered by Senator Douglas to the ultimate 1967 version, the bill was basically designed to cover one subject—disclosure of the costs and true annual percentage rate of finance charges in credit transactions. Opposition to the legislation was substantial, and, until 1968, successful. The truth-in-lending law, as passed, was designed to affect all persons who are regularly engaged in the business of extending credit, both retailers and lending institutions. It applies to any seller or lender who extends credit to consumers who will use the money, goods, or services for personal, family, household, or agricultural purposes. And it applies to any such creditor, regardless of whether his activities may be wholly intrastate in character. The intent of the law is to enable consumers to shop around for the best credit terms. It was designed to let borrowers know in writing and in clear terms exactly how much they would pay on a loan, a mortgage, or on the installment purchase of a car, washing machine, or any other item.

No fewer than nine federal agencies share responsibility for finding and prosecuting violators, who may be fined up to $5,000 and jailed for as long as a year. In addition, a victim may sue for twice the amount of any misrepresented finance charge and collect damages up to $1,000, plus court costs. The heaviest enforcement burden falls on the FTC, which was given an additional appropriation by Congress for this purpose. Federal agencies that already exercise general regulatory authority over certain sectors of the economy enforce the Act as to those sectors, including most banks and certain other financial institutions, and such specialized activities as packers, stockyards, railroads, and airlines. All creditors not so regulated are subject to the jurisdiction of the FTC.

Congress provided that the Board of Governors of the Federal Reserve System, which was aided by FTC staff members, promulgate the regulations to carry out the purposes of the Act. The final product—Regulation Z, as it is known— was a reflection of the sum of the Board's consideration of all the comments received. Regulation Z has the force and effect of law. On March 3, 1969, the Commission announced plans for distribution of the Consumer Credit Protection Act along with Regulation Z. The Commission estimated that its mailing went to more than 750,000 creditors. A series of meetings was also held with various trade and consumer groups to explain the Act and the Regulation. The consumer credit staff of the FTC held itself in readiness to answer questions and to meet with groups across the country in an effort to promote creditor and consumer understanding of the new law.

The FTC obviously can never marshal sufficient resources to inspect the credit advertising and practices of each of the

1.7 million retailers and of the thousands of finance companies subject to its jurisdiction. Successful compliance calls for a high degree of cooperation by business. With this in mind, the FTC has developed a simplified procedure whereby numerous firms are brought into compliance merely by an exchange of letters.

The Commission is continuing to place increased emphasis on consumer-protection activities. When Caspar Weinberger left, after only five months on the job, to assume new duties in the Administration, his efforts to reorient the agency toward consumer concerns were hailed by no less an authority than Ralph Nader. In addition to concentrating all consumer-protection activities (as contrasted with antitrust work) in one bureau, Chairman Weinberger moved to make FTC field offices into centers of regional action. As "little FTC's," they were to originate cases and stimulate coordinated efforts by the multitude of federal, state, and local agencies that share responsibility for policing the market place. In an address to the antitrust section of the American Bar Association on April 9, 1970, Weinberger said that, if Congress gives the FTC the broadened powers President Nixon has requested, the "little Old Lady of Pennsylvania Avenue will have doffed her tennis shoes and put on cleats." The Commission of the 1970's will, without question, he said, "be judged by what it can and will contribute to consumer protection."

XIV

The Public, Congress, and the Executive Circle

The public is entitled to certain information about government agencies as a matter of right, but where that right to know begins and ends has always been a controversial subject. Since the dissemination of information is a primary function of the FTC in its dual role as governess and policeman of the free enterprise system, this problem is a particularly knotty one for the agency. The FTC must seek to satisfy not only the public at large, but also the business community, the communications media, Congress, and the current Presidential Administration while still retaining the integrity to pursue regulation of business as it thinks best. In short, it must balance credibility and effectiveness against the pressures of special interests and the occasional need to maintain secrecy.

THE PRESS RELEASE

At the very beginning of its history, the FTC was faced with having to decide how far it should go in publicizing complaints lodged by business competitors against each other. It came as a distinct surprise to the business world that parties

202

charged could be named. Pressure built up against such revelations. The Commission decided, at first, not to publicize the offenders by name but to proceed with the case and issue orders without publicity. This procedure proved wholly ineffectual. Business interests that had filed applications for complaints were irritated that they could not have the protection of publicity when a competitor had violated the law. This irritation was conveyed to congressmen and senators, who soon demanded that the FTC name respondents publicly. Hence, issuing news releases at the time a complaint is lodged became part of FTC procedure.

By 1924, when Gerard Henderson wrote his treatise on the agency, the opposite cry was heard. Businessmen and attorneys practicing before the Commission complained about the injustice of a government tribunal's publicly charging serious offenses against reputable citizens based merely upon tentative belief that the charges were true. "The complaint is given to the newspapers and naturally attracts much attention," Henderson wrote. "Many months later it may be withdrawn or dismissed, but the injury to the respondent's reputation has already been done."

Nevertheless, challenges to the legality of the news release have failed. In an early case, a company, claiming injury because public notice of the agency's complaint against it was published in trade journals, sought an injunction against the Commission. In the absence of an allegation that the FTC acted unfairly or arbitrarily, the District of Columbia Circuit Court of Appeals said, in 1933, "We find nothing in the [FTC] Act which will warrant this limitation on the Commission's powers, or indeed anything which would indicate that this was the intention of Congress." Again, in 1967, the policy of issuing press releases was challenged. The case arose out of an FTC deceptive advertising complaint. The Cinderella Career College and Finishing School of the District of Columbia went to court seeking an order barring the FTC from issuing news releases and alleging that issuance of the release had damaged its business unfairly since the case had not been adjudicated. The judge ruled against the FTC, ordering it to stop the practice of issuing press releases, but the District of Columbia Court of Appeals reversed that order in 1968, upholding the FTC's right to issue factual press releases describing events that have taken place.

How Much Secrecy?

Traditionally, FTC complaints and orders as well as major interlocutory actions were summarized in news releases soon after the actions were taken. As a lure to prospective respondents to voluntarily redress illegalities, the FTC decided in the early 1960's to notify them of the FTC's intent to issue a complaint. If, within a reasonable period of time, they agreed to enter a consent order, only a single release would be disseminated, containing the complaint and the order.

When the Freedom of Information Act was passed in 1966, the FTC announced that it was making broad revisions in its rules and policies to bring them in line with the new law. It was, in fact, the first federal agency to announce revision of its public information policies to conform to the law's requirements. But the House Subcommittee on Government Information, under the chairmanship of California Democrat John E. Moss, expressed dissatisfaction with the changes made by the FTC in a November, 1968, report on the effectiveness of the new law.

The FTC took a new look at the problem and, in October, 1969, made further changes. During the previous months, the American Bar Association had joined the chorus decrying the agency for secretiveness, asserting that secret proceedings foster political wheeling-dealing and deprive both businessmen and consumers of information they need. "The lack of any definite published standards on this subject has created

an atmosphere of uncertainty and suspicion that is damaging
to the prestige of the FTC," the ABA said in its report on the
agency. The issue came to a head in May of 1969, when the
Commission reversed itself on a merger application of two
major department stores: Broadway-Hale of Los Angeles and
Neiman-Marcus of Dallas, Texas. The Commission at first
vetoed the proposed mergers, 3 to 2, but eventually reversed
itself after Commissioner Jones changed her vote. In the
department store case, for the first time, the Commission made
its decision on a merger clearance public and presented opinions from the Commissioners.

The first rule change followed a few days later. For firms
under orders to get FTC approval for mergers, the Commission agreed to make public a provisional decision that would
be liable to reversal if any significant opposition developed
within 30 days. Later in the year, the Commission announced
its determination to issue complaints publicly at the time they
are sent to the respondents for the negotiation of possible consent orders rather than defer release of the complaints until
such time as consent orders are executed or the complaints
are formally served on the respondents. The public can now
know that a complaint is pending against a particular respondent and what practices are being held illegal at the same time
that the respondent first receives notice of the Commission's
intention to issue a complaint.

Under rules issued in October, 1969, similar to procedures
already existing in most other regulatory agencies, the Commission agreed to announce publicly any application of firms
to merge or obtain advisory opinions about business practices.
Previously, these matters were decided off-the-record. The
new rule provides that advisory opinions themselves and the
requests for them will be made public when the opinions are
rendered by the FTC and will include the names of the
requesting parties and details of the request. "To an increasing degree, the Commission is publicizing its actions as fully

and speedily as possible, giving the public opportunity to submit views on various proposals, and taking these views into consideration in making its rulings," the FTC said in announcing its liberalized public information disclosure policies.

THE PUBLIC INFORMATION ROLE OF FIELD OFFICES

Although FTC field staff generally perform the basic law enforcement function of investigation, they also provide a link to the public at large, and their role as local information officers is being expanded.

In early 1970, the FTC announced that it would make use of field offices located in key cities throughout the United States to wage a broad attack against fraud and deception practiced against consumers. As a result of a meeting with field representatives on January 28, 1970, Chairman Weinberger announced plans to establish consumer advisory boards under the auspices of existing FTC field offices to serve as sounding boards for consumer complaints and to provide for more effective coordination of the efforts of all three levels of government. "Where state and local governments do not have adequate laws to protect consumers, the FTC will furnish guidelines, on request, and assist local officials in securing new legislation and adopting local consumer programs, if they wish," he said in his announcement. The FTC's role in this effort is essentially cooperative since its responsibility extends only to situations involving interstate commerce.

INFORMATION FOR THE PUBLIC

The FTC classifies as confidential a variety of information, including official minutes of Commission meetings, records related solely to the internal personnel rules and practices of the Commission, trade secrets and names of customers, and commercial or financial information obtained in the investigative stages of a proceeding. Some of this information will be made public or disclosed under certain circumstances to members of the public or other government agencies, but any employee of the Commission who makes public any information contained in confidential records, without authorization of the Commission, unless directed by a court, is guilty of a misdemeanor, and, upon conviction, may be punished by a fine of not more than $5,000 or by imprisonment of one year, or both, at the discretion of the court.

With the exception of its confidential material, all of the Commission's records are available for inspection, and facilities are provided for copying at the FTC's main office. Copies of some records are made available at field offices and field stations. At the end of each fiscal year, the Commission makes a report to Congress and the public summarizing its work during the year. These annual reports are available for inspection and copies may be obtained from the Government Printing Office. The Commission also publishes in the *Federal Register* descriptions of its organization and statements of its rules, procedures, policies, and administrative interpretations.

The Commission periodically publishes its official reports under the title *Federal Trade Commission Decisions.* This material includes the initial decisions of hearing examiners in adjudicative proceedings, with statements of the reasons or basis for action and any concurring and dissenting opinions; significant orders and opinions on interlocutory matters in adjudicative proceedings, the decisions of the Commission in proceedings disposed of by the entry of consent orders to cease and desist, and tests or digests of selected advisory opinions.

Also in the public records of the Commission are a current index of opinions, orders, statements of policy and interpretations, staff manuals and instructions that affect any member of the public; records of the final votes of each member of the Commission in every agency proceeding; petitions, applications, pleadings, briefs, and other records filed by the Commission with the courts in connection with adjudicative, injunctive, and condemnation proceedings; opinions and orders of the courts and the Commission in disposition thereof; pleadings, motions, certifications, orders, and the transcripts of hearings, including public conferences, testimony, oral arguments, and exhibits and all documents received in evidence or made a part of the record in adjudicative proceedings.

Available for reference are some 800 court opinions rendered since 1914 in the interpretation of the FTC Act. The decisions of the Commission and the courts are available also in loose-leaf notebook form and are kept up to date by services such as the Commerce Clearing House *Trade Regulation Reporter*. The rules and guides issued by the Commission are in the Code of Federal Regulations, Title 16, entitled *Commercial Practices* and may be obtained at nominal cost from the Government Printing Office.

In addition to the records available to the public, the FTC maintains an Office of Public Information to respond to requests about Commission actions and to keep the public informed generally about its activities. Several mailing lists are maintained for persons desiring different types of Commission materials. The office also disseminates speeches by Commissioners and bureau personnel and puts out a number of publications. *Advertising Alerts* are sent to advertising media summarizing Commission decisions and actions of interest to the advertising world and the consuming public. Pamphlets describing the role of the Commission in consumer protection include *This is Your FTC* and *Fight Back: The Ungentle Art of Self-Defense*. The Information Office also issues consumer bulletins such as *Pitfalls to Watch Out for in Mail Order Insurance Policies* and *Unordered Merchandise: Shipper's Obligations and Consumer's Rights* to alert members of the consuming public to particular problems.

RELATIONS WITH BUSINESS

The FTC maintains relations with the wide spectrum of business it regulates in many ways. Guides and other publications are distributed to businessmen. Field office representatives attempt to serve an educational function by making speeches to local business and consumer groups. The Commissioners themselves maintain a heavy schedule of speeches to industry groups and see industry representatives in their offices on an informal basis. But, on the whole, industry tends to think of the FTC as a nuisance, or, at best, a necessary evil. The agency's cumbersome procedures come in for ridicule from many businessmen, who refuse to concede that Washington bureaucrats can possibly understand how business really operates.

In the latter part of the 1960's, however, business organizations and representatives began to get worried about the consumer movement. They took some steps to come to grips with the situation. By 1968, Better Business Bureaus in ten states had established their first consumer affairs councils designed to bring business and consumers together to discuss common problems. Many industry trade associations have been newly established or have given renewed emphasis to consumer relations. Their attorneys, in conjunction with other members of the private bar, are organizing special bar association programs to explore the many legal questions involving consumers. Most recently, the U.S. Chamber of Commerce announced the launching of a pilot program to stimulate direct business-consumer contacts through the creation of local business-consumer-relations committees by selected local chambers of commerce.

The FTC relates to business in another way, of course—as legal adversary. Antitrust lawyers represent firms in trouble with the FTC, and these relations have a certain Byzantine complexity almost incomprehensible to the layman. Charges that Washington law firms are part of a "lobbying infrastructure" that works to the disadvantage of consumers were made by Ralph Nader on March 20, 1969, before the Senate Subcommittee on Executive Reorganization. Nader said the law firms "are the masters of the *ex parte* contract, the private deals and trade-offs, the greasing of the corporate wheels and the softening of the bureaucrats' will." These allegations were denied by partners of such prestigious Washington law firms as Covington & Burling and Arnold & Porter. H. Thomas Austern of Covington & Burling, whose firm has represented the tobacco manufacturers in their fight against FTC regulation of cigarette advertising and the makers of Geritol in their ten-year struggle with the agency, told the *Washington Post* on September 20, 1969: "I do not engage in lobbying. . . . I have never talked, alone, to a Congressman or Senator about pending legislation." Members of congressional committee staffs are equally adamant in their insistence that they do not talk privately to lawyers about pending legislation or matters involving the regulatory commissions.

Since the Commission regulates no particular industry, it theoretically remains freer of direct business influence than, say, the Federal Communications Commission or the Federal Power Commission. Business influence on the agency is felt indirectly through the political process, including actions by Congress and appointments by the President.

CONGRESSIONAL OVERSIGHT

Because of the size of Congress and its diffuse responsibilities, supervision and evaluation of administrative agency performance has been left to those congressional committees responsible for the same areas of commerce as the agencies in question. The House Select Committee on Small Business and the Antimonopoly Subcommittee of the Senate Committee on the Judiciary have consistently expressed special interest in the FTC. This interest has centered on antitrust activity. The regulatory commissions also come under the scrutiny of the Subcommittee on Legislative Oversight of the House Committee on Interstate and Foreign Commerce and the Subcommittee on Administrative Practice and Procedure of the Senate Committee on the Judiciary.

FTC officials must also testify before appropriations subcommittees of both Houses of Congress and comment on pending bills. The Executive Director handles appropriations and receives recommendations from Congress for the hiring of agency personnel.

Congressmen also pass consumer complaints from constituents on to the FTC for action or referral to another government agency. The secretary of the FTC, who acts as congressional liaison officer in these matters, estimates that in 1969 the FTC received some 4,000 letters from congressmen, most of which related to queries from constituents regarding questionable trade practices. With the rise of the consumer movement, this work has increased tremendously.

CONGRESSIONAL PRESSURE

According to Daniel Jay Baum, associate professor at the School of Law, Indiana University, writing in the fall, 1964, issue of the *Federal Bar Journal,* the basing-point experience left the FTC with "a nerve that is oversensitive to the will of Congress." He went on to explain that

> the Commission is sensitive to the mood of particularly important committees and Congressmen who possess the ultimate power of persuading the legislative branch to act. And, in this respect the Commission also is sensitive to the Executive through whose hands all appropriations are presented to Congress. The question no longer is, to put it bluntly, what the agency acting independently has the power to do under statute, but rather, recognizing the sweep of its power, how far the agency can go without incurring the wrath of Congress.

In September, 1969, despite vigorous dissents from his colleagues, Commissioner Elman supported Baum's analysis. He told a Senate group that congressional pressure "corrupts the atmosphere" in which his agency works. He charged that congressmen make private, unrecorded calls on behalf of companies seeking FTC approval of million-dollar mergers. He said he received none himself, but called this a "subtle, insidious and destructive" intrusion on the regulatory process. Commissioner Jones flatly denied the existence of congressional intervention. "I may be naive," she told the senators, "but I don't think there is any [pressure] at all." Outside the hearing room, Chairman Dixon also disputed Elman's testimony. "There has not been a senator, a congressman or anybody . . . in the Executive Branch that has threatened me on any decision," he told *Washington Post* reporter Bernard D. Nossiter. The September 13 session was the first of a series of hearings by the subcommittee chaired by Senator Edward Kennedy to determine the extent to which regulatory bodies are responsive to public needs. The subcommittee did not press Commissioner Elman to cite cases. But, in response to the *Post* reporter's questions, Elman observed that the two Democratic senators from West Virginia had both appealed to Chairman Dixon for approval of a bid by Occidental Petroleum Corporation to buy the ailing Maust Coal and Coke Corporation of West Virginia. The FTC approved the purchase on August 7, 1969, by a 3 to 2 vote with Commissioners Elman and Jones dissenting. The Commission's docket shows that Senators Jennings Randolph and Robert Byrd sent wires to Dixon urging speedy and favorable action. Randolph said the merger was of great importance to his state's economy.

The White House

The President has two forms of direct control over the FTC. He has the power to appoint the Commissioners and the

Chairman and, through the Office of Management and Budget, he has the power of budget review. Yet the degree of the President's authority has never been clearly demarcated by case law or statute.

In the 1920's, the Republican Presidents were not inclined to test the limits of their prerogatives. When Franklin Roosevelt came to office, he attempted to change the policies of the FTC through changes in personnel, but his efforts were frustrated. Nevertheless, the notion that an administrative agency can be an effective instrument for the achievement of public policy only if it is led by men whose thinking is consistent with that of the incumbent administration did not end with FDR's heavy-handed maneuvering.

This matter of Presidential control has been discussed and debated publicly. The 1937 report of the President's Committee on Administrative Management suggested that

> no administrative reorganization worthy of the name can leave hanging in the air more than a dozen powerful, irresponsible agencies free to determine policy and administer law. Any program to restore our constitutional ideal of a fully coordinated Executive Branch responsible to the President must bring within the reach of that responsible control all work done by these independent commissions which is not judicial in nature.

The 1960 Landis Report on regulatory agencies prepared for President-elect Kennedy observed that previous Presidents had failed to employ their power over agency chairmanships as an effective instrument for furthering administration policies. The report, advocating a broader role for the President than that implicit in the appointive power, contended that FTC policy "should be keyed to whatever overall program is then the administration's prime concern." It continued: "The responsibility for concentration on a particular area should be the responsibility of the Executive and not the Federal Trade Commission."

At a White House press conference on February 8, 1961, however, President Kennedy commented that he believed Congress had special responsibility for the independent agencies, and that he was not sure it would be wise to change that arrangement. At the White House swearing-in ceremony of Chairman Weinberger on January 13, 1969, President Nixon made a pointed reference to the FTC's nonexecutive status when he remarked that the new Chairman probably would never have another opportunity to talk to him because he was about to assume duties as head of an "independent" agency. Nixon had given his Chairman clear instructions to revitalize the agency, however.

THE SHERMAN ADAMS AFFAIR

There has been one blatant example of White House interference in the affairs of the FTC. That was the Sherman Adams affair, which shook the Eisenhower Administration to its foundations. The story became public in 1958, when the House Subcommittee on Legislative Oversight discovered that Adams, President Eisenhower's top White House aide, had intervened on several occasions with both the FTC and the Securities and Exchange Commission to elicit information of interest to his friend, New England textile manufacturer Bernard Goldfine.

On July 30, 1956, the FTC had issued a complaint charging Goldfine's company, Northfield Mills, Goldfine, and four other individual respondents with violating the Wool Products Labeling Act and the FTC Act by falsely stamping, tagging, and labeling the constituent fibers contained in a certain fabric. The FTC alleged that the textiles in question had been labeled 70 per cent Guanaco (second cousin to the Vicuna) and 30 per cent wool when the fabrics contained "substantially less than 70% Guanaco." The examiner's initial decision, issued on December 18, 1956, upheld the complaint, and, on February 7, 1957, the Commission issued a cease-and-desist order. An FTC attorney subsequently negotiated a consent order under which Northfield Mills agreed to cease and desist from the practices alleged in the FTC complaint.

However, it came out in the 1958 congressional hearings that sometime between 1953, when Northfield Mills had been founded, and the time the FTC issued its complaint, Sherman Adams had had conversations with FTC Chairman Edward Howrey about the reports that the Goldfine firm was falsely labeling fabrics. It was also reported that Goldfine talked to Howrey in his office in a meeting arranged by Adams. In addition, Adams had occasionally received gifts of clothing, including a Vicuna coat, and had frequently accepted payment of hotel bills for himself and his family from Goldfine. Adams appeared on June 17 before the subcommittee, where he acknowledged that he might have acted with "a little more prudence." The whole incident raised such a storm of controversy that Adams resigned shortly thereafter.

Justice Department's Concurrent Jurisdiction

"The most cordial relations have existed and are maintained between the Commission and the Department of Justice" said the 1916 annual report of the FTC. "Each refers to the other complaints primarily within the other's jurisdiction." According to this rosy view, all Sherman Act cases were referred to the Department of Justice and those involving unfair methods of competition, to the FTC. But jurisdiction was not clear-cut, and misunderstandings and friction soon developed to prevent the easy cooperation specified by the terms of the FTC statute. For example, when Justice sought to prosecute a combination of newsprint manufacturers while the Commission was attempting to work out a reform of their business procedure, the Commission claimed that those accused had been assured immunity in return for voluntary cooperation with the FTC. It was not until 1948 that a formal liaison arrangement was established between the Commission and the Justice Department under which one agency or the other obtains priority in particular actions through a system of clearances.

The FTC and Justice now have a formal working arrangement whereby each clears with the other its plans in overlapping areas. This arrangement includes referral of outside complaints, notification of proposed investigations or rulemaking procedures, and the exchange of information by the examination of files and by supplying copies of documents. Each agency formulates its own program. If they coincide, it is by accident rather than design, since there is no central direction. If criminal action can be sustained, action will be brought by Justice. Both agencies have tended to develop expertise on certain industries and products and have divided cases accordingly. In the merger field, for instance, the FTC has become the recognized authority in the milk industry. Justice has taken the steel industry for its particular domain.

FOOD AND DRUG ADMINISTRATION

The FTC is only one of several agencies having jurisdiction over false advertising and deception. The Food and Drug Administration is another. Efforts have been made to coordinate activities between the two agencies and to prevent duplication. Some commentators have suggested that control over both labeling and false advertising of foods, drugs, and cosmetics should be unified in either the FDA or the FTC because there is so much overlap. Actually, FDA achieves practical control over drug advertising claims through the broadly construed definition of labeling and through the requirement of "adequate directions for use" on labels, which has been interpreted to require labeling claims to be consistent with advertising claims. The FTC has sometimes been able to proceed against false labeling under Section 5 of the FTC Act.

The two agencies entered into a "working agreement" in 1954 to coordinate their activities. That agreement was updated in 1968, with special reference to the Commission's proposed trade regulation rule regarding advertising of non-prescription and analgesic drugs. The 1968 agreement also spelled out lines of jurisdiction resulting from the 1962 amendments to the Pure Food and Drug Act. Officials of the two agencies meet once a month to thrash out mutual problems.

POST OFFICE DEPARTMENT

The Post Office has jurisdiction over any fraudulent sales practices perpetrated on the public through the use of the mails. But because Post Office jurisdiction is limited to frauds cognizable under criminal law, fewer deceptive sales practices are subject to its jurisdiction than to the FTC's. Nevertheless, the jurisdiction of the Post Office Department is important because of the criminal sanctions comprising either jail terms or fines, or both, which can be imposed on the merchant who attempts to defraud the consumer. FTC field offices check with postal inspectors to put them on notice that the FTC is investigating a particular firm. If an investigation develops indications of mail fraud, the FTC continues consultation with postal authorities. Although there is no formal consultation agreement, FTC officials have asked the Post Office to inform them when its investigations turn up possible violations of Section 5 of the FTC Act lacking the elements of a fraud.

OTHER FEDERAL AGENCIES

The Federal Communications Commission (FCC), by virtue of its licensing power, recognizes that radio and television stations have a responsibility to avoid broadcasting false advertisements. Although the FCC probably has the power to take effective action against a licensee who fails to fulfill this responsibility, it has been reluctant to make use of this power except by advising stations of complaints and by occasional exhortation. The FCC and FTC made a liaison agreement in 1957 under which the FTC furnishes information to the FCC about questionable advertising aired over radio or television and provides copies of relevant cease-and-desist orders to its sister agency.

The Commission also has a practice of notifying the Federal Housing Administration (FHA) of any deceptive practices involving a home improvement enterprise that utilizes FHA financing, thus enabling FHA to proceed if it desires. In addition, the Commission maintained close contact with the Board of Governors of the Federal Reserve System during the drafting of Regulation Z under the Consumer Credit Protection Act and takes part in meetings of representatives of all the federal departments and agencies affected by the Act.

State Consumer Protection

The problems of consumers are fundamentally local in nature and it is to local organizations that the consumer is first inclined to turn. In 1967, for example, the Better Business Bureau in metropolitan New York received about 260,-000 complaints from consumers while the FTC received only about 10,000 complaints. But it is to the credit of both Congress and the FTC that they have addressed themselves to fraudulent practices, because, if they had not, few states would have provided relief. In 1950, most states had laws of the so-called "printers ink" type, which declare false advertising and certain deceptive practices to be misdemeanors. However, most of these statutes are applicable only to categorical misrepresentations of fact and are, therefore, easily circumvented and practically incapable of outlawing any but the most blatant falsehoods.

In 1966, Chairman Dixon, on behalf of the FTC, publicly urged the states to adopt legislation similar to the Commission's own authority to prevent false advertising and deceptive acts and practices. By doing so, he suggested, the states could draw on the Commission's experience and the 800-plus court decisions interpreting unlawful advertising and marketing practices. The Commission proposed a program of cooperation with other interested federal agencies and with relevant departments in the states.

By late 1969, twenty-eight states had adopted laws generally similar to the FTC Act. In five of the states, the law reads exactly like the Act, prohibiting use of "unfair methods of competition and unfair or deceptive acts or practices" in the conduct of any trade or commerce. The other twenty-three states have slightly different laws that achieve approximately the same results, at least with regard to preventing consumer deception. Seven additional states have set up consumer fraud bureaus, consumer complaint clearinghouses, or study committees to determine the need for new legislation. After a Commission recommendation made in April of 1969, three states enacted legislation providing for private or class actions to redress complaints about deceptive and unfair trade practices with minimum recovery of $200.

The FTC maintains active liaison with state attorneys general and local consumer-protection officials so that if it receives complaints about deceptive or other illegal practices that are not within its jurisdiction, it attempts to forward the complaint to the appropriate local official for action under local law.

The Commission has an informal arrangement with the National Association of Insurance Commissioners, under which complaints involving insurance matters are referred to the appropriate state insurance commissioner in cases in which the FTC does not have jurisdiction. The arrangement contemplates similar referrals by those state authorities to the FTC.

XV

An Embattled FTC Faces
the Future

Herbert Hoover called the FTC "the noble experiment of
1914." Other commentators have been less kind. The FTC
building at the apex of the Federal Triangle is embraced on
one side by the National Archives and on the other by the
National Galley of Art. "Our three museums," wits remark,
pointing to a gallery of photographs of Commission Chairmen
enshrined on the walls of an FTC corridor.

Over the more than fifty years of FTC history, a succession
of independent scholars and analysts have consistently found
the Commission wanting in the performance of its duties.
Recent critics have come close to saying that the agency is
incapable of discharging its basic responsibilities, and some
have concluded not only that the Commission is incapable of
significant action but that it is beyond reform and should be
scrapped.

Criticism of the FTC has been, in fact, an integral part of
the agency's history, beginning in 1924 when Gerard C. Henderson
wrote *The Federal Trade Commission.* Henderson
scored the Commission then for concentrating on trivia, failing
to set up any system of priorities, and failing to assure a high

level of professional competence on the staff. These and other criticisms have been leveled at the agency repeatedly over the years.

In 1949, a Hoover Commission task force in its *Report on Regulatory Commissions* found the FTC's record "disappointing." Recognizing that the Commission has been hampered by inadequate funds, hostile court rulings, and mediocre appointments, the report nevertheless concluded:

As the years have progressed, the Commission has become immersed in a multitude of petty problems; it has not probed into new areas of anticompetitive practices; it has become increasingly bogged down with cumbersome procedures and inordinate delays in disposition of cases. Its economic work— instead of being the backbone of its activities—has been allowed to dwindle almost to none. The Commission has largely become a passive judicial agency, waiting for cases to come up on the docket, under routinized procedures, without active responsibility for achieving the statutory objectives.

A report submitted at about the same time by Representative Estes Kefauver of the House Small Business Committee came to a similar conclusion. Analyzing the extent to which the FTC has brought proceedings involving the 121 most highly concentrated products in the economy (products with annual shipments of more than $10 million), the report found that between 1932 and 1947 fewer than one-third of the products had been covered by FTC antitrust actions, although the leading four producers accounted for more than 75 per cent of the output. In another test, the report matched the FTC case record against the names of manufacturers and discovered that action had been taken against only 15 of the 107 largest industrial corporations.

In 1951, the House Small Business Committee spoke of the generally low level of the morale among FTC employees, citing as evidence:

The internal strife and office politics that pervade the agency. . . . The many small cliques and groups whose chief interest is in personal authority and advancement. . . . The pronounced feeling of unrest and dissatisfaction in many segments of the Commission. . . . Among the older employees an attitude of indifference toward the work of the agency, a reluctance to face new issues.

Former Commissioner James M. Landis, serving then as Chairman of the Committee on Cartels and Monopoly of the Twentieth Century Fund, scathingly disagreed with the committee's recommendation that the Commission be strengthened. "Reference must be made to what I would call the utter bankruptcy of the FTC. As a practical matter, the deterioration of that Commission has gone beyond redemption. If duties of this kind are to be thrust on some agency, there is really only one thing to do, wipe out the FTC completely and start afresh."

Recently, the FTC has been hit by a series of broadsides. In January, 1969, Ralph Nader's young investigators issued a 185-page report calling for the resignation of Chairman Dixon and a sweeping overhaul of the agency's policies, practices, and staff. The group had spent three months during the summer of 1968 checking FTC files and interviewing officials. The student investigators claimed that during their summer's work many documents were withheld from them and at least one door, the Chairman's, was slammed in their faces.

The Nader group concluded that Chairman Dixon's "chief and perhaps only contribution to the Commission's improvement would be to resign from the agency." The students asserted that Dixon had neglected his responsibilities to consumers, had favored big business, and had led the agency into a swamp of "political and regional cronyism." They said also that he had become "notorious" for dunning the FTC's civil service personnel for political contributions in violation of federal law, that the agency was marked by incompetence and discrimination against employment of Ivy League lawyers and blacks, that the Commission had become a "deceptive practice unto itself" by busying itself with trivial cases. The report contained a list of twenty-six recommendations for change, the majority of which were quite specific. They included such standard prescriptions for bureaucratic self-renewal as setting rational priorities, making full use of the Commission's legal powers, expediting the processing of cases, and securing a larger appropriation from Congress.

The image of the FTC evoked by the Nader Report was that of a county courthouse in the South, most particularly, in Tennessee. Since the 1930's, the report said, the FTC has been the property of what remains of Boss Crump's Memphis Democratic machine. After Estes Kefauver succeeded Kenneth McKellar in the Senate, the hold of the Tennessee Gang hardened. The only favor Senator Kefauver ever asked of President Kennedy, reportedly, was the appointment of Paul Rand Dixon as FTC Chairman. Chairman Dixon, according to the Nader group, got along by doing the bidding of influential members of Congress such as Representative Joe L. Evins, a fellow Tennessean and chairman of the House subcommittee that passes on appropriations for the regulatory agencies. At Representative Evins's request, Dixon even went so far as to establish a branch office in Oak Ridge, Tennessee (even though cities as large as Philadelphia and Detroit were represented only by Textile and Fur investigators) to take care of a Tennessee politico who had come to the end of the road in local politics. The Oak Ridge office was created without the knowledge of Dixon's fellow Commissioners.

This was the most outstanding example of cronyism on the Commission cited by the Nader group, but Nader's Raiders traced numerous appointments of FTC supergrade employees to political connections. "Of the nearly five hundred lawyers working for the Commission only about forty are now Republicans with approximately twenty of these being located in the central office. At the present time only one Republican holds a position of any prominence in the operating bureaus of the FTC," the report claimed.

Nader's team was frank in stating that its report was a critique, not an appraisal, of FTC strengths and weaknesses. Nevertheless, the report panicked Dixon into making a public tirade. In an 8-page statement bristling with anger, the Chairman rejected the "arrogant demand for my resignation" made by the group of law students as a "summer vacation smear project." He called the report "a hysterical, anti-business diatribe and a scurrilous, untruthful attack on the career personnel of the Commission." In response, Nader said that Dixon had "failed to answer the documented charges" in the report and that congressional investigation would show it was "truly an understatement." Partly as a result of Dixon's reaction, the Nader Report reached network television audiences on numerous occasions for a month or more. And the *Washington Post* said in an editorial dated January 9, 1969: "Perhaps, as the students suggest, the FTC can be saved by an infusion of money and personnel. . . . But it may be that the FTC, at least in its present form, is not worth saving."

Moves to Reform

The Nader Report proved to be a point of departure for political action. Commenting later, Commissioner Jones conceded that when Nader issued his report on the Federal Trade Commission, "my first feeling was irritation. But I feel now that the Commission has pulled itself together more, and faster, than if it had not come out." In spotlighting the agency's deficiencies, Nader's Raiders succeeded in winning a majority of the Commission over to their view that things were radically wrong. Commissioners Jones, Elman, and Nicholson moved to make certain changes. This "cabal" of three, as Nebraska Republican Senator Carl T. Curtis called them, claimed that the Commission, not the Chairman, had the right to hire and fire top personnel and to oversee administration of the agency. They requested authority to approve appointments of sixty top officials. Dixon refused this request, asserting that the Commission was entitled to pass only on "major administrative" positions far fewer in number. The Civil Service Commission later came to the same conclusion. Although this first attempt to change the make-up of the FTC staff failed, the mood of reform was on the Commission—or, at least, on some of its members.

Early in 1969, a few weeks after Senator Edward Kennedy assumed its chairmanship, the Senate Subcommittee on Administrative Practice and Procedure sent a questionnaire to the federal regulatory agencies that was to serve as the basis for a wide-ranging inquiry into agency practices. Senator Kennedy announced that because "some of the most penetrating self-criticism and the broadest spectrum of replies" came from the FTC, that agency would be the subject of an immediate hearing.

Commissioner MacIntyre, testifying at the hearings in September, 1969, blamed the FTC's troubles on dissension among the Commissioners. "There is at this time no meaningful agreement among the FTC's members as to the legislative goals, namely, the public policies which this agency is to pursue." Although Commission members agree on the goal of preserving competition and protecting consumers from fraud and deception, he said, disagreement comes in the practical sphere—over the objectives of particular statutes, their importance, and, finally, their application in concrete instances. "One of the most serious obstacles to coherent Commission antitrust activity," he said, "is a basic disagreement of some members of the Commission with the public policy declared by Congress in Section 2 of the Clayton Antitrust Act, as amended by the Robinson-Patman Act." He noted that Robinson-Patman "is again under severe attack on the ground that the prevention of price discrimination is action against price competition."

Commissioner Elman made a statement to the Kennedy subcommittee expounding his general theory that the Commission "should not expend its limited resources on the prosecution of *per se* and hard-core cases for which its remedies are inadequate and its expertise unnecessary. It should concentrate, instead, on the pressing but more subtle problems which call for the judgment, skills, and flexible powers of an expert administrative body." Elman also criticized the FTC's "preoccupation with secrecy, its failure to plan a program in which the trivial is carefully distinguished from the important and its reluctance to accord greater weight to the findings and procedural rulings of its hearing examiners." All these combine, in Elman's view, to produce "intolerable" delays in Commission procedures. As of June 30, 1969, "over one-half of the pending investigations in deceptive practice and restraint of trade matters were more than two years old," he said, "and the backlog increases."

On April 24, 1969, Chairman Dixon, sore and bruised by the Nader Report, defended the FTC's performance in protecting consumers and laid the agency's problem at the door of Congress itself. He told a Senate subcommittee on executive reorganization that Congress had been "one of the chief constraints." To meet public demands for relief from an unhappy situation, he said, Congress passes a law but, at the same time, satisfies "the demands of special industry groups for freedom from real regulation by the simple expedient of appropriating only token amounts of money for the actual enforcement of the law."

In criticizing Congress, Dixon said that in no year since 1962 had the Bureau of the Budget given the FTC a significant increase in appropriations, and "what little it did recommend was invariably cut by Congress." Although the Commission staff has remained almost unchanged in size for six years, Congress has continued to add to the FTC's workload. As an example of congressional reluctance to support the activities of the Commission, Dixon cited the study begun in 1962, less than two years after he took office, of intercorporate relations between the nation's one thousand largest corporations. Funds for the study, which Dixon said would have better equipped the FTC to deal with the merger movement that "threatens to engulf us," were approved by the Bureau of the Budget. But Congress not only refused to approve funds for the study for three years in a row; it also tacked a "rider" on the FTC's appropriations bill prohibiting the agency from spending any of its money on this inquiry, which was halted as a result.

Less than a year after release of the Nader Report, there were signs that it had made a real impact, in stimulating reform of the FTC and in calling public attention to the regulatory agencies. Largely as a result of the Nader findings, President Nixon called for an investigation of the FTC by the American Bar Association. The findings of the 16-member ABA study group headed by Philadelphia lawyer Miles W. Kirkpatrick, in effect, endorsed the major findings of the Nader Report. The ABA's 84-page report made few references to Commission activities on the plus side. In unusually blunt and unequivocal language for such a document, it summed up the Commission's performance as "a failure on many counts." Failures included "incompetence" of many top staff members, heavy reliance on complaints from the public, undue reliance on voluntary procedures, mismanagement of resources. The ABA report proposed that the FTC shift the main emphasis of its activities toward detection and eradication of frauds against the consumer and concentrate on "particularly vulnerable groups such as the poor, the uneducated and the elderly." Fifteen members signed the ABA report. The sixteenth, Professor Richard A. Posner of the Stanford

Law School, took a more critical view than his cohorts and even questioned whether the agency could be made to function effectively.

The ABA report said that revitalization of the FTC would depend on the ability of the Chairman appointed by Nixon, who had given the ABA a September 15 deadline so he would have time to review its report before making his selection. A vacancy on the Commission, enabling Nixon to make an appointment, was due to come up the end of September when Commissioner James M. Nicholson's term expired. Following the recommendation of the ABA study group, Nixon decided to appoint a Chairman who had had no prior connection with the FTC. He chose Caspar W. Weinberger.

In the meantime, the Nixon Administration had presented to Congress a program for "consumerism in the America of the 70s." In his first consumer message to Congress, Nixon asked for legislation to make the President's special assistant for consumer affairs statutory, to create a new consumer-protection division in the Justice Department, and to provide for "reactivation and revitalization" of the FTC. The President asked Congress to enact legislation under which the FTC could move against consumer abuses "affecting" interstate commerce, a move to broaden the jurisdiction of the FTC in line with that of other regulatory statutes. Congress was also asked, as it had been by previous administrations, to grant the FTC power to seek and obtain preliminary injunctions against unfair or deceptive business practices. This could decrease by months and even years, the President said, the "unacceptable delay between the time a harmful practice is discovered and the time it is ended." Later, the Administration proposed that the federal courts be made available for individual and class consumer actions after termination of a successful government suit, either by the Justice Department or the FTC, against the perpetrator of a fraudulent or deceptive practice.

After he took office in January, Chairman Weinberger moved to bring consumer protection down to the local level by beefing up the operations of FTC field offices, asked for regulation of automobile standards, and requested Congress to pass legislation covering warranties. He also reorganized the agency before he was suddenly and unexpectedly, after only five months in office, picked by President Nixon to be deputy director of the new Office of Management and Budget. A set-back in the revitalization of the agency was feared, and it was generally conceded that much depended on who succeeded Weinberger. That it should turn out to be none other than Miles W. Kirkpatrick, who headed the ABA study group, came as a surprise.

The dismay in consumer circles over Weinberger's removal began to dwindle as the new Chairman moved to pick up where Weinberger had left off. Consumer interests were encouraged by Kirkpatrick's strong consumer-protection stance and his early activities, which included a successful effort to retire some of the older men on the FTC staff and replace them with outstanding young lawyers from private practice.

Early in the Kirkpatrick regime, the Commission agreed, for the first time in its history, to permit consumer groups to intervene in agency proceedings on behalf of the public as a whole. At issue in this test case is whether an advertiser should be made to disclose in its future advertising that its past advertising had been found to be deceptive. In an address before the National Food Sales Conference in New York on December 5, 1970, Kirkpatrick said that the agency was developing new rules that would have dramatic effect on the market place. He added, in support of pending legislation to give the FTC increased powers, that "a stronger FTC is the best insurance policy both businessmen and consumers can have for continued existence of the free enterprise system."

Appendix A

Careers in Trade Regulation

As a law enforcement agency, the Federal Trade Commission employs attorneys in many phases of its operations. In fact, lawyers make up the largest single category in a staff of about 1,330. There are approximately 500 attorneys, the largest number of whom are assigned to field offices. Since most of the legal casework of the Commission originates in the field, these attorneys are responsible for obtaining evidence as to whether a law violation has occurred, evaluating this evidence, and making the initial recommendations as to action to be taken by the Commission. They also negotiate informal settlements and try cases of local significance.

Attorneys in the Consumer Protection and Competition bureaus in Washington coordinate the work of the field offices, prepare and review complaints, conduct the trial of cases having a national impact, and supervise compliance with cease-and-desist orders. Attorneys in the General Counsel's Office represent the Commission in court proceedings.

The FTC actively recruits law school graduates for its attorney positions. A recent graduate who has been admitted to the bar of any state or the District of Columbia may receive an appointment as an attorney at grade GS-9 or GS-11. The FTC does not limit its attorney recruitment program to appointments at the junior levels, but, because of the FTC's policy of promotion from within, few appointments are made at grades above GS-12.

The FTC employs about forty-five economists on its staff who develop case theory and conduct and analyze industry surveys. The agency is particularly interested in graduate students with knowledge of industrial economics and hires some economists at the bachelor's degree level, particularly if they plan to continue their academic studies. The entrance level for an economist with a Ph.D. is at GS-11 or GS-12.

The FTC has recently created a new job category—that of consumer protection specialist. These men work out of the field offices as part of a newly strengthened attack on fraud and deception practiced against consumers. To qualify, applicants must have civil service status or pass a civil service examination.

In addition, the agency hires a small number of specialists such as physical science technicians, advertising examiners, medical officers, general physical scientists, business analysts, textile technologists, photographers, computer specialists, and chemists, and it is always looking for accountants. The large secretarial staff numbers more than 400.

Appendix B

The Federal Trade Commission Act

As Amended by the Wheeler-Lea Act of 1938

The statutory objectives of the FTC are set forth in the Federal Trade Commission Act, as amended by the Wheeler-Lea Act; the Clayton Act, as amended by the Robinson-Patman Act and the Celler-Kefauver Antimerger Act; the Wool Products Labeling Act; the Fur Products Labeling Act; the Flammable Fabrics Act; and the Textile Fiber Products Identification Act. The Commission also has responsibilities under the Packers and Stockyards Act, the Webb-Pomerene Export Trade Act, the Lanham Trade-Mark Act, the Oleomargarine Act, the Fair Packaging and Labeling Act, and the Consumer Credit Protection Act. Additional statutes and court decisions have further refined the FTC's responsibilities. The text of the FTC Act follows:

Be it enacted by the Senate and House of Representatives of the United States of America in Congress assembled, That a commission is hereby created and established, to be known as the Federal Trade Commission (hereinafter referred to as the commission), which shall be composed of five commissioners, who shall be appointed by the President, by and with the advice and consent of the Senate. Not more than three of the commissioners shall be members of the same political party. The first commissioners appointed shall continue in office for terms of three, four, five, six, and seven years, respectively, from the date of the taking effect of this Act, the term of each to be designated by the President, but their successors shall be appointed for terms of seven years, except that any person chosen to fill a vacancy shall be appointed only for the unexpired term of the commissioner whom he shall succeed: *Provided, however,* That upon the expiration of his term of office a commissioner shall continue to serve until his successor shall have been appointed and shall have qualified. The commission shall choose a chairman from its own membership. No commissioner shall engage in any other business, vocation, or employment. Any commissioner may be removed by the President for inefficiency, neglect of duty, or malfeasance in office. A vacancy in the commission shall not impair the right of the remaining commissioners to exercise all the powers of the commission.

The commission shall have an official seal, which shall be judicially noticed.

SEC. 2. That each commissioner shall receive a salary of $10,000 a year, payable in the same manner as the salaries of the judges of the courts of the United States. The commission shall appoint a secretary, who shall receive a salary of $5,000 a year, payable in like manner, and it shall have authority to employ and fix the compensation of such attorneys, special experts, examiners, clerks and other employees as it may from time to time find necessary for the proper performance of its duties and as may be from time to time appropriated for by Congress.

With the exception of the secretary, a clerk to each commissioner, the attorneys, and such special experts and examiners as the commission may from time to time find necessary for the conduct of its work, all employees of the commission shall be a part of the classified civil service, and shall enter the service under such rules and regulations as may be prescribed by the commission and by the Civil Service Commission.

All of the expenses of the commission, including all necessary expenses for transportation incurred by the commissioners or by their employees under their orders, in making any investigation, or upon official business in any other places than in the city of Washington, shall be allowed and paid on the presentation of itemized vouchers therefor approved by the commission.

Until otherwise provided by law, the commission may rent suitable offices for its use.

The Auditor for the State and Other Departments shall receive and examine all accounts of expenditures of the commission.

SEC. 3. That upon the organization of the commission and election of its chairman, the Bureau of Corporations and the offices of Commissioner and Deputy Commissioner of Corporations shall cease to exist; and all pending investigations and proceedings of the Bureau of Corporations shall be continued by the commission.

All clerks and employees of the said bureau shall be transferred to and become clerks and employees of the commission at their present grades and salaries. All records, papers, and property of the said bureau shall become records, papers, and property of the commission, and all unexpended funds and appropriations for the use, and maintenance of the said bureau, including any allotment already made to it by the Secretary of Commerce from the contingent appropriation for the Department of Commerce for the fiscal year nineteen hundred and fifteen, or from the departmental printing fund for the fiscal year nineteen hundred and fifteen, shall become funds and appropriations available to be expended by the commission in the exercise of the powers, authority, and duties conferred on it by this Act.

The principal office of the commission shall be in the city of Washington, but it may meet and exercise all its powers at any other place. The commission may, by one or more of its members, or by such examiners as it may designate, prosecute any inquiry necessary to its duties in any part of the United States.

SEC. 4. The words defined in this section shall have the following meaning when found in this Act, to wit:

"Commerce" means commerce among the several States or with foreign nations, or in any Territory of the United States or in the District of Columbia, or between any such Territory and another, or between any such Territory and any State or foreign nation, or between the District of Columbia and any State or Territory or foreign nation.

"Corporation" shall be deemed to include any company, trust, so-called Massachusetts trust, or association, incorporated or unincorporated, which is organized to carry on business for its own profit or that of its members, and has shares of capital or capital stock or certificates of interest, and any company, trust, so-called Massachusetts trust, or association, incorporated or unincorporated, without shares of capital or capital stock or certificates of interest, except partnerships, which is organized to carry on business for its own profit or that of its members.

"Documentary evidence" includes all documents, papers, correspondence, books of account, and financial and corporate records.

"Acts to regulate commerce" means the Act entitled "An Act to regulate commerce," approved February 14, 1887, and all Acts amendatory thereof and supplementary thereto and the Communications Act of 1934 and all Acts amendatory thereof and supplementary thereto.

"Antitrust Acts" means the Act entitled "An Act to protect trade and commerce against unlawful restraints and monopolies," approved July 2, 1890; also sections 73 to 77, inclusive, of an Act entitled "An Act to reduce taxation, to provide revenue for the Government, and for other purposes," approved August 27, 1894; also the Act entitled "An Act to amend sections 73 and 76 of the Act of August 27, 1894, entitled 'An Act to reduce taxation, to provide revenue for the Government, and for other purposes,'" approved February 12, 1913; and also the Act entitled "An Act to supplement existing laws against unlawful restraints and monopolies, and for other purposes," approved October 15, 1914.

SEC. 5. (a) (1) Unfair methods of competition in commerce, and unfair or deceptive acts or practices in commerce, are hereby declared unlawful.

(2) Nothing contained in this Act or in any of the Antitrust Acts shall render unlawful any contracts or agreements prescribing minimum or stipulated prices, or requiring a vendee to enter into contracts or agreements prescribing minimum or stipulated prices, for the resale of a commodity which bears, or the label or container of which bears, the trade-mark, brand, or name of the producer or distributor of such commodity and which is in free and open competition with commodities of the same general class produced or distributed by others, when contracts or agreements of that description are lawful as applied to intrastate transactions under any statute, law, or public policy now or hereafter in effect in any State, Territory, or the District of Columbia in which such resale is to be made, or to which the commodity is to be transported for such resale.

(3) Nothing contained in this Act or in any of the Antitrust Acts shall render unlawful the exercise or the enforcement of any right of action created by any statute, law, or public policy now or hereafter in effect in any State, Territory, or the District of Columbia, which in substance provides that willfully and knowingly advertising, offering for sale, or selling any commodity at less than the price or prices prescribed in such contracts or agreements whether the person so advertising, offering for sale, or selling is or is not a party to such a contract or agreement, is unfair competition and is actionable at the suit of any person damaged thereby.

(4) Neither the making of contracts or agreements as described in paragraph (2) of this subsection, nor the exercise or enforcement of any right or right of action as described in paragraph (3) of this subsection shall constitute an unlawful burden or restraint upon, or interference with, commerce.

(5) Nothing contained in paragraph (2) of this subsection shall make lawful contracts or agreements providing for the establishment or maintenance of minimum or stipulated resale prices on any commodity referred to in paragraph (2) of this subsection, between manufacturers, or between producers, or between wholesalers, or between brokers, or between factors, or between retailers, or between persons, firms, or corporations in competition with each other.

(6) The Commission is hereby empowered and directed to prevent persons, partnerships, or corporations, except banks, common carriers subject to the Acts to regulate commerce, air carriers, and foreign air carriers subject to the Federal Aviation Act of 1958, and persons, partnerships, or corporations insofar as they are subject to the Packers and Stockyards Act, 1921, as amended, except as provided in section 406(b) of said Act, from using unfair methods of competition in commerce and unfair or deceptive acts or practices in commerce.

(b) Whenever the Commission shall have reason to believe that any such person, partnership, or corporation has been or is using any unfair method of competition or unfair or deceptive act or practice in commerce, and if it shall appear to the Commission that a proceeding by it in respect thereof would be to the interest of the public, it shall issue and serve upon such person, partnership, or corporation a complaint stating its charges in that respect and containing a notice of a hearing upon a day and at a place therein fixed at least thirty days after the service of said complaint. The person, partnership, or corporation so complained of shall have the right to appear at the place and time so fixed and show cause why an order should not be entered by the Commission requiring such person, partnership, or corporation to cease and desist from the violation of the law so charged in said complaint. Any person, partnership, or corporation may make application, and upon good cause shown may be allowed by the Commission to intervene and appear in said proceeding by counsel or in person. The testimony in any such proceeding shall be reduced to writing and filed in the office of the Commission. If upon such hearing the Commission shall be of the opinion that the method of competition or the act or practice in question is prohibited by this Act, it shall make a report in writing in which it shall state its findings as to the facts and shall issue and cause to be served on such person, partnership, or corporation an order requiring such person, partnership, or corporation to cease and desist from using such method of competition or such act or practice. Until the expiration of the time allowed for filing a petition for review, if no such petition has been duly filed within such time, or, if a petition for review has been filed within such time then until the record in the proceeding has been filed in a court of appeals of the United States, as hereinafter provided, the Commission may at any time, upon such notice and in such manner as it shall deem proper, modify or set aside, in whole or in part, any report or any order made or issued by it under this section. After the expiration of the time allowed for filing a petition for review, if no such petition has been duly filed within such time, the Commission may at any time, after notice and opportunity for hearing, reopen and alter, modify, or set aside, in whole or in part, any report or order made or issued by it under this section, whenever in the opinion of the Commission conditions of fact or of law have so changed as to require such action or if the public interest shall so require: *Provided, however,* That the said person, partnership, or corporation may, within sixty days after service upon him or it of said report or order entered after such a reopening, obtain a review thereof in the appropriate court of appeals of the United States, in the manner provided in subsection (c) of this section.

(c) Any person, partnership, or corporation required by an order of the Commission to cease and desist from using any method of competition or act or practice may obtain a review of such order in the court of appeals of the United States, within any circuit where the method of competition or the act or practice in question was used or where such person, partnership, or corporation resides or carries on business, by filing in the court, within sixty days from the date of the service of such order, a written petition praying that the order of the Commission be set aside. A copy of such petition shall be forthwith transmitted by the clerk of the court to the Commission, and thereupon the Commission shall file in the court the record in the proceeding, as provided in Section 2112 of Title 28, United States Code. Upon such filing of the petition the court shall have jurisdiction of the proceeding and of the question determined therein concurrently with the Commission until the filing of the record and shall have power to make and enter a decree affirming, modifying, or setting aside the order of the Commission, and enforcing the same to the extent that such order is affirmed, and to issue such writs as are ancillary to its jurisdiction or are necessary in its judgment to prevent injury to the public or to competitors pendente lite. The finding of the Commission as to the facts, if supported by evidence, shall be conclusive. To the extent that the order of the Commission is affirmed, the court shall thereupon issue its own order commanding obedience to the terms of such order of the Commission. If either party shall apply to the court for leave to adduce additional evidence, and shall show to the satisfaction of the court that such additional evidence is material and that there were reasonable grounds for the failure to adduce such evidence in the proceeding before the Commission, the court may order such additional evidence to be taken before the Commission and to be adduced upon the hearing in such manner and upon such terms and conditions as to the court may seem proper. The Commission may modify its findings as to the facts, or make new findings, by reason of the additional evidence so taken, and it shall file such modified or new findings, which, if supported by evidence, shall be conclusive, and its recommendation, if any, for the modification or setting aside of its original order, with the return of such additional evidence. The judgment and decree of the court shall be final, except that the same shall be subjected to review by the Supreme Court upon certiorari, as provided in section 240 of the Judicial Code.

(d) Upon the filing of the record with it the jurisdiction of the court of appeals of the United States to affirm, enforce, modify, or set aside orders of the Commission shall be exclusive.

(e) Such proceedings in the court of appeals shall be given precedence over other cases pending therein, and shall be in every way expedited. No order of the Commission or judgment of court to enforce the same shall in anywise relieve or absolve any person, partnership, or corporation from any liability under the Antitrust Acts.

(f) Complaints, orders, and other processes of the Commission under this section may be served by anyone duly authorized by the Commission, either (a) by delivering a copy thereof to the person to be served, or to a member of the partnership to be served, or the president, secretary, or other executive officer or a director of the corporation to be served; or (b) by leaving a copy thereof at the residence or principal office or place of business of such person, partnership, or corporation; or (c) by mailing a copy thereof by registered mail or by certified mail addressed to such person, partnership, or corporation at his or its residence or principal office or place of business. The verified return by the person so serving said complaint, order, or other process setting forth the manner of said service shall be proof of the same, and the return post office receipt for said complaint, order, or other process mailed by registered mail or by certified mail as aforesaid shall be proof of the service of the same.

(g) An order of the Commission to cease and desist shall become final—

(1) Upon the expiration of the time allowed for filing a petition for review, if no such petition has been duly filed within such time; but the Commission may thereafter modify or set aside its order to the extent provided in the last sentence of subsection (b); or

(2) Upon the expiration of the time allowed for filing a petition for certiorari, the order of the Commission has been affirmed, or the petition for review dismissed by the court of appeals, and no petition for certiorari has been duly filed; or

(3) Upon the denial of a petition for certiorari, if the order of the Commission has been affirmed or the petition for review dismissed by the court of appeals; or

(4) Upon the expiration of thirty days from the date of issuance of the mandate of the Supreme Court, if such Court directs that the order of the Commission be affirmed or the petition for review dismissed.

(h) If the Supreme Court directs that the order of the Commission be modified or set aside, the order of the Commission rendered in accordance with the mandate of the Supreme Court shall become final upon the expiration of thirty days from the time it was rendered, unless within such thirty days either party has instituted proceedings to have such order corrected to accord with the mandate, in which event the order of the Commission shall become final when so corrected.

(i) If the order of the Commission is modified or set aside by the court of appeals, and if (1) the time allowed for filing a petition for certiorari has expired and no such petition has been duly filed, or (2) the petition for certiorari has been denied, or (3) the decision of the court has been affirmed by the Supreme Court, then the order of the Commission rendered in accordance with the mandate of the court of appeals shall become final on the expiration of thirty days from the time such order of the Commission was rendered, unless within such thirty days either party has instituted proceedings to have such order corrected so that it will accord with the mandate, in which event the order of the Commission shall become final when so corrected.

(j) If the Supreme Court orders a rehearing; or if the case is remanded by the court of appeals to the Commission for a rehearing, and if (1) the time allowed for filing a petition for certiorari has expired; and no such petition has been duly filed, or (2) the petition for certiorari has been denied, or (3) the decision of the court has been affirmed by the Supreme Court, then the order of the Commission rendered upon such rehearing shall become final in the same manner as though no prior order of the Commission had been rendered.

(k) As used in this section the term "mandate," in case a mandate has been recalled prior to the expiration of thirty days from the date of issuance thereof, means the final mandate.

(l) Any person, partnership, or corporation who violates an order of the Commission to cease and desist after it has become final, and while such order is in effect, shall forfeit and pay to the United States a civil penalty of not more than $5,000 for each violation, which shall accrue to the United States and may be recovered in a civil action brought by the United States. Each separate violation of such an order shall be a separate offense, except that in the case of a violation through continuing failure or neglect to obey a final order of the commission each day of continuance of such failure or neglect shall be deemed a separate offense.

SEC. 6. That the commission shall also have power—

(a) To gather and compile information concerning, and to investigate from time to time the organization, business, conduct, practices, and management of any corporation engaged in commerce, excepting banks and common carriers subject to the Act to regulate commerce, and its relation to other corporations and to individuals, associations, and partnerships.

(b) To require, by general or special orders, corporations engaged in commerce, excepting banks, and common carriers subject to the Act to regulate commerce, or any class of them, or any of them, respectively, to file with the commission in such form as the commission may prescribe annual or special, or both annual and special reports or answers in writing to specific questions, furnishing to the commission such information as it may require as to the organization, business, conduct, practices, management, and relation to other corporations, partnerships, and individuals of the respective corporations filing such reports or answers in writing. Such reports and answers shall be made under oath, or otherwise, as the commission may prescribe, and shall be filed with the commission within such reasonable period as the commission may prescribe, unless additional time be granted in any case by the commission.

(c) Whenever a final decree has been entered against any defendant corporation in any suit brought by the United States to prevent and restrain any violation of the antitrust Acts, to make investigation, upon its own initiative, of the manner in which the decree has been or is being carried out, and upon the application of the Attorney General it shall be its duty to make such investigation. It shall transmit to the Attorney General a report embodying its findings and recommendations as a result of any such investigation, and the report shall be made public in the discretion of the commission.

(d) Upon the direction of the President or either House of Congress to investigate and report the facts relating to any alleged violations of the antitrust Acts by any corporation.

(e) Upon the application of the Attorney General to investigate and make recommendations for the readjustment of the business of any corporation alleged to be violating the antitrust Acts in order that the corporation may thereafter maintain its organization, management, and conduct of business in accordance with law.

(f) To make public from time to time such portions of the information obtained by it hereunder, except trade secrets and names of customers, as it shall deem expedient in the public interest; and to make annual and special reports to the Congress and to submit therewith recommendations for additional legislation; and to provide for the publication of its reports and decisions in such form and manner as may be best adapted for public information and use.

(g) From time to time to classify corporations and to make rules and regulations for the purpose of carrying out the provisions of this Act.

(h) To investigate, from time to time, trade conditions in and with foreign countries where associations, combinations, or practices of manufacturers, merchants, or traders, or other conditions, may affect the foreign trade of the United States, and to report to Congress thereon with such recommendations as it deems advisable.

Sec. 7. That in any suit in equity brought by or under the direction of the Attorney General as provided in the antitrust Acts, the court may, upon the conclusion of the testimony therein, if it shall be then of opinion that the complainant is entitled to relief, refer said suit to the commission, as a master in chancery, to ascertain and report an appropriate form of decree therein. The commission shall proceed upon such notice to the parties and under such rules of procedure as the court may prescribe, and upon the coming in of such report such exceptions may be filed and such proceedings had in relation thereto as upon the report of a master in other equity causes, but the court may adopt or reject such report, in whole or in part, and enter such decree as the nature of the case may in its judgment require.

Sec. 8. That the several departments and bureaus of the Government when directed by the President shall furnish the commission, upon its request, all records, papers, and information in their possession relating to any corporation subject to any of the provisions of this Act, and shall detail from time to time such officials and employees to the commission as he may direct.

SEC. 9. That for the purposes of this Act the commission, or its duly authorized agent or agents, shall at all reasonable times have access to, for the purpose of examination, and the right to copy any documentary evidence of any corporation being investigated or proceeded against; and the commission shall have power to require by subpoena the attendance and testimony of witnesses and the production of all such documentary evidence relating to any matter under investigation. Any member of the commission may sign subpoenas, and members and examiners of the commission may administer oaths and affirmations, examine witnesses, and receive evidence.

Such attendance of witnesses, and the production of such documentary evidence, may be required from any place in the United States, at any designated place of hearing. And in case of disobedience to a subpoena the commission may invoke the aid of any court of the United States in requiring the attendance and testimony of witnesses and the production of documentary evidence.

Any of the district courts of the United States within the jurisdiction of which such inquiry is carried on may, in case of contumacy or refusal to obey a subpoena issued to any corporation or other person, issue an order requiring such corporation or other person to appear before the commission, or to produce documentary evidence if so ordered, or to give evidence touching the matter in question; and any failure to obey such order of the court may be punished by such court as a contempt thereof.

Upon the application of the Attorney General of the United States, at the request of the commission, the district courts of the United States shall have jurisdiction to issue writs of mandamus commanding any person or corporation to comply with the provisions of this Act or any order of the commission made in pursuance thereof.

The commission may order testimony to be taken by deposition in any proceeding or investigation pending under this Act at any stage of such proceeding or investigation. Such depositions may be taken before any person designated by the commission and having power to administer oaths. Such testimony shall be reduced to writing by the person taking the deposition, or under his direction, and shall then be subscribed by the deponent. Any person may be compelled to appear and depose and to produce documentary evidence in the same manner as witnesses may be compelled to appear and testify and produce documentary evidence before the commission as hereinbefore provided.

Witnesses summoned before the commission shall be paid the same fees and mileage that are paid witnesses in the courts of the United States, and witnesses whose depositions are taken, and the persons taking the same shall severally be entitled to the same fees as are paid for like services in the courts of the United States.

No person shall be excused from attending and testifying or from producing documentary evidence before the commission or in obedience to the subpoena of the commission on the ground or for the reason that the testimony or evidence, documentary or otherwise, required of him may tend to criminate him or subject him to a penalty or forfeiture. But no natural person shall be prosecuted or subjected to any penalty or forfeiture for or on account of any transaction, matter, or thing concerning which he may testify, or produce evidence, documentary or otherwise, before the commission in obedience to a subpoena issued by it: *Provided,* That no natural person so testifying shall be exempt from prosecution and punishment for perjury committed in so testifying.

SEC. 10. That any person who shall neglect or refuse to attend and testify, or to answer any lawful inquiry, or to produce documentary evidence, if in his power to do so, in obedience to the subpoena or lawful requirement of the commission, shall be guilty of an offense and upon conviction thereof by a court of competent jurisdiction shall be punished by a fine of not less than $1,000 nor more than $5,000, or by imprisonment for not more than one year, or by both such fine and imprisonment.

Any person who shall willfully make, or cause to be made, any false entry or statement of fact in any report required to be made under this Act, or who shall willfully make, or cause to be made, any false entry in any account, record, or memorandum kept by any corporation subject to this Act, or who shall willfully neglect or fail to make, or to cause to be made, full, true, and correct entries in such accounts, records, or memoranda of all facts and transactions appertaining to the business of such corporation, or who shall willfully remove out of the jurisdiction of the United States, or willfully mutilate, alter, or by any other means falsify any documentary evidence of such corporation, or who shall willfully refuse to submit to the commission or to any of its authorized agents, for the purpose of inspection and taking copies, any documentary evidence of such corporation in his possession or within his control, shall be deemed guilty of an offense against the United States, and shall be subject, upon conviction in any court of the United States of competent jurisdiction, to a fine of not less than $1,000 nor more than $5,000 or to imprisonment for a term of not more than three years, or both such fine and imprisonment.

If any corporation required by this Act to file any annual or special report shall fail so to do within the time fixed by the commission for filing the same, and such failure shall continue for thirty days after notice of such default, the corporation shall forfeit to the United States the sum of $100 for each and every day of the continuance of such failure which forfeiture shall be payable into the Treasury of the United States, and shall be recoverable in a civil suit in the name of the United States brought in the district where the corporation has its principal office or in any district in which it shall do business. It shall be the duty of the various United States attorneys, under the direction of the Attorney General of the United States, to prosecute for the recovery of forfeitures. The costs and expenses of such prosecution shall be paid out of the appropriation for the expenses of the courts of the United States.

Any officer or employee of the commission who shall make public any information obtained by the commission without its authority, unless directed by a court, shall be deemed guilty of a misdemeanor, and, upon conviction thereof, shall be punished by a fine not exceeding $5,000, or by imprisonment not exceeding one year, or by fine and imprisonment, in the discretion of the court.

SEC. 11. Nothing contained in this Act shall be construed to prevent or interfere with the enforcement of the provisions of the antitrust Acts or the Acts to regulate commerce, nor shall anything contained in the Acts be construed to alter, modify, or repeal the said antitrust Acts or the Acts to regulate commerce or any part or parts thereof.

SEC. 12. (a) It shall be unlawful for any person, partnership, or corporation to disseminate, or cause to be disseminated, any false advertisement—

(1) By United States mails, or in commerce by any means, for the purpose of inducing, or which is likely to induce, directly or indirectly the purchase of food, drugs, devices, or cosmetics; or

(2) By any means, for the purpose of inducing, or which is likely to induce directly or indirectly, the purchase in commerce of food, drugs, devices, or cosmetics.

(b) The dissemination or the causing to be disseminated of any false advertisement within the provisions of subsection (a) of this section shall be an unfair or deceptive act or practice in commerce within the meaning of section 5.

SEC. 13. (a) Whenever the Commission has reason to believe—

(1) that any person, partnership, or corporation is engaged in, or is about to engage in, the dissemination or the causing of the dissemination of any advertisement in violation of section 12, and

(2) that the enjoining thereof pending the issuance of a complaint by the commission under section 5, and until such complaint is dismissed by the Commission or set aside by the court on review, or the order of the Commission to cease and desist made thereon has become final within the meaning of section 5, would be to the interest of the public,

the Commision by any of its attorneys designated by it for such purpose may bring suit in a district court of the United States or in the United States court of any Territory, to enjoin the dissemination or the causing of the dissemination of such advertisement. Upon proper showing a temporary injunction or restraining order shall be granted without bond. Any such suit shall be brought in the district in which such person, partnership, or corporation resides or transacts business

(b) Whenever it appears to the satisfaction of the court in the case of a newspaper, magazine, periodical, or other publication, published at regular intervals—

(1) that restraining the dissemination of a false advertisement in any particular issue of such publication would delay the delivery of such issue after the regular time therefor, and

(2) that such delay would be due to the method by which the manufacture and distribution of such publication is customarily conducted by the publisher in accordance with sound business practice, and not to any method or device adopted for the evasion of this section or to prevent or delay the issuance of an injunction or restraining order with respect to such false advertisement or any other advertisement,

the court shall exclude such issue from the operation of the restraining order or injunction.

SEC. 14. (a) Any person, partnership, or corporation who violates any provision of section 12(a) shall, if the use of the commodity advertised may be injurious to health because of results from such use under the conditions prescribed in the advertisement thereof, or under such conditions as are customary or usual, or if such violation is with intent to defraud or mislead, be guilty of a misdemeanor, and upon conviction shall be punished by a fine of not more than $5,000 or by imprisonment for not more than six months, or by both such fine or imprisonment; except that if the conviction is for a violation committed after a first conviction of such person, partnership, or corporation, for any violation of such section, punishment shall be by a fine of not more than $10,000 or by imprisonment for not more than one year, or by both such fine and imprisonment: *Provided,* That for the purposes of this section meats and meat food products duly inspected, marked, and labeled in accordance with rules and regulations issued under the Meat Inspection Act approved March 4, 1907, as amended, shall be conclusively presumed not injurious to health at the time the same leave official "establishments."

(b) No publisher, radio-broadcast licensee, or agency or medium for the manufacturer, packer, distributor, or seller of the commodity to which the false advertisement relates, shall be liable under this section by reason of the dissemination by him of false advertisement, unless he has refused, on the request of the Commission, to furnish the Commission the name and post-office address of the manufacturer, packer, distributor, or advertising agency, residing in the United States, who caused him to disseminate such advertisement. No advertising agency shall be liable under this section by reason of the causing by it of the dissemination of any false advertisement, unless it has refused, on the request of the Commission, to furnish the Commission the name and post-office address of the manufacturer, packer, distributor, or seller, residing in the United States, who caused it to cause the dissemination of such advertisement.

SEC. 15. For the purposes of sections 12, 13, and 14—

(a) (1) The term "false advertisement" means an advertisement, other than labeling, which is misleading in a material respect; and in determining whether any advertisement is misleading, there shall be taken into account (among other things) not only representations made or suggested by statement, word, design, device, sound, or any combination thereof, but also the extent to which the advertisement fails to reveal facts material in the light of such representations or material with respect to consequences which may result from the use of the commodity to which the advertisement relates under the condi-- tions prescribed in said advertisement, or under such conditions as are customary or usual. No advertisement of a drug shall be deemed to be false if it is disseminated only to members of the medical profession, contains no false representation of a material fact, and includes, or is accompanied in each instance by truthful disclosure of, the formula showing quantitatively each ingredient of such drug.

(2) In the case of oleomargarine or margarine an advertisement shall be deemed misleading in a material respect if in such advertisement representations are made or suggested by statement, word, grade designation, design, device, symbol, sound, or any combination thereof, that such oleomargarine or margarine is a dairy product, except that nothing contained herein shall prevent a truthful, accurate, and full statement in any such advertisement of all the ingredients contained in such oleomargarine or margarine.

(b) The term "food" means (1) articles used for food or drink for man or other animals, (2) chewing gum, and (3) articles used for components of any such article.

(c) The term "drug" means (1) articles recognized in the official United States Pharmacopoeia, official Homoeopathic Pharmacopoeia of the United States, or official National Formulary, or any supplement to any of them; and (2) articles intended for use in the diagnosis, cure, mitigation, treatment, or prevention of disease in man or other animals; and (3) articles (other than food) intended to affect the structure or any function of the body of man or other animals; and (4) articles intended for use as a component of any article specified in clause (1), (2), or (3); but does not include devices or their components, parts, or accessories.

(d) The term "device" (except when used in subsection (a) of this section) means instruments, apparatus, and contrivances, including their parts and accessories, intended (1) for use in the diagnosis, cure, mitigation, treatment, or prevention of disease in man or other animals; or (2) to affect the structure or any function of the body of man or other animals.

(e) The term "cosmetic" means (1) articles to be rubbed, poured, sprinkled, or sprayed on, introduced into, or otherwise applied to the human body or any part thereof intended for cleansing, beautifying, promoting attractiveness, or altering the appearance, and (2) articles intended for use as a component of any such article; except that such term shall not include soap.

(f) For the purposes of this section and section 407 of the Federal Food, Drug, and Cosmetic Act, as amended, the term "oleomargarine" or "margarine" includes—

(1) all substances, mixtures, and compounds known as oleomargarine or margarine;

(2) all substances, mixtures, and compounds which have a consistence similar to that of butter and which contain any edible oils or fats other than milk fat if made in imitation or semblance of butter.

Sec. 16. Whenever the Federal Trade Commission has reason to believe that any person, partnership, or corporation is liable to a penalty under section 14 or under subsection (1) of section 5, it shall certify the facts to the Attorney General, whose duty it shall be to cause appropriate proceedings to be brought for the enforcement of the provisions of such section or subsection.

Sec. 17. If any provision of this Act, or the application thereof to any person, partnership, corporation, or circumstance, is held invalid, the remainder of the Act and the application of such provision to any other person, partnership, corporation, or circumstance, shall not be affected thereby.

Sec. 18. This Act may be cited as the "Federal Trade Commission Act."

Organic Act approved September 26, 1914.

Wheeler-Lea Amendment approved March 21, 1938.

"Permissible Scope of Cease and Desist Orders: Legislation and Adjudication by the FTC." *University of Chicago Law Review* 29 (1962):706–27.

ROCKEFELLER, EDWIN S., and R. L. WALD. "Antitrust Enforcement by the Federal Trade Commission and the Department of Justice: A Primer for Small Business." *Dickinson Law Review* 66 (1962): 251–67.

ROWE, FREDERICK M. "The Federal Trade Commission's Administration of the Anti–Price Discrimination Law: A Paradox of Antitrust Policy." *Columbia Law Review* 64 (1964):415–38.

"Television Advertising and the FTC." *Notre Dame Lawyer*, Part 1: (1962):524–44. Part 2: 38 (1963):350–54.

ZIMMERMAN, EDWIN M. "The Federal Trade Commission and Mergers." *Columbia Law Review* 64 (1964):500–523.

LAW JOURNAL SPECIAL ISSUES

Columbia Law Review, March, 1964. FTC Fiftieth Anniversary Issue.
Federal Bar Journal, Fall, 1964. FTC Fiftieth Anniversary Issue.
George Washington Law Review, January–February, 1940. Federal Trade Commission Silver Anniversary Issue, S. CHESTERFIELD OPPENHEIM, special editor.
Indiana Law Journal, Spring, 1963. Proceedings of a symposium on the Federal Trade Commission.
St. John's Law Review, Spring, 1970. Entire issue devoted to conglomerate mergers and acquisitions.

FEDERAL TRADE COMMISSION PUBLICATIONS AND REPORTS

Advisory Opinion Digest, Nos. 1–313 (June 1, 1962, to December 31, 1968).
Annual Report of the Federal Trade Commission, 1965–68.
Current Trends in Merger Activity, 1969, Statistical Report No. 6, 1970.
Economic Report on Mergers and Vertical Integration in the Cement Industry, 1966.
Economic Report on the Use of Games of Chance in Food and Gasoline Retailing, 1968.
Federal Trade Commission Report to Congress Pursuant to the Federal Cigarette Labeling and Advertising Act, 1968.
FTC Staff Report on Automobile Warranties, 1968.
National Consumer Protection Hearings, 1968.
Organization, Procedures and Rules of Practice, 1970.
Report of Ad Hoc Committee on Franchising, 1969.
Report on Anticompetitive Practices in the Marketing of Gasoline, 1967.

OTHER DOCUMENTS

American Bar Association. *Antitrust Development from 1956 to 1968,* a supplement to the Report of the Attorney General's National Committee to Study the Antitrust Laws, March 31, 1955. Chicago, 1968.

————. Section of Antitrust Law. *Proceedings at the Spring Meeting, Washington, D.C., April, 1966.* "The Robinson-Patman Act: 1936–1966; Antitrust Report from Official Washington; FTC Practice, Policies and Problems." Chicago, 1966.

————. ————. *Report of the ABA Commission to Study the Federal Trade Commission.* Chicago, 1969.

AUSTERN, H. THOMAS. "Five Thousand Dollars a Day: An Inquiry into the Civil Penalty Consequences of Violation of a Federal Trade Commission Cease and Desist Order." American Bar Association, section in Antitrust Law. Proceedings 21 (1962) : 285 ff.

BOCK, BETTY. *Mergers and Markets: A Guide to Economic Analysis of Case Law.* 3d ed. Studies in Business Economics, No. 85. National Industrial Conference Board. New York, 1964.

LANDIS, JAMES M. *Report on Regulatory Agencies to the President-Elect.* Issued by the Senate Committee on the Judiciary, Subcommittee on Administrative Practice and Procedure. 86th Congress, 2d session. December, 1960.

Report of the Attorney General's National Committee to Study the Antitrust Laws. Washington: D.C.: Government Printing Office, 1955.

U.S. Commission on the Organization of the Executive Branch of the Government (Hoover Commission Report). Washington, D.C.: Government Printing Office, 1949.

U.S. House of Representatives. Committee on Interstate Commerce. *Control of Corporations, Persons and Firms Engaged in Interstate Commerce.* Report No. 1326. 62nd Congress, 3d session. February 26, 1913.

————. ————. *Interstate Trade Commission.* Report No. 533. 63d Congress, 2d session. April 14, 1914.

————. Committee on the Judiciary. *Antitrust Legislation.* Report No. 627. 63d Congress, 2d session. May 12, 1914.

————. ————. *The Antitrust Laws: A Basis for Economic Freedom.* Washington, D.C.: Government Printing Office, 1959.

————. ————. *The Celler-Kefauver Act: Sixteen Years of Enforcement.* Washington, D.C.: Government Printing Office, 1967.

————. Select Committee on Small Business. *Mergers and Superconcentration: Acquisitions of 500 Largest Industrial and 50 Largest Merchandising Firms.* Washington, D.C.: Government Printing Office, 1962.

U.S. Senate. *Antitrust Legislation.* Conference Report on H.R. 15657 to Supplement Existing Laws Against Unlawful Restraints and Monopolies and for Other Purposes. Senate Document No. 585. 63d Congress, 2d session. September 4, 1914.

————. Committee on Interstate Commerce. *Federal Trade Commission.* Report No. 597. 63d Congress, 2d session. June 13, 1914.

————. Committee on the Judiciary. *Administered Prices; A Compendium on Public Policy: The Celler-Kefauver Act; A Review of Enforcement Policy.* Washington, D.C.: Government Printing Office, 1963.

————. ————. *Mergers, Superconcentration, and the Public Interest.* Washington, D.C.: Government Printing Office, 1963.

————. Select Committee on Small Business. A *Seminar Discussion of the Question: "Are Planning and Regulation Replacing Competition in the New Industrial State?"* Washington, D.C.: Government Printing Office, 1967.

————. ————. *The Status and Future of Small Business in the American Economy.* Washington, D.C.: Government Printing Office, 1967.

Index

257

353.00826 W125f